Praise for Seminex in Print

No other event of the last century, including changes of policy about sexuality in the Evangelical Lutheran Church in America, shook and rearranged the trajectory of North American Lutheranism as did the conflict over the inerrancy of Scripture and the third use of the Law in The Lutheran Church—Missouri Synod in the 1970s. This exhaustive bibliography will serve as the definitive go-to resource about this conflict for decades to come.

Mark Mattes
Lutheran Bible Institute Chair in Bible and Theology, Grand View University, Des Moines, Iowa

This is a wonderful and much-needed book! This bibliography of materials on the Seminex episode in American Lutheran history is an invaluable service to the field, and David Berger is to be commended for his accomplishment. The definitive historical work on this era has yet to be written, but with this bibliography it is much more likely that such a volume eventually will be produced. Kudos to Berger and to the Concordia Historical Institute for this important new volume.

Mark Granquist
Lloyd and Annelotte Svendsbye Professor of the History of Christianity, Luther Seminary, Saint Paul, Minnesota

Seminex in Print is a remarkable achievement serving to index books, occasional papers, articles from both the religious and secular press, and other documents reflecting both sides of the controversy. It is an indispensable guide for research. Those who want to understand the dynamics that led to theological and institutional conflict and, finally, the shift of direction within The Lutheran Church—Missouri Synod will find in this volume a useful resource.

John T. Pless
Assistant Professor of Pastoral Ministry and Missions, Concordia Theological Seminary, Fort Wayne, Indiana

Bibliography lays the foundation for all historical research. Berger's meticulous work demonstrates the librarian's knowledge of the nooks and crannies in which relevant documents may lie hidden. His sensitive sleuthing for related publications has created a *vademecum* for all future historians who wish to explore the critical events surrounding the founding of Seminex and the larger ecclesiastical environment in which the developments of 1974 took place. "Berger" will become the handbook to which countless students and scholars turn for gathering the primary sources for their studies of the critical events surrounding the divide within The Lutheran Church—Missouri Synod, which reflected trends of the times in the wider North American church landscape.

Robert Kolb
Professor Emeritus of Systematic Theology, Concordia Seminary, Saint Louis

Although I only touched on the split in a peripheral way in my dissertation, *A Tale of Two Synods,* I would have welcomed a volume such as this. *Seminex in Print* provides helpful but brief introductions, a time line, and sources from a wide variety of publications and perspectives. Especially on this topic, secondary sources written on the source have frequently been supportive of one side or the other. The balance in this volume will give later historians a better chance to evaluate all the information and arrive at their own conclusions.

Mark Braun

Retired professor, Wisconsin Lutheran College, Milwaukee

Seminex in Print is an indispensable tool for examining one of the most significant turning points in American Christianity of the twentieth century. With a distinguished career as a research librarian and archivist at Concordia Seminary, Saint Louis, David O. Berger has produced a meticulously detailed bibliography documenting the broad range of sources available in various media forms pertaining to the controversy among Lutherans in the 1960s and 1970s. This is an immensely helpful resource for historians, theologians, librarians, and archivists seeking to investigate the key questions involved in this critical period in church history.

Gerhard Bode

Associate Professor of Historical Theology, Seminary Archivist, Concordia Seminary, Saint Louis

Seminex in Print

A Comprehensive Bibliography of Published Material and Selected Archival Resources for Historical Research

Seminex in Print

A Comprehensive Bibliography of Published Material and Selected Archival Resources for Historical Research

Compiled by

David O. Berger

with Daniel N. Harmelink

concordia historical institute monograph series

Concordia Publishing House • Saint Louis

Published by Concordia Publishing House
3558 S. Jefferson Ave., St. Louis, MO 63118-3968
1-800-325-3040 • cph.org

Manufactured in the United States of America

LIBRARY OF CONGRESS CATALOGING-IN-PUBLICATION DATA

Names: Berger, David O., editor. | Harmelink, Daniel Nathan, 1959- editor. | Concordia Historical Institute editor.
Title: Seminex in print : a comprehensive bibliography of published material and selected archival resources for historical research / compiled by David O. Berger ; with Daniel N. Harmelink.
Description: Saint Louis : Concordia Publishing House, 2022. | Series: Concordia Historical Institute monograph series | Includes bibliographical references and index. | Summary: "In this bibliography, David O. Berger, longtime librarian at Concordia Seminary, St. Louis, catalogs the published materials produced in the immediate context of the conflict within the Missouri Synod in the 1960s and '70s. Mr. Berger has painstakingly surveyed the extensive literature, organized it in a usable fashion, and thereby opened a window into the materials surrounding the conflict and the various interpretations that were offered by people affected by the events of this difficult period. Citations frequently include related matters—theological and practical, previous and subsequent—that cannot be divorced from the main events and people involved in 1974"-- Provided by publisher.
Identifiers: LCCN 2021046475 (print) | LCCN 2021046476 (ebook) | ISBN 9780758672216 (paperback) | ISBN 9780758672223 (ebook)
Subjects: LCSH: Christ Seminary-Seminex--History--Bibliography. | Lutheran Church--Missouri Synod--History--20th century--Bibliography. | Church controversies--Lutheran Church--Missouri Synod--History--Bibliography.
Classification: LCC Z7778.U6 B47 2022 BV4070.C555 (print) | LCC Z7778.U6 BV4070.C555 (ebook) | DDC 273--dc23
LC record available at https://lccn.loc.gov/2021046475
LC ebook record available at https://lccn.loc.gov/2021046476

3 4 5 6 7 8 9 10 30 29 28 27 26 25 24

Table of Contents

The Concordia Historical Institute Monograph Series

Concordia Historical Institute has always been driven to trumpet the historical treasures that it has been called to steward. Only months after its incorporation in 1927, the Institute began publishing historical articles and notices in its *Quarterly*. A year later a nationwide campaign began to finance the building of a museum. Major building projects to enhance the sharing of the growing number of books, documents, photographs, artifacts, audiovisual material, and fine art were undertaken in 1951 and again in 1978. A museum housing a permanent display of the history of the Missouri Synod was dedicated in 2009.

Under the belief that Concordia Historical Institute is called to treasure and trumpet Christ's redeeming work in the life of the Lutheran Church, this monograph series has been established to broadcast pertinent historical materials necessary for meaningful historical study, research, and discussion.

Concordia Historical Institute is thankful for the support expressed by many historians, archivists, and church leaders—especially the members of the Institute—for this intentional effort to advance the study of Lutheranism in North America.

Special funding for this volume has been made possible by the Eugene E. and Nell S. Fincke Memorial Trust; in thankfulness for this gift, this book is produced to the glory of God and in honor of Ewald J. Otto, Edwin C. Weber, Charles H. Burmeister, Alfred W. Briel, and Walter C. Dissen—majority members who served on the Concordia Seminary Board of Control at the time of the "walkout."

Photograph by Paul Ockrassa

Concordia Seminary students gather after the "walkout" on February 18, 1974.

FOREWORD

Mark A. Noll

This remarkably thorough bibliography opens a wide door to anyone concerned about one of the most dramatic moments in the recent history of North American Christianity. The formation of Seminex in early 1974 by students and faculty departing from the LCMS's Concordia Seminary (Saint Louis) came after several years of escalating tension. The many levels represented by that tension underscored the devisive character of Seminex's founding and the subsequent rearrangement of American Lutheranism that this founding helped precipitate. Although popular media focused on the leading personalities involved, much more was in play. How should confessional standards inherited from the European Reformation function in circumstances greatly altered from Martin Luther's day? Which aspects of modern biblical scholarship could be constructively incorporated into historic Lutheranism? Where in the American landscape would Lutherans find their most helpful partners for conversation, counsel, and cooperation? Would forces of cohesion keep American Lutherans together as German and Scandinavian heritages continued to fade? Was there a distinctive contribution that Lutherans could make to the cause of the Gospel in the United States and to American civic life?

By providing so much useful information on the history of Seminex, this bibliography also illuminates the first-order questions that lurked in the background as Missouri leaders squared off against each other. The value of *Seminex in Print* for Lutheran scholars, pastors, and interested laity is obvious. But it should also be useful for non-Lutherans like myself who, as an example, have learned much from trying to understand why Samuel Schmucker and C. F. W. Walther chose the contrasting paths they pursued in the nineteenth century. Or how, as faithful confessional Lutherans, Walter Maier and Oswald Hoffmann could contribute so much to the general Christian cause in the twentieth century. By seeing more clearly how Lutherans involved in the complex Seminex drama sought to understand the Gospel, honor the historical Lutheran Confessions, and act responsibly in the modern situation, all readers should be aided to themselves understand the Gospel better, increase their respect for believers who have gone before, and live more responsibly today.

Mark A. Noll, McAnaney Professor of History Emeritus (University of Notre Dame), is the author of *The Old Religion in a New World: The History of North American Christianity* (Eerdmans, 2002), "America Has Honoured Luther—But not the Lutheran Point of View," in *Martin Luther 500* (Belfast, 2017); and other works.

Photograph by Paul Ockrassa

Boarded-up arches under the east side of Luther Tower on the campus of Concordia Seminary, February 18, 1974.

PREFACE

Lawrence R. Rast Jr.

"Synod's Attic"—that's how some have occasionally referred to Concordia Historical Institute. It brings up images of a dusty, cobweb-filled space into which people rarely venture. I know that's not a fair description of CHI, having served on the Board of Governors in various capacities and at various times over the course of more than a quarter century now. But in one sense the "attic motif" does hold. For, as is often the case in a beloved home, the attic houses the memories of the family. There one may find the love letters of grandparents and great-grandparents, family Bibles in another language that hold genealogical keys to the clan's story, and photographs of known and unknown ancestors. All of these artifacts—and many others—invite the adventurous historian to delve into a world that is often only known in outline, and the details that emerge from such an engagement can transform understanding and life.

For those who do risk the allergens and creepy-crawling things, Concordia Historical Institute holds wonders aplenty to explore. Not merely an "attic"—a simple storage facility—CHI holds within its collections the stories of God at work through His people as they fulfill the Great Commission to "go therefore and make disciples of all nations, baptizing them in the name of the Father and of the Son and of the Holy Spirit, teaching them to observe all that I have commanded you" (Matthew 28:19–20). These stories are written in broad strokes and also painted down to the last detail. And what they consistently reveal is God's working through His Word and Sacraments as faithful, sometimes struggling, Christian people seek to carry out His will in challenging historical circumstances.

Making these stories available to the larger church is part of the mission of Concordia Historical Institute. Synod's Bylaws tell us that CHI is "the official Department of Archives and History of the Synod." As such the Synod directs it to "promote interest in the history of Lutheranism in America, particularly of The Lutheran Church—Missouri Synod" and to "serve as an advisory and correlating agency for historical interests within the Synod and shall collect and preserve articles of historical value" (*LCMS Handbook* [2019], Bylaw 3.6.2, pages 124–26). One can almost hear the attic stairs creaking as we climb them at this point.

But, again, there is more to CHI than merely collecting! For Synod also directs the Institute to "stimulate historical research, publish its results." That is the purpose of the Concordia Historical Institute Monograph Series and specifically of this first volume in that series: *Seminex in Print: A Comprehensive Bibliography of Published Material and Selected Archival Resources for Historical Research*. True, bibliographies may not necessarily provide a life-changing, scintillating narrative. However, they can point the reader and researcher to those places where such stories may be found and motivate them to share the stories that the materials collected tell.

In this particular bibliography, David O. Berger, longtime librarian at Concordia Seminary, Saint Louis, catalogs the published materials produced in the immediate context of the conflict within the Missouri Synod in the 1960s and 1970s. This conflict disrupted Concordia Seminary, The Lutheran Church—Missouri Synod, and ultimately resulted in the formation of Christ Seminary—Seminex and the Association of Evangelical Lutheran Churches. Mr. Berger has painstakingly surveyed the extensive literature, organized it in a usable fashion, and thereby opened a window into the materials surrounding the conflict and the various interpretations that were offered by people affected by the events of this difficult period.

A collection of this sort suggests many avenues for further study, and it is the hope of the Editorial Committee of the CHI Monograph Series that this will lead many to engage the materials that eventuated in the "walkout" of February 19, 1974, the fiftieth anniversary of which will be upon us in just a few years. But like any attic exploration, we may find materials that challenge our assumptions about these events. Stories have been told, but perhaps they have lacked detail or nuance. In the immediate wake of the "walkout" a spate of books appeared interpreting it. Now that we enjoy nearly a half century of historical distance from the emotional events of the mid-1970s, it is time to take up the historical challenge and to remind ourselves of our family's story—difficult as that may be.

In the end, we do so knowing that historical interpretation is limited by the context of the interpreter him/herself. No human telling of history is the final word. At the same time, it is important that we struggle to tell that story in a faithful, well-researched, and plausible way. This volume of sources will help make that happen. The necessity of continuing to explore and retell the story in the years to come remains, even as we hold fast to God's promise that "I am with you always, to the end of the age" (Matthew 28:20).

Introduction

Scope and Chronology

This bibliography focuses on the February 1974 student and faculty "walkout" at Concordia Seminary, Saint Louis, and the subsequent establishment of Seminex / Christ Seminary—Seminex. Citations, however, frequently include related matters—theological and practical, previous and subsequent—that cannot be divorced from the main events and people involved in 1974. It is impossible to examine Seminex in isolation. In fact, the "walkout" and the establishment of Seminex might be called the "Grand Symptoms" or simply the culmination of the many theological and church political issues roiling The Lutheran Church—Missouri Synod from the 1960s into the 1980s. The chronological span of the bibliography is primarily the early 1970s to the early 1980s. (Christ Seminary—Seminex moved from Saint Louis to three other locations in 1983.) In publications outside Lutheran circles, interest in the controversy began with the 1973 LCMS convention in New Orleans, peaked at the suspension of President John Tietjen and the "walkout" in early 1974, and waned quickly after the 1975 Anaheim convention. For Lutheran publications, the controversy and related issues held interest over a longer time span.

The actions regarding the Concordia Seminary faculty at LCMS conventions beginning at Milwaukee (1971) and culminating at New Orleans (1973); the "walkout" at Concordia Seminary, Saint Louis, Missouri, in February 1974; the subsequent creation of Seminex; and the effects of Seminex on the Missouri Synod and related church bodies are intricately connected via several concurrent issues that preclude distinct start and ending dates and clear limits of scope. The issues comprise:

1. **Theological matters**, such as the relationship between the Gospel and Holy Scripture, the inspiration and inerrancy of Scripture, and use of the historical-critical method of biblical interpretation. Early manifestations extend back at least to questions raised about the teaching of several faculty members at Concordia Seminary in the late 1950s. In October 1960, the faculty of Concordia Seminary issued "A Statement on the Form and Function of the Holy Scriptures" (*Concordia Theological Monthly* 31:10, pages 626–27), which was excerpted and discussed in a "Special Report" in *The Lutheran Witness* (80:7, April 4, 1961, pages 14–22). A Counselors Conference at Valparaiso University in

1960 dealt in part with the emerging issues. (Concordia Publishing House published *A Symposium of Essays and Addresses Given at the Counselors Conference*, several essays of which focus on the relevant topics.) Several "unpublished" overtures to the 1965 LCMS convention singled out two Concordia Seminary faculty members for their teachings (Martin Scharlemann and Gilbert Thiele) and called for the removal of President Alfred Fuerbringer. Closer to the event, Resolutions 2-01 to 2-06 of the 1969 convention of the LCMS in Denver revealed continuing growing concerns for doctrinal discipline in the Synod. (See the Appendix for evidence of the ongoing controversy in overtures to and resolutions at LCMS conventions from 1962 to 1975.)

2. **PRACTICAL QUESTIONS**, such as the binding nature of the Synod's doctrinal resolutions and statements as well as the matter of congregational autonomy vis-à-vis the Synod. Also in the air was the issue of academic freedom and how or whether it applies to a seminary faculty, or any Lutheran faculty, in a confessional setting. Convention adoption in 1973 of *A Statement of Scriptural and Confessional Principles* served as a flash point. *In Touch* (Lutheran Faculty Federation, Valparaiso, Indiana), for example, featured articles on *A Statement* and its application to faculties at other LCMS institutions of higher education.

3. **LCMS RELATIONSHIPS WITH OTHER LUTHERAN BODIES** at a time when major changes were taking place, such as the ordination of women and plans to adopt a common hymnal. More than a quarter century before, "A Statement [of the Forty-Four]" served as a harbinger; more recently, the LCMS had approved fellowship with the ALC in 1969.

4. **THE REACTIVE CREATION OF INDEPENDENT CHURCH BODIES AND ORGANIZATIONS** in the 1970s, such as Evangelical Lutherans in Mission (ELIM) and the Association of Evangelical Lutheran Churches (AELC).

5. **THE PUBLICATION AND CONVENTION ADOPTION OF *THE MISSION AFFIRMATIONS*** in 1965 and the eventual dismissal and resignations of some mission personnel around the time of the "walkout" and establishment of Seminex.

Relevant, but not included in this bibliography, are the culture-rending events of the late 1960s and the 1970s. Student activism was widespread. The atmosphere at Concordia Seminary was primed, for example, by a moratorium on classes in the spring of 1969. Student demands included an end to requiring specific Seminary IV courses and to the practice of sending course grades to parents.

Types of Material Included

The bibliography includes two major types of analyzed sources: published materials attributed to a specific author and materials that are the product of unnamed authors or editors. Context will guide the researcher in determining if individual entries are the reporting of news or editorial pieces or if they are sanctioned by individual church bodies or institutions. When available in the source, news articles and editorials are so identified.

1. **Signed materials**

Major stand-alone works (books, documents, pamphlets); reviews of major books on the controversy; editorials and articles in periodicals; academic and conference papers; audiovisual productions; also archival collections (not exclusively "published" materials).

Since the issues at dispute are often dealt with in the faculty journals of the respective institutions—namely, *Concordia Theological Monthly* and *Concordia Journal* (Concordia Seminary), *Currents in Theology and Mission* (Seminex), and even *The Springfielder* and *Concordia Theological Quarterly* (Concordia Theological Seminary)—the journals are selectively analyzed for articles related to the issues in dispute in the years surrounding the time of the "walkout." Citations are found in **3.1 *Signed Articles and Editorials.***

2. **News reports and editorials, signed and unsigned**

a. Official LCMS periodicals (2.1): *The Lutheran Witness*, *Lutheran Witness Reporter*, *Lutheran Witness Reporter Edition*, and *Reporter.*

b. Other Lutheran periodicals (2.2): *The Lutheran* (Lutheran Church in America), *The Lutheran Standard* (ALC), *The Lutheran Layman* (Lutheran Laymen's League [an auxiliary of the LCMS]), *The Northwestern Lutheran* (WELS), *The Lutheran* (Lutheran Church of Australia), *Lutherans Alert National* (ALC protest group), and *The Lutheran Spokesman* (CLC).

c. Assorted periodicals, both religious and secular, e.g., *The Christian Century*, *Christianity Today*, and *Time.*

Other official denominational publications—mostly Protestant, many of them not indexed or incompletely indexed—also provide some coverage of the "walkout," Seminex, and related controversies. For example, several citations from the *Presbyterian Journal* and the Seventh-Day Adventist *Review and Herald* are included in categories 3.1 and 3.2. Further research of this category would require identifying more such publications and locating holdings at relevant institutions.

Similar content often appears in news articles in official and unofficial church body publications. Such similarities may result from a common source of information, e.g., press releases from a communications department. The astute researcher will be alert to differences in how the same information is presented.

Organization

Categories that include mostly signed materials—books, book reviews, audiovisual productions, academic papers, some journal articles, and archive collections—are listed alphabetically by the last name of the author or subject. News articles in various manifestations of *The Lutheran Witness* and *Reporter* are of two kinds: signed articles and news articles. Given the number and frequency of the news articles in the various Lutheran publications, even those with authors identified, the citations are in chronological order. (Mostly) unsigned news articles and editorials in assorted periodicals (3.2) are organized chronologically within each source. The organization of each category is identified in the bibliography. *Note that for clarity and convenience in searching, the compiler has enhanced many titles, especially of news articles and editorials. Clarifying words and names added to titles are enclosed in brackets [ ].*

Table of Bibliography Categories

This comprehensive bibliography is organized into twenty-six different categories in eight groupings with an appendix. Note that 6.0 contains lists of publications rather than analyzed sources.

Print Sources for Further Investigation and Research

1. The long list of ***Independent, Unofficial Lutheran Publications*** (7.1)—some national, some regional or LCMS District—that contain much information and commentary on Seminex and related matters of doctrine and practice should also be investigated by the researcher, who will find something in almost every issue in the relevant years: ca. 1969–83, and most notably 1973–79. Holdings at Concordia Historical Institute are noted in the bibliography after each title; some of the publications may also be held in other Lutheran archives and academic libraries.

a. **National:** *Affirm*; *Confessional Lutheran* (although ceasing before the 1969 LCMS convention, the *Confessional Lutheran* provides a thorough historical overview of theological issues culminating in Christ Seminary—Seminex.); *Lutheran News* / (later) *Christian News*; *Missouri in Perspective* / (later) *Lutheran Perspective.*

b. **Regional:** A group of more than sixty independent periodicals, often lay initiated and limited in time, deal almost exclusively with the issues preceding and surrounding Seminex. Overlapping content in such periodicals results from common sources, e.g., ELIM, Doctrinal Concerns Program / Organization.

2. Publications of LCMS institutions, Districts, and local Lutheran entities

a. **INSTITUTIONS**
Publications for both internal and external constituencies of Seminex, Concordia Seminary, and Concordia Senior College are listed, along with holdings at CHI. They should be considered primary source material on Seminex and related issues during the decade of focus.

Note that Senior College graduates were choosing between Concordia Seminary and Seminex in the fall of 1974.

b. **DISTRICTS** (examples below are not analyzed or listed in the bibliography)
District editions of *The Lutheran Witness* for the years of the controversy, e.g., English District (also *Lutheran Accent*, 1975–78), Southern Illinois (also *Contact*, 1973–75), Atlantic District, California-Nevada District. Many of these regional editions are held at CHI, along with District convention proceedings from the relevant years.

Note that not all District publications reflect the controversy in significant detail.

c. **LOCAL LUTHERAN ENTITIES** (one publication analyzed)
Examples include *St. Louis Lutheran*, *Badger Lutheran*, and *Cleveland Lutheran*. Not all such publications deal with the controversy in significant detail. Exception: Individual articles from the *St. Louis Lutheran* are included in the bibliography (see 2.2.3), since this periodical provides the most complete local record of events and issues revolving around Seminex and seems to have published many or most of the Seminex press releases.

Online Tools and Resources for Locating Cited Materials and Additional Materials for Investigation

1. **WORLDCAT**

Most public and academic libraries provide access to OCLC's WorldCat (the free public version) or to WorldCat via FirstSearch (a paid subscription by libraries). The public version is readily available online at **www.worldcat.org**.

In different ways, both versions of WorldCat display holding libraries of the publications searched, whether books or periodicals.

Note that CHI cataloged library holdings display in FirstSearch WorldCat but not in the public (free) version.

2. **ATLA RDB and ATLAS[ERIES] PLUS**

The American Theological Library Association Religion Database (ATLA RDB or ATLAS[eries] Plus) indexes a wide range of religious periodicals and essay collections. Many articles are provided in full text (PDF). Many of the signed journal articles in the bibliography can be found here.

In addition to the availability of the ATLA RDB at most theological schools and seminaries, seminary alumni—including those of Concordia Seminary, Saint Louis, and Concordia Theological Seminary, Fort Wayne, Indiana—may receive access to the database on request to the libraries of their alma mater.

Denominational publications, such as *The Lutheran Witness* and *The Lutheran*, are generally not found in this database; however, WorldCat will provide names and locations of libraries holding the paper or microform volumes of these "house organs." Also, institutions are increasingly digitizing their print publications to make them available online.

3. **Digitized resources**

At the time of compiling this bibliography, online access to at least two major categories of cited resources was available:

a. Wisconsin Lutheran Seminary (WELS), Mequon: Faculty and student papers at **www.wls.wels.net/resources/essay-files**

b. Concordia Seminary, Saint Louis: Selected print and audiovisual resources at **scholar.csl.edu**

The process of digitizing print, sound, and video recordings is ongoing at Concordia Seminary Library as well as at other Lutheran university and seminary libraries likely to hold relevant materials.

4. **Various resources available online** (both print and nonprint)

For example, to access contemporary interviews and news programs on local television, users of YouTube, the popular online source of audio and video, can search relevant terms such as "Seminex" or prominent individuals in the controversy such as "John Tietjen."

5. **Local newspapers**

Coverage may be searched, for example, at **www.newspapers.com**, a comprehensive, indexed digital archive of more than 11,000 newspapers (requiring a paid subscription to access). Many newspapers provide their own online archives, but searchability and cost vary.

Note: For online researchers using the keyword "seminex": A Peabody, Massachusetts, corporation named "SemiNex" manufactures high-powered diode lasers.

Resources Available at Concordia Historical Institute

1. Many of the relevant **PUBLISHED MONOGRAPHS AND DOCUMENTS** in the Concordia Historical Institute Library are discoverable at: **bridges.searchmobius.org/search**

2. **PERIODICALS** in the Concordia Historical Institute Library can be searched by typing the title of the periodical (in quotation marks) at: **concordiahistoricalinstitute.libraryhost.com**

3. **ARCHIVAL DOCUMENTS, CORRESPONDENCE, AUDIOVISUAL MATERIALS, ARTIFACTS, AND PHOTOGRAPHS**, including many items previously closed for research, can be searched at: **concordiahistoricalinstitute.libraryhost.com**

   (See also **8.1** ***Concordia Historical Institute***)

Conclusion

The primary focus of the bibliography is on published sources, admittedly some quite obscurely or privately published. Any bibliography is, to be sure, a work in progress, as more resources are "out there," known or yet to be discovered by others. In its ongoing goal of keeping future editions of this bibliography as comprehensive as possible, Concordia Historical Institute will be most grateful to learn of other published works, articles, etc., as well as archival materials, directly related to the subject of Seminex.

David O. Berger
Feast of All Saints 2019

Acknowledgments

Appreciation is expressed for the assistance given by the Executive Director of Concordia Historical Institute, Dr. Daniel Harmelink, in the organization and editing of the material in this publication. Appreciation is also expressed for the Reference and Research staff at Concordia Historical Institute, especially Mark Bliese and Todd D. Zittlow (CHI archivist), as well as Donna Church (Public Services Librarian) and Wayne Seitz (Coordinator, Digital Services) at Concordia Seminary Library.

Acronyms and Abbreviations Used

AAL – Aid Association for Lutherans

AATS – American Association of Theological Schools (later **ATS**)

AAUP – American Association of University Professors

ACDC – [LCMS] Advisory Committee on Doctrine and Conciliation

AELC – Association of Evangelical Lutheran Churches

ALC – American Lutheran Church

ATLA – American Theological Library Association

ATS – Association of Theological Schools (previously **AATS**)

BoC – Board of Control (of LCMS higher education institutions)

CCM – [LCMS] Committee / Commission on Constitutional Matters

CHI – Concordia Historical Institute (LCMS Department of Archives and History)

CLC – Church of the Lutheran Confession

CNLC – Commission for a New Lutheran Church

CoP – [LCMS] Council of [District] Presidents

CRM – *Candidatus reverendi ministerii*

CTCR – [LCMS] Commission on Theology and Church Relations

CTM – *Concordia Theological Monthly* (faculty journal, Concordia Seminary)

ELCA – Evangelical Lutheran Church in America

ELIM – Evangelical Lutherans in Mission

FFC – [LCMS] Fact Finding Committee

IELC – India Evangelical Lutheran Church

LAHE – Lutheran Association of Higher Education (Saint Louis)

LCA – Lutheran Church in America

LCA – Lutheran Church of Australia

LCM – Lutheran Church in Mission

LCMS – The Lutheran Church—Missouri Synod

LCUSA – Lutheran Council in the United States of America

LLL – Lutheran Laymen's League

LSTC – Lutheran School of Theology at Chicago

NCA – North Central Association (higher education accrediting agency)

SDA – Seventh-Day Adventists

WELS – Wisconsin Evangelical Lutheran Synod

Note: A key document in the controversy—A Statement of Scriptural and Confessional Principles—*is often referred to simply as* A Statement.

Photograph by Paul Ockrassa

Prof. Robert Bertram reports on the decision of the Faculty Advisory Committee to an assembly of students and faculty in Wyneken Chapel during the moratorium in January 1974.

Chronology of Events

Christ Seminary—Seminex

Adapted from John H. Tietjen, *Memoirs in Exile: Confessional Hope and Institutional Conflict.* Minneapolis: Fortress Press, 1990. Pages xiii–xvi. Used with permission.

May 19, 1969	John Tietjen elected president of Concordia Seminary, Saint Louis
June 12, 1969	J. A. O. Preus elected president of The Lutheran Church—Missouri Synod
May 17, 1970	Preus publicly announces his intention to take action on alleged departures from the Missouri Synod's doctrinal position
September 9, 1970	Preus announces appointment of a Fact Finding Committee (FFC) to investigate the Concordia Seminary faculty
December 11, 1970	Interviews of the Concordia Seminary faculty begin
January 5, 1971	Concordia Seminary faculty announces its decision to continue participation in the FFC interviews, but under protest
March 6, 1971	Interviews of Concordia Seminary faculty by FFC conclude
June 15, 1971	Report of the FFC submitted to Preus
July 15, 1971	LCMS convention in Milwaukee defeats effort to require submission to convention-adopted doctrinal statements
July 15, 1971	LCMS convention in Milwaukee turns FFC report over to Concordia Seminary Board of Control (BoC)
September 20, 1971	Concordia Seminary BoC begins its review of the FFC report
December 13, 1971	Concordia Seminary BoC declines the reappointment of faculty member Arlis J. Ehlen
January 4, 1972	Concordia Seminary faculty asks to meet with Preus regarding the BoC decision concerning Ehlen
January 11, 1972	Preus advises of impending disciplinary action against Tietjen
January 18, 1972	Tietjen and Preus meet to work out a compromise
February 18, 1972	Preus withdraws from the compromise agreement and gives the Concordia Seminary BoC *A Statement of Scriptural and Confessional Principles* to serve as the standard for doctrinal review
March 5, 1972	Tietjen refuses to implement Preus's demand that Ehlen be barred from teaching exegetical courses
June 17, 1972	Concordia Seminary BoC issues its progress report to Preus, stating that it has not yet found false doctrine in the faculty

September 1, 1972	Preus issues his "Blue Book," a report condemning numerous unnamed Concordia Seminary faculty for teaching false doctrine
September 8, 1972	Tietjen issues *Fact Finding or Fault Finding?* to counter the "Blue Book"
September 20, 1972	LCMS Council of Presidents (CoP) announces a compromise to the controversy
October 26, 1972	Preus acts against CoP compromise
November 3, 1972	LCMS Commission on Theology and Church Relations (CTCR) issues a positive evaluation of *A Statement*
November 1972	Concordia Seminary faculty issues the document *Faithful to Our Calling, Faithful to Our Lord*
January 15, 1973	Concordia Seminary BoC completes its interviews with faculty, clearing all of the charge of false doctrine
July 10, 1973	LCMS convention in New Orleans affirms that convention-adopted doctrinal statements are binding
July 11, 1973	LCMS convention in New Orleans adopts *A Statement of Scriptural and Confessional Principles* as a binding doctrinal statement
July 12, 1973	LCMS convention in New Orleans condemns the Concordia Seminary faculty for teaching false doctrine
July 13, 1973	LCMS convention in New Orleans requires newly elected Concordia Seminary BoC to deal with future of Tietjen as president
July 23, 1973	Concordia Seminary faculty issues "A Declaration of Protest and Confession"
August 18, 1973	Concordia Seminary BoC suspends Tietjen as president and faculty member but then delays implementation of its action
August 28–29, 1973	Conference of Evangelical Lutherans meets in Chicago and organizes (later incorporated as Evangelical Lutherans in Mission [ELIM])
September 29, 1973	Concordia Seminary BoC "vacates" Tietjen suspension
December 13, 1973	Concordia Seminary faculty member A. C. Piepkorn dies
January 20, 1974	Concordia Seminary BoC suspends Tietjen as president
January 21, 1974	A majority of Concordia Seminary students announces a moratorium on classes
January 21, 1974	A majority of Concordia Seminary faculty members announce that they consider themselves to be suspended

February 17, 1974	Concordia Seminary BoC requires faculty decision to return to class or to be held in breach of their contract
February 18, 1974	A majority of faculty takes no action on the Concordia Seminary BoC demand
February 18, 1974	A majority of faculty and students stage "walkout" procession off the Concordia Seminary campus
February 19, 1974	A majority of students join faculty in resuming seminary education "in exile"
February 20, 1974	Classes of Concordia Seminary in Exile (Seminex) begin at Saint Louis University and Eden Seminary
April 10, 1974	William Kohn resigns as executive secretary of LCMS Board for Missions
May 11, 1974	Partners in Mission begins functioning as the mission arm of ELIM
May 24, 1974	First class graduates from Seminex
June 21, 1974	Concordia Seminary in Exile is legally incorporated
August 26–28, 1974	Second ELIM Assembly is held in Chicago
October 12, 1974	Concordia Seminary BoC removes Tietjen from office as president and faculty member
February 1, 1975	Seminex governing board elects Tietjen as president
April 14, 1975	A theological convocation is held to try to effect reconciliation
June 29, 1975	Missouri District official Oscar Gerken clears Tietjen of charges of false doctrine
July 4–11, 1975	LCMS convention in Anaheim, California, condemns ELIM, censures eight District presidents for ordaining uncertified Seminex graduates, and authorizes Preus to remove them from office
August 13–15, 1975	Third ELIM Assembly in Chicago authorizes formation of "a new association"
August 15, 1975	Seminex moves into its own facilities in the University Club Building at 607 N. Grand Blvd. in Saint Louis
February 28, 1976	A Coordinating Council for a new church organization is created
April 2, 1976	Preus removes four LCMS District presidents from office
June 19, 1976	English Synod is established out of the LCMS English District
August 18–20, 1976	Fourth ELIM Assembly is held in Chicago
December 3–4, 1976	Association of Evangelical Lutheran Churches (AELC) is organized with five constituent synods

May 12, 1977	Decision of the Seminex board to reduce staff precipitates crisis
August 19–20, 1977	Fifth ELIM Assembly is held in Chicago
September 28, 1977	LCMS vice president Theodore Nickel declares Tietjen removed from the LCMS ministerial roster
December 28, 1977	Concordia Seminary in Exile changes its name to Christ Seminary—Seminex
April 14–16, 1978	AELC issues "A Call for Lutheran Union"
October 13–14, 1978	Sixth ELIM Assembly is held in Saint Louis
January 22–23, 1979	AELC joins American Lutheran Church-Lutheran Church in America Committee on Lutheran Unity
December 14, 1979	AELC is invited to join ALC-LCA Consultation on Theological Education
June 20, 1980	William Lesher of the Lutheran School of Theology at Chicago (LSTC) meets with Tietjen in Denver to propose move of Seminex to the LSTC campus
October 3, 1981	Seminex board proposes merger of LSTC and Seminex
November 30, 1981	Representatives of Seminex and LSTC boards consider proposals for closer relations between the two schools
January 14, 1982	Seminex moves to new facilities at 539 N. Grand Blvd. in Saint Louis
January 29, 1982	Plan for three-way deployment of Seminex resources is proposed
May 1982	LSTC, Pacific Lutheran Theological Seminary, Lutheran Seminary Program in the Southwest / Wartburg Theological Seminary, and Seminex boards agree to a three-way deployment of Seminex resources
September 8, 1982	ALC, AELC, LCA conventions agree to unite and authorize a union process
September 1982	Commission for a New Lutheran Church (CNLC) begins its work
May 1983	Last Seminex commencement is held in Saint Louis
August 1983	Seminex students and staff disburse to Chicago; Berkeley, California; and Austin, Texas
August 29, 1986	ALC, AELC, LCA conventions agree to form the Evangelical Lutheran Church in America (ELCA)
April 30, 1987	Constituting convention of the ELCA begins
December 31, 1987	Seminex ceases to exist as an educational institution

1.0 Major Works and Documents

1.1 Books, Reports, Documents, and Pamphlets

(alphabetical order by author)

(* = See also corresponding book reviews identified under **5.0 *Reviews of Major Books on the Controversy***)

*Adams, James E. *Preus of Missouri and the Great Lutheran Civil War.* New York: Harper & Row, 1977. 237 pages.

Fourteen chapters: 1. Options at New Orleans; 2. The Missouri Waltz; 3. Synodical Cynicism; 4. Young Man Preus; 5. Awesome Seminarian Preus; 6. Scholar, Teacher, and Pastor; 7. From Norway to Missouri; 8. Eager-Beaver Seminary Builder; 9. Coyness Becomes Jack; 10. President Preus; 11. Doing It the Preus Way; 12. "Gospel" Preachers Versus "Bible" Teachers; 13. Preus at the Brink; 14. Preus Triumphant? Followed by Index.

Adams, an "outsider" journalist (religion editor of *The St. Louis Post-Dispatch*), presents biographical material "with a viewpoint" (x). J. A. O. Preus is presented as "this 'immoderate' man and his 'immoderate' church" (ix). In summarizing the place of J. A. O. Preus in the history of the LCMS, Adams concludes that "enforcing an inerrant Bible from now on will be more a church-wrecking than a church-building premise. An epoch is ending. It is unlikely that Jacob Aall Ottesen Preus of the Missouri Synod will do much in the long run to stop it, but he is not going to be ushered away without putting up a good fight" (237).

Note: A significant amount of James Adams's own research files and his hand-corrected copy of the published book are available for research in the Concordia Historical Institute collection.

Atlantic District, Lutheran Church—Missouri Synod, The. *Proceedings of the Special Convention.* Bronxville, New York: Atlantic District, 1974.

This special convention was held March 1–2, 1974, at Concordia, Bronxville, New York.

Baker, Tom [Thomas A.]. *Watershed at the Rivergate: 1,400* [the number of signatures to the document "Declaration of Determination"] *vs. 250,000* [the number of endorsements to the document "Crossroads"]. Sturgis, Michigan: Tom Baker, 1973. 120 pages.

An examination of events leading up to the 50th Regular Convention of the LCMS (1973) in New Orleans at the Rivergate Convention Center. Baker dedicates his work to "The Faithful Faculty Minority Five." Book presents material in three sections: 1. The Historical-Critical

Method; 2. The Neoliberal Political Organization; 3. The Future. Followed by Index.

Copies of this book were mailed to all delegates of the LCMS convention in New Orleans two months before the convention convened. The book is now in its third printing.

"[T]his book attempts to uncover and bring into the open the terribly sad fact that the polarization of the synod is not on account of personality conflicts or political power plays; instead, our synod is experiencing one of the most crucial and basic doctrinal disputes in its 125-year history" (5). "I have attempted to be as fair and honest as possible in arranging the material in order that issues rather than personalities remain the prime concern. . . . My prime concern has been to defend those who have been unjustly attacked and slandered because of their desire to maintain a united witness to the Gospel as the synod has believed, taught and confessed during its 125-year history" (5).

Baker, Tom [Thomas A.]. *Fellowship Principles of E.L.I.M.* [s.l., s.n.], 1975. 23 pages.

Available only at Concordia Seminary Library.

[Bertram, Robert W., et al.] *The Promising Tradition: A Reader in Law-Gospel Reconstructionist Theology.* Saint Louis: Concordia Seminary, 1973, 1974 (2nd ed.). 202 pages.

Articles by Robert W. Bertram, Walter R. Bouman, Werner Elert, Wenzel Lohff, Edward H. Schroeder, Robert C. Schultz, C. F. W. Walther, and Andrew M. Weyermann—some reprinted from other sources.

Bohlmann, Ralph A. *Principles of Biblical Interpretation in the Lutheran Confessions.* Revised edition. Saint Louis: Concordia Publishing House, 1968, 1983. 163 pages.

Contents presented in two parts: 1. The Confessional View of Holy Scripture; 2. Confessional Principles of Biblical Interpretation. With Introduction, Notes, and Bibliography.

From the Preface: "The subject matter of this volume was initially treated in a modest essay delivered to a meeting of seminary faculties and District Presidents of The Lutheran Church—Missouri Synod in November 1965" (11).

*Braaten, Carl. *Because of Christ: Memoirs of a Lutheran Theologian.* Grand Rapids: Eerdmans, 2010. 210 pages.

See especially his comments about Seminex on pages 118–21. Braaten believes the merging of Seminex into LSTC served as a catalyst for a theological and moral shift at LSTC.

Bretscher, Paul G. *After the Purifying.* River Forest, Illinois: Lutheran Education Association, 1975. 108 pages.

Contents in four chapters with Epilogue: 1. The Purifying; 2. The Word of Spirit and Life; 3. Stumbling Blocks and Unbelief; 4. The Use of Scripture in Lutheran Education.

From the Prologue by Paul W. Lange, chairman of the Lutheran Education Association Editorial Committee: "This unity is to be found in fidelity to the 'Word of God' and the administration of the Sacraments; fidelity not to a Book, a tradition, a legislative authority, or an elected leader, but unreservedly to the 'Word of God'" (v). From the Prologue: "The conflict which has been tearing The Lutheran Church—Missouri Synod for the past several years has overwhelming significance for the future of education in our church" (xi). "Our title embodies a vision. It suggests that what is happening in the Missouri Synod now is a purifying" (3).

Bretscher, Paul G. *The Sword of the Spirit.* Saint Louis: Evangelical Lutherans in Mission, 1979. 27 pages.

Contents presented in three sections: 1. The Sharpening of the Sword; 2. The Sword at War against a Falsified Word; 3. The Sword at War against a Falsified Church.

Dedicated to Richard and Dorothy Caemmerer and presented at the 1978 Assembly of ELIM on October 13–14, 1978. The booklet ends with a quote from 2 Corinthians 4:16–18 and the words: "No ox is so stubborn that he will not turn if only the goads of truth keep pricking him long enough."

*Burkee, James C. *Power, Politics, and the Missouri Synod: A Conflict that Changed American Christianity.* Minneapolis: Fortress Press, 2011. 256 pages.

Footnoted contents in four sections: 1. Change and Reaction in the LCMS: 1938–1965; 2. Countermovement: 1965–1969; 3. Power, Politics, and the Purge: 1969–1974; 4. Genie on the Loose: 1974–1981. With Photographs, Abbreviations, Bibliography, and Index.

Burkee writes in his Introduction: "I argue here what I believe everyone knows but few will confess: the schismatic history of the Lutheran Church—Missouri Synod is about more than just theology. I readily concede that theological language dominated the conflict as the synod polarized in the postwar years around the questions of truth: those who saw biblical truth in part as subjective, through historical and cultural lenses, and those who viewed it as definable and untouchable, transcending time and interpretation" (4). Burkee argues that the Seminex conflict marks the beginning of the long-term decline of the LCMS as a church body and comes to the conclusion that "Herman Otten was the single most influential conservative in the synod before 1969" (7).

Childs, James M., Robert D. Preus, Ralph W. Klein, Harold H. Buls, Harry A. Huth, and Robert Bertram. *The Nature and Function of Holy Scripture: Responses to the Essayists at the Theological Convocation Held at the Concordia Seminary, St. Louis, April 14–18, 1975.* Saint Louis: [s.n.], 1975. 79 pages.

1. Responding to Howard Tepker's "Inspiration and Inerrancy of the Holy Scriptures," James M. Childs and Robert Preus; 2. Responding to Martin Franzmann's "Historical-Critical Method," Ralph W. Klein and Harold H. Buls; 3. Responding to Fred Kramer's "Gospel-Scripture Relationship," Harry Huth and Robert W. Bertram.

*Concordia Seminary, Saint Louis, Board of Control. *Exodus from Concordia: A Report on the 1974 Walkout.* Saint Louis: Concordia College [Concordia Seminary], 1977. 186 pages.

Preface, followed by contents in ten sections, and nine appendices: 1. Doctrinal Concerns in the Sixties; 2. The Deepening Crisis, 1969–1973; 3. The New Orleans Convention, 1973; 4. Response to New Orleans; 5. The Year of Crisis Begins; 6. The Tension Heightens; 7. Suspension and Moratorium; 8. Outreach, Outrage, and Exodus; 9. Dealing with Exiles; 10. Epilogue. Includes photographs.

Concordia Seminary, Saint Louis, Faculty. *Faithful to Our Calling, Faithful to Our Lord: An Affirmation in Two Parts by the Faculty of Concordia Seminary, St. Louis, Missouri. Part I: A Witness to Our Faith: A Joint Statement and Discussion of Issues.* [Part 1 of 2.] Saint Louis: Concordia Seminary Office of Seminary Relations, [1973]. 43 pages.

First of two parts. Preamble and text of "Affirmations," followed by nine points of discussion (each discussion is followed by Scripture passages, citations from the Lutheran Confessions, and "secondary literature" references).

The "Affirmations" were adopted by Concordia's faculty on November 21, 1972. Those signing the document are listed on pages 10 and 11. ["Professors Mark Bangert, Ralph Bohlmann, and Martin Scharlemann were on leave and off campus at the time of the publication of these documents" (43).]

Concordia Seminary, Saint Louis, Faculty. *Faithful to Our Calling, Faithful to Our Lord: An Affirmation in Two Parts by the Faculty of Concordia Seminary, St. Louis, Missouri. Part II: I Believe: Personal Confessions of Faith and Discussion of Issues.* [Part 2 of 2.] Saint Louis: Concordia Seminary Office of Seminary Relations, [1973]. 156 pages.

Second of two parts. Introduction by John H. Tietjen, president, followed by personal confessions of faith by John H. Tietjen, John S. Damm, Kenneth H. Breimeier, Robert R. Bergt, Robert W. Bertram, Herbert J. A. Bouman, Richard R. Caemmerer Sr., Robert L. Conrad, John W. Constable, Frederick W. Danker, William J. Danker, David E. Deppe, Arlis J. Ehlen, Alfred O. Fuerbringer, Paul F. Goetting, Carl Graesser, Robert A. Grunow, Norman C. Habel, H. Lucille Hager, George W. Hoyer, Holland H. Jones, Everett R. Kalin, Wi Jo Kang, Richard Klann, Ralph W. Klein, Edgar M. Krentz, Paul G. Lessmann, Erwin L. Lueker, Herbert T. Mayer, Duane P. Mehl, Carl S. Meyer, Eldon E. Pederson, Arthur Carl Piepkorn, Robert D. Preus, Arthur C. Repp, Alfred von Rohr Sauer, Edward H. Schroeder, Kenneth J. Siess, Robert H. Smith, Gilbert A. Thiele, Arthur M. Vincent, Carl A. Volz, Walter Wegner, Robert J. Werberig, Andrew M. Weyermann, Leonhard C. Wuerffel, Lorenz Wunderlich. ["Professors Mark Bangert, Ralph Bohlmann, and Martin Scharlemann were on leave and off campus at the time of the publication of these documents" (156).]

Concordia Seminary, Saint Louis, Faculty and Executive Staff. *Response of the Faculty of Concordia Seminary, St. Louis, April 4, 1972* [to *A Statement of Scriptural and Confessional Principles*]. Saint Louis: [s.n.], 1972. 4 pages.

Danker, Frederick W. *Under Investigation.* [1st ed.] Saint Louis: [F. W. Danker], 1971. x, xxxiv leaves.

Danker, Frederick W. *Under Investigation.* [2nd ed.] Saint Louis: [F. W. Danker], 1971. x, xxxvi leaves.

*Danker, Frederick W., assisted by Jan Schambach. *No Room in the Brotherhood: The Preus-Otten Purge of Missouri.* Saint Louis: Clayton Publishing House, 1977. 378 pages.

Contexts in twenty-eight chapters with Foreword, Chapter Notes, and four pages of photographs by Steven M. Dietrich. 1. "Tietjen Must Go"; 2. Corporate Ego; 3. Gathering Storm; 4. Drill for Consensus; 5. Radical Integrity vs. Open Integrity; 6. Under Investigation; 7. Double Jeopardy; 8. "A Statement"; 9. "A Statement" Critique; 10. "Blue Book"; 11. "The War Is On!" 12. Battle of New Orleans—Stage I; 13. Battle of New Orleans—Stage II; 14. Protest; 15. Aborted Suspension; 16. The Goetting Case; 17. Mission under Fire; 18. Moratorium; 19. Indecision; 20. Moratorium Endorsed; 21. Showdown; 22. Dismissed! 23. "No Deal!" 24. Outreach; 25. Case of Appendix 6; 26. Exiled; 27. Death and Resurrection; 28. Conclusion.

Title page quote: "Truth is not decided by majority vote." According to the Foreword, there was to be a succeeding volume, detailing "the establishment of Seminex, the decisions of the English District, and the founding of the Association of Evangelical Lutheran Churches and subsequent developments. . . . As a third-generation member of the Lutheran Church—Missouri Synod, I am a partisan. As one who came under fire from my own church body for questioning it on certain issues, I can claim non-partisan objectivity."

Documents surrounding "A Statement [of the Forty-Four]." (1945–47), various paginations.

"A Statement [of the Forty-Four]" was signed by forty-four subscribers on September 7, 1945, at the Stevens (Conrad Hilton) Hotel in Chicago, with accompanying correspondence and related editorials.

Evangelical Lutherans in Mission. *Responses to Presentations Delivered at Theological Convocation, Concordia Seminary, St. Louis, Missouri: The Nature and Function of Holy Scripture: A Study Document Offered to the Members of The Lutheran Church—Missouri Synod.* Saint Louis: ELIM, 1975. 39 pages.

Heming, Carol Piper. "Elfrieda von Rohr Sauer: A Life Reinterpreted." Pages 119–38 in *Feminist Frontiers.* Kirksville, Missouri: Truman State University Press, 2010.

Hunter, Julius K. Pages 17–19 in *TV One-on-One.* [Saint Louis]: Gashouse Books, 2008.

Includes a short account of interview with J. A. O. Preus by a television news reporter who grew up in the LCMS but eventually joined an AELC congregation.

Knight, C. R. *For the Sake of the Gospel: A Historical Reader concerning the People and Events which Have Created Seminex.* Saint Louis: Student Coordinating Committee, Concordia Seminary in Exile, 1974. 90 pages.

Krentz, Edgar. *The Historical-Critical Method.* Guides to Biblical Scholarship. Edited by Gene M. Tucker. Philadelphia: Fortress Press, 1975. 88 pages.

Contents, with Editor's Foreword, presented in five chapters: 1. Introduction; 2. The Rise of Historical Criticism; 3. Goals and Techniques; 4. Presuppositions and Achievements; 5. Historical Criticism in Theological Discussion since 1945.

"The author makes clear how new developments have initially been regarded as threats to established intellectual and ecclesiastical interests, only to become common coin as time has moved on" (back cover). "The consensus was not reached without casualties. Many scholars, even in recent times, have paid the price of personal privation and suffering for their convictions. Historical criticism 'has throughout its history almost always stood in the cross-fire of a generally less than joyful polemic from the side of unenlightened orthodox zealots'" (3).

Lueker, Erwin L. *Confessing Movements.* [Saint Louis: Seminex], 1977. 23 pages.

Lueking, F. Dean. *Mission in the Making: The Missionary Enterprise among Missouri Synod Lutherans: 1846–1963.* Saint Louis: Concordia Publishing House, 1964.

"The thesis of the book is that Missouri Synod Lutherans shaped their missionary motives and practices from three main sources. These are called American evangelicalism, scholastic confessionalism, and evangelical confessionalism" (4). Lueking was one of the five finalists for the position of president of Concordia Seminary, Saint Louis, in 1969 and a public opponent of the Preus administration.

Lutheran Church—Missouri Synod, The. *A Brief Statement of the Doctrinal Position of the Missouri Synod.* Saint Louis: Concordia Publishing House, [1932]. 22 pages. [1947]. 23 pages.

Lutheran Church—Missouri Synod, The. *Convention Workbook / Reports and Overtures* and *Proceedings* of LCMS conventions (from 1969–77).

Lutheran Church—Missouri Synod, The. *The Mission Affirmations: Adopted at the 46th Convention of The Lutheran Church—Missouri Synod, June 1965.* Saint Louis: The Lutheran Church—Missouri Synod, 1965. 7 pages.

Lutheran Church—Missouri Synod, The. *Nature and Function of Holy Scripture: Theological Convocation, St. Louis, Missouri, April 14–18, 1975.* Saint Louis: Concordia Publishing House, 1975. 87 pages.

Following a Preface by J. A. O. Preus, five papers are presented: 1. "The Inspiration and Inerrancy of the Holy Scriptures," by Howard W. Tepker; 2. "Historical-Critical Method," by Martin H. Franzmann; 3. "The Church under the Scriptures," by Ralph A. Bohlmann; 4. "The Church under the Scriptures," by Herbert J. A. Bouman; 5. "Gospel-Scripture Relationship," by Fred P. Kramer.

"In December 1974 the Council of Presidents called for a theological convocation to discuss current theological concerns in our church. Jointly sponsored by the Council of Presidents, the Board of Directors of Synod, and the President of Synod, this convocation will bring together over 300 participants from all parts of the Lutheran Church—Missouri Synod" (3).

Lutheran Church—Missouri Synod, The. *Report of the Advisory Committee on Doctrine and Conciliation.* Saint Louis: Concordia Publishing House, 1976. 147 pages.

Contents in two sections: 1. Position Papers and Responses; 2. Proposals for Dealing with the Issues. Each of four parts under section 1 (a. Inspiration and Inerrancy; b. Gospel and Scripture; c. Historical-Critical Method; d. Third Use of the Law) is organized in four parts: 1. Moderate Position Paper; 2. Conservative Position Paper; 3. Moderate Response to Conservative Position Paper; 4. Conservative Response to Moderate Position Paper. "Moderate Proposals" and "Conservative Proposals" make up the two parts under section 2. Appendix: Moderate Caucus Evaluation of The Report of the Advisory Committee on Doctrine and Conciliation (145–47).

From the Foreword by LCMS President J. A. O. Preus: "For many years, going back to the administration of President Behnken and President Harms, The Lutheran Church—Missouri Synod has been involved in doctrinal controversy. Charges and counter charges of doctrinal difference within the Synod have abounded. These matters came to a head and were the central focus of attention at the 1973 synodical convention. At this convention 'A Statement of Scriptural and Confessional Principles' was adopted by the Synod as a 'more formal and comprehensive statement of belief' (1973 Resolution 3-01), and that which has been referred to as a 'faculty majority position' was rejected. Following the 1973 convention, charges, including charges of false doctrine, were brought against the president of Concordia Seminary and he was suspended from office.

"Because some confusion seemed to characterize the doctrinal discussions which have gone on for many years and most especially which followed in the wake of the New Orleans convention, in January 1974, after discussions with the Council of Presidents, the Board of Directors, and the Commission on Theology and Church Relations, I appointed the Advisory Committee on Doctrine and Conciliation. To this committee were appointed 15 well-known and articulate theologians representing the diverse theological positions within the Synod and a journalistic consultant. Two tasks were assigned to this committee: 1) delineate the issues, and 2) develop proposals for dealing with the issues in such a way that the Synod can under God and by His grace achieve doctrinal consensus."

The committee began its work in January 1974. It was hoped this report would be published and distributed before the LCMS convention in Anaheim (July 1975). Members of the committee: Karl L. Barth, William T. Eggers, Arthur F. Graudin, H. Armin Moellering, Robert D. Preus, Don Ridgeway, Lorenz Wunderlich, James [M.] Childs Jr., Walter A. Christopher, Carl A. Gaertner, Lloyd H. Goetz, Ralph W. Klein, Richard A. Lischer, Samuel J. Roth.

Lutheran Church—Missouri Synod, The. *A Statement of Scriptural and Confessional Principles.* [Saint Louis: The Lutheran Church—Missouri Synod], 1973. 5 pages.

Lutheran Church—Missouri Synod, The, Commission on Theology and Church Relations. *Gospel and Scripture: The Interrelationship of the Material and Formal Principles in Lutheran Theology. A Report of the Commission on Theology and Church Relations: The Lutheran Church—Missouri Synod: November 1972.* Saint Louis: LCMS Commission on Theology and Church Relations, 1972. 23 pages.

"As the President of The Lutheran Church—Missouri Synod noted in his address to the 1971 Synodical Convention there has been increasing confusion within Lutheranism in recent years concerning the proper interrelationship of Gospel and Scripture" (4). "New impetus to the study was given in 1970 when the English District referred to the CTCR a memorial calling for a reaffirmation of the primacy of the Gospel" (4–5).

Lutheran Church—Missouri Synod, The, Commission on Theology and Church Relations. *Guiding Principles for the Use of* A Statement of Scriptural and Confessional Principles*: With Special Reference to the Expression of Dissent. A Report of the Commission on Theology and Church Relations: The Lutheran Church—Missouri Synod: November 1973.* Saint Louis: LCMS Commission on Theology and Church Relations, 1973. 13 pages.

This booklet was drafted at the request of LCMS President Preus, discussed with the LCMS Council of Presidents (July and September 1973), and submitted to the CTCR (September 1973) for "further consideration" (3). "After discussion and revision in two meetings of the commission, it was formally adopted for distribution throughout the Synod" (3). Note that the full text of Resolution 3-01 is included as a footnote.

Ralph Bohlmann was executive secretary of the CTCR at the time this report was written and published.

Lutheran Church—Missouri Synod, The, Commission on Theology and Church Relations. *Report on Dissent from* A Statement of Scriptural and Confessional Principles *and Other Doctrinal Resolutions of The Lutheran Church—Missouri Synod. September 1974.* Saint Louis: LCMS, 1974. 24 pages.

Contents presented under three sections: 1. Survey of Materials Received [at the New Orleans convention in opposition to *A Statement*]; 2. General Criticisms; 3. Specific Criticism. Includes one-page Conclusion.

"[A]n examination of the major criticisms of the theological formulations and content of '*A Statement*' has shown no cause why the Commission on Theology and Church Relations should alter its opinion of November 21, 1972" (23).

Lutheran Church—Missouri Synod, The, Counselor's Conference. *A Symposium of Essays and Addresses Given at the Counselors Conference: Valparaiso, Indiana, September 7–14, 1960.* Saint Louis: Concordia Publishing House, [1960].

Note especially "The State of the Church," by John W. Behnken; "Revelation-Scripture-Interpretation," by Martin H. Franzmann; "Scripture, Confessions, and Doctrinal Statements," by Arthur C. Repp; "Our Newest Frontier: Theology," by Alfred O. Fuerbringer. Franzmann, Repp, and Fuerbringer were on the faculty of Concordia Seminary.

Lutheran Council in the U.S.A. *The Function of Doctrine and Theology in Light of the Unity of the Church: A Report Plus 15 Papers from an Official Study Conducted by the Division of Theological Studies, Lutheran Council in the USA, during 1972–77.* Studies series. New York: Lutheran Council in the U.S.A., 1978. 93 pages.

Report and Articles on "Definitions of Gospel, Doctrine, Theology, and Consensus," "Consensus in the Gospel as the Basis for Fellowship," "The Interrelatedness of the Gospel," "Biblical Interpretation," and "Theological Diversity in a Confessional Church," by Warren A. Quanbeck, Robert C. Schultz, Roland A. Hopmann, Edgar M. Carlson, Ralph A. Bohlmann, Charles S. Anderson, H. George Anderson, Robert D. Preus, Duane A. Priebe, Albert M. Marcis.

Lutherans for Openness and Trust. *A Call to Openness and Trust.* Saint Louis: Lutherans for Openness and Trust, 1970. 6 pages.

*Marquart, Kurt E. *Anatomy of an Explosion: Missouri in Lutheran Perspective.* Concordia Seminary Monograph Series 3. Fort Wayne, Indiana: Concordia Theological Seminary Press, 1977. 170 pages.

Introduction by Robert D. Preus, president, Concordia Theological Seminary. Contents in four parts with Epilogue: 1. Needed: A Realistic "Model" of the Missouri Synod Conflict; 2. The Basic Principles; 3. The Counter-Confessional (Ecumenical) Attack; 4. The Counter-Biblical (Critical) Attack. Appendix A: Church Fellowship; Appendix B: Fellowship in Its Necessary Context of the Doctrine of the Church.

*Marquart, Kurt E. *Anatomy of an Explosion: A Theological Analysis of the Missouri Synod Conflict.* Grand Rapids: Baker Book House, 1978. 176 pages.

Montgomery, John Warwick. *Crisis in Lutheran Theology: The Validity and Relevance of Historic Lutheranism vs. Its Contemporary Rivals.* Volume 1 of 2 volumes. Grand Rapids: Baker, 1967. 133 pages.

Preface by J. A. O. Preus, president, Concordia Theological Seminary, Springfield, Illinois.

In this volume Montgomery first uses vocabulary that would later be referred to by others as "Gospel Reductionism" (120).

Mueller, Richard E. *What God Hath Joined Together. . . .* Saint Louis: ELIM, 1981. 15 pages.

Nelson, Jeffrey S. *The Theology of Inexpedience: Two Case Studies in "Moderate" Congregational Dissent in The Lutheran Church—Missouri Synod.* Lanham, Maryland: University Press of America, 1998. 160 pages.

Otten, Herman. *Marquart's Legacy: Kurt Marquart, "the International Luther."* New Haven, Missouri: Lutheran News, 2006. 74 pages.

Preus, Jacob A. O. *The Authority of Scripture.* Springfield, Illinois: Concordia Seminary Printshop, 1969. 71 pages.

Convention essay, Alberta-British Columbia District, LCMS, Calgary, Alberta, February 14–17, 1966.

Preus, Jacob A. O. *Bethany College Reformation Lectures.* 1973.

Uses term "Gospel reductionism" in describing Luther vs. Zwingli.

Preus, Jacob A. O. *Keynote Address: Theological Convocation, St. Louis, Missouri.* Saint Louis: Concordia Seminary, 1975. 10 pages.

Preus, Jacob A. O. *A Letter to the Members of The Lutheran Church—Missouri Synod: Congregations, Pastors, Teachers.* Saint Louis: LCMS, Office of the President, 1972. 4 pages.

March 3, 1972, communique concerning developments at Concordia Seminary sent to all LCMS pastors, teachers, and professors. Attached was a copy of *A Statement of Scriptural and Confessional Principles.*

Preus, Jacob A. O. *Report of the Synodical President to The Lutheran Church—Missouri Synod in Compliance with Resolution 2-28 of the 49th Regular Convention of the Synod, Held at Milwaukee, Wisconsin, July 9–16, 1971: Upon Receipt of Progress Report of the Board of Control of Concordia Seminary, St. Louis, Missouri, Relative to Its Action Taken on the Basis of the Report of the Fact Finding Committee Appointed by the Synodical President, September 1, 1972.* Saint Louis: LCMS, Office of the President, 1975. 160 pages.

Contents presented in eight parts: 1. Preface; 2. Historical Introduction; 3. Summary of the Findings; 4. Table of Divergent Positions Held by Various Members of the Faculty; 5. The Findings by Topics (eleven subpoints: The Holy Scriptures; The Inerrancy of the Scriptures; The Authority of the Scriptures; The Gospel; The Historical-Critical Method; Permissiveness; The Ordination of Women to the Pastoral Ministry; The Third Use of the Law; Commitment to the Lutheran Confessions; The Seminary's Responsibility toward the Synod's Doctrinal Stance; Conversations with Seminary Students); 6. The Report of the Board of Control of Concordia Seminary, St. Louis, Missouri; 7. Statement by the Synodical President; 8. Epilog. Appendices in six parts.

Preus, Jacob A. O. *Report to the Church.* Saint Louis: LCMS, Office of the President, 1975. 19 pages.

Preus, Jacob A. O. *A Study Edition of* A Statement of Scriptural and Confessional Principles. Saint Louis: [s.n.], 1972. 47 pages.

Contents under six sections and Conclusion: 1. Christ as Savior and Lord; 2. Law and Gospel; 3. Mission and the Church; 4. Holy Scripture (subsections: a. The Inspiration of Scripture; b. The Purpose of Scripture; c. The Gospel and Holy Scripture; d. The Authority of Scripture; e. The Canonical Text of Scripture; f. The Infallibility of Scripture; g. The Unity of Scripture; h. Old Testament Prophecy; i. Historical Methods of Biblical Interpretation); 5. Original Sin; 6. Confessional Subscription.

Includes Preface by CTCR Executive Secretary Ralph Bohlmann and reprint of Resolution 3-01 (1973 *Proceedings* at New Orleans).

Preus, Robert D. *"Fellowship Reconsidered": An Assessment of Fellowship between the LCMS and the ALC in the Light of Past, Present and Future.* Casper, Wyoming: Mount Hope Lutheran Church, 1971. 24 pages.

Printing of an essay given at the April 13–15, 1971, Wyoming District Pastors Conference.

Preus, Robert D. "The Hermeneutics of the Lutheran Confessions and the Historical-Critical Method." Pages 65–75 in *The Function of Doctrine and Theology in Light of the Unity of the Church: Materials Distributed by the Division of Theological Studies, Lutheran Council in the USA, for Study and Discussion.* New York: Lutheran Council in the USA, 1978.

Repp, Arthur C. *Letter to Herman C. Scherer and Ralph A. Bohlmann.* Typescript / Mimeograph copy, 1973. 13 pages.

Regarding *A Statement of Scriptural and Confessional Principles*

Sauer, Alfred von Rohr, and Eleanor F. Sauer. *Adam, Look Not Back: A Commemorative Booklet of Sauer Family History.* [Saint Louis: Office of Seminary Relations, Christ Seminary—Seminex], 1981. 60 pages.

Personal accounts under three sections: 1. Personal Remembrances; 2. Chapel Addresses; 3. Historical Reminiscences.

Includes photographs of the Christ Seminary—Seminex faculty, explanations of the stained-glass windows dedicated to Alfred and Eleanor, and a Norman C. Habel hymn commemorating Alfred's seventieth birthday. Five hundred copies were printed; the copy in the Concordia Historical Institute collection is personally signed and numbered "Number 181 of 500."

Scaer, David P. "John Tietjen, John Damm, and Seminex." Pages 129–42 in *Surviving the Storms: Memoirs of David P. Scaer.* [S. l.]: Luther Academy, 2018.

Scharlemann, Martin H. (Martin Henry). "The Inerrancy of Scripture." (unpublished essay). 1958. 15 pages.

Scharlemann, Martin H. *The Making of a Theologian: Selected Works of Martin H. Scharlemann.* Edited by Richard P. Lieske, with an introduction by Richard Klann. Saint Louis: Student Association of Concordia Seminary, 1984. 182 pages.

A collection of previously unpublished works. See "The Pastor as Scholar" (61–76); "Biography" (177–78); "An Appreciation" (179–82).

Schmidt, Stephen A. "American Education: A Lutheran Footnote." Pages 168–93 in *The Lutheran Church in North American Life, 1776–1976.* Edited by John E. Groh and Robert H. Smith. Saint Louis: Clayton Publishing House, 1979. [See also pages 190–91.]

Schroeder, Edward H., and Paul A. Zimmerman. *The Wars of Missouri That Led to Seminex: A Retrospective.* Parts 1–3. Saint Louis: Concordia Seminary Library, 2007. [printed from website]

Handout from Thursday Theology, 482–484. Crossings website. Also at https://crossings.org/?s=zimmerman

"A Statement [of the Forty-Four]." [S.l., s.n.], 1945.

Signed September 7, 1945, at the Stevens (Conrad Hilton) Hotel, Chicago, with accompanying correspondence and editorials concerning the issuance of "A Statement [of the Forty-Four]." Available at Concordia Seminary Library: microfiche 91-120.

Contents: A. "A Statement"; B. Letter accompanying "A Statement," sent to all pastors of the Synod, dated September 20, 1945 / [Evangelical Lutheran Synod of Missouri, Ohio and Other States Continuation Committee]; C. A pamphlet of correspondence between Dr. J. W. Behnken and Rev. E. J. Friedrich / J. W. Behnken; D. Editorial page of *The Lutheran Witness* 65:11, May 21, 1946, containing caption titles: "The district presidents and the Chicago Statement" and "Formulating Six points"; E. Letter to the clergy of the Synod dated July 3, 1946 / The President's Committee of Ten; F. Letter to the clergy of the Missouri Synod, date written in (8/5/46) / The Continuation Committee; G. Letter to the clergy of the Synod from the Office of the President, with caption title: "Meetings of the 'Ten and Ten,'" date written in (12/10/46) / J. W. Behnken; H. Letter to the clergy of the Synod from the Office of the President, giving an overview of the situation concerning "A Statement," dated January 18, 1947 / J. W. Behnken; I. An agreement / E. W. A. Koehler; released at the request of a number of men from seven districts of Synod. [Contents described from Concordia Seminary Library catalog record.]

Tietjen, John H. *Fact Finding or Fault Finding? An Analysis of President J. A. O. Preus' Investigation of Concordia Seminary.* Saint Louis: Concordia Seminary, 1972. 35 pages.

Contents presented in two parts with introduction and conclusion. 1. General Analysis of the Seminary Investigation; 2. Detailed Analysis of the Fact Finding Report.

Tietjen presents his judgment that the investigation of Concordia Seminary faculty by J. A. O. Preus through a Fact Finding Committee was unfair and prejudiced and the results of the investigation were unreliable, distorted, and "less than Lutheran" (2).

*Tietjen, John H. *Memoirs in Exile: Confessional Hope and Institutional Conflict.* Minneapolis: Fortress Press, 1990. 368 pages.

Contents presented in fifteen chapters in three parts: 1. "If Your Brother Sins against You"; 2. "If He Will Not Listen to You"; 3. "For Where Two or Three Come Together." Includes Preface and Epilogue, Abbreviations, Chronology of Events, and Index.

"My first intention . . . is to tell what happened as I experienced it. I make no pretense at writing a definitive history of the events and the period I am describing. I was after all a partisan in the struggle . . . and confess that I am a partisan still. I tell the story from my perspective, as I saw it happen. What I write belongs, therefore, to the category of memoirs" (vi). Tietjen chronicles his personal experiences during and after the controversy, believing he was the lightning rod for unjust persecution by J. A. O. Preus and his minions over what he believed to be an authentic Lutheran confession of "the gospel." Despite feeling victimized, Tietjen sees himself as a driving force in bringing new life from death in establishing Christ Seminary—Seminex and ultimately the formation of the ELCA. The last words of his memoir: "God brings life out of death."

Todd, Mary. *Authority Vested: A Story of Identity and Change in The Lutheran Church—Missouri Synod.* Grand Rapids: Eerdmans, 2000. 336 pages.

Contents in six chapters with Abbreviations, Introduction, Appendix, Bibliography, and Index. 1. Defining the Decade, 1831–1841: The Formative Years; 2. Establishing an Identity: The Nineteenth Century; 3. Identity Redefined: A Twentieth-Century Church? 4. The Issue of Authority: Woman Suffrage; 5. "Not in God's Lifetime": The Significance of the Ordination of Women; 6. The Problem of Authority. Note: See pages 218–47 for discussions related to the Seminex controversy.

"Todd chronicles the history of this struggle for identity in the LCMS, critically examining the central—often contentious—issue of authority in relation to Scripture, ministry, and the role of women in the church."

Todd, Mary. "The Curious Case of the Missouri Synod." Pages 26–44 in *Lutherans Today: American Lutheran Identity in the Twenty-First Century.* Edited by R. P. Cimino. Grand Rapids: Eerdmans, 2003.

Wangerin, Walter, and Paul Manz. *Una Sancta: A Mass in Thanksgiving for the Unity of the Body of Christ.* Chicago: Christ Seminary—Seminex, 1986. 39 pages.

Performed with the Seminex Chorus in 1986 and 1987. Title page verso: "Presented for use at the uniting of Lutheran churches in 1988."

*Zimmerman, Paul A. *A Seminary in Crisis: The Inside Story of the Preus Fact Finding Committee.* Saint Louis: Concordia Publishing House, 2007. 444 pages.

Contents presented in ten chapters with Foreword, Preface, Notes, Bibliography, and Supplements: 1. Storm Clouds Gathering; 2. President J. A. O. Preus Seeks a Solution; 3. The Committee in Action; 4. Initial Report of the Fact Finding Committee; 5. The Plot Thickens; 6. Finally—The Facts Emerge; 7. The New Orleans Convention; 8. The Counterattack that Failed; 9. The Storm Slowly Passes; 10. Lessons for the Present and Future.

Zimmerman is "one of two living members of the Fact Finding Committee appointed by LCMS President J. A. O. Preus to investigate charges of false doctrine being taught at Concordia Seminary in the 1970s" (back cover). "Beginning with the 1947 division over church fellowship, Zimmerman sheds light on the numerous controversies that culminated in charges against the faculty for teaching contrary to the LCMS position on biblical authority. Zimmerman shares his personal account of the Fact Finding Committee interviews, coupled with pertinent passages from convention documents, bylaws, and findings of the committee. This book includes the full report of the Fact Finding Committee, never before made public, and the 'Blue Book,' the complete 1972 report of the synodical president" (back cover).

1.2 Academic Theses, Dissertations, Student and Conference Papers

(alphabetical order by author)

Barnhart, Melody Ruth. *Heresy vs. Orthodoxy: The Preus / Tietjen Controversy.* MS thesis, University of North Texas, Denton, 1991. 187 leaves.

Becker, Siegbert W. *The Historical-Critical Method of Biblical Interpretation.* Faculty paper, Wisconsin Lutheran Seminary, Mequon, [1976 or 1977 ?]. 36 pages.

Note: Wisconsin Lutheran Seminary (WELS) essays and papers available at http://essays.wls.wels.net/

Bolwerk, Jeffery. *Trinity Evangelical Lutheran Church, Jackson, Wisconsin: Their Split with The Lutheran Church—Missouri Synod.* Student paper for Modern Christianity course, Wisconsin Lutheran Seminary, Mequon, December 2006. 32 pages.

Burkee, James Christian. *Pastors and Politics: The Conservative Movement in The Lutheran Church—Missouri Synod, 1956–1981.* PhD dissertation, Northwestern University, Evanston, Illinois, 2003. 329 pages.

Carter, John. *A History of Good Shepherd Ev[angelical] Lutheran Church, Downers Grove, Illinois.* Student paper for Senior Church History course, Wisconsin Lutheran Seminary, Mequon, May 1986. 23 pages.

Cohen, Mark David. *Taking God Seriously: A Study of a Lutheran Church.* MS thesis, University of Wisconsin, Madison, 1989. 70 leaves.

Fuliga, Jose B. *The Historical-Critical Method: Dividing Wall between Moderates and Conservatives in The Lutheran Church—Missouri Synod Controversy.* ThD dissertation, Concordia Seminary, Saint Louis, 1982. 291 leaves.

Grönberg, Erik K. J. *Adaptive Leadership in Crisis: John Tietjen, Concordia Seminary, and The Lutheran Church—Missouri Synod Crisis of 1969 to 1975.* PhD dissertation, Dallas Baptist University, Gary Cook School of Leadership, 2017. 212 pages.

Hayes, Laurie A. S. *The Rhetoric of Controversy in The Lutheran Church—Missouri Synod with Particular Emphasis on the Years 1969–1976.* PhD dissertation, University of Wisconsin–Madison, 1980. 2 volumes, 610 leaves.

LaBore, Richard D. *Traditions and Transitions: A Study of the Leadership of The Lutheran Church—Missouri Synod during a Decade of Theological Change, 1960–1969.* PhD dissertation, Saint Louis University, 1980. 427 pages.

Lentner, Charles David. *The Use of Authority in Church Conflict Management.* STM thesis, Concordia Seminary in Exile, Saint Louis, 1977. 84 leaves.

Lotz, David W. *An Appraisal of the Theological Crisis in the Missouri Synod.* Prepared for a Special Atlantic District (LCMS) Convention (March 1–2, 1974). 8 leaves. Also published in *In Touch* (June or July 1974).

Held in the "1974 Atlantic District Special Convention" materials at Concordia Historical Institute.

Lotz, David W. *A Brief Synopsis of the Major Theological-Doctrinal Issues* [in the LCMS]. Prepared for a Special Atlantic District (LCMS) Convention (March 1–2, 1974). 14 leaves. Also published in *In Touch* (June or July 1974).

Held in the "1974 Atlantic District Special Convention" materials at Concordia Historical Institute.

*Lotz, David W. *A Critical Appraisal of* "A Statement of Scriptural and Confessional Principles." Prepared for a Special Atlantic District (LCMS) Convention (March 1–2, 1974). 13 pages.

See also **3.1 *Signed Articles and Editorials***, Scaer, David P. "A Response to David Lotz' Writings." *The Springfielder* 38:3 (December 1974), pages 226–31.

Meitner, Paul S. *Martin Scharlemann: A Journey Back to Orthodoxy.* MDiv thesis, Wisconsin Lutheran Seminary, Mequon, 2002. 58 pages.

Mielens, Scott C. *"A House Divided": Theological Unrest in The Lutheran Church—Missouri Synod which Led to the Formation of the Association of Evangelical Lutheran Churches.* Student paper for Church History course, Wisconsin Lutheran Seminary, Mequon, May 1990. 13 pages.

Mueller, Daniel P. *The Politicalization of a Voluntary Organization: The Case of The Lutheran Church—Missouri Synod.* Paper for Sociology of Organizations course, 1973. 50 pages.

Held in the "LCMS General History: Dissertations" materials at Concordia Historical Institute.

Neeb, Larry W. (Larry William). *Historical and Theological Dimension of a Confessing Movement within The Lutheran Church—Missouri Synod.* DMin, Eden Theological Seminary, Saint Louis, 1975. 181 leaves.

Nickel, Ronald Paul. *Professional Autonomy in the Denominational Seminary: A Vulnerability Model: History and Analysis of the Conflict between The Lutheran Church—Missouri Synod and Concordia Seminary, St. Louis, 1969–1974.* PhD dissertation, Washington University, Saint Louis, 1977. 593 leaves.

Pless, Joel. *Cancer at Concordia: An Examination of How the Historical-Critical Method of Biblical Interpretation Was Introduced to the Classroom Teaching at Concordia Seminary, St. Louis, Missouri, and What Were the Subsequent Effects.* Student thesis, Wisconsin Lutheran Seminary, Mequon, May 1986. 112 pages.

Reko, H. Karl. *Determinative Factors in the Ability of Christ Seminary—Seminex Graduates to Conduct Worker-Priest Ministries in the United States.* DMin, Eden Theological Seminary, Saint Louis, 1980.

Riebe, Kimberly Kay. *Christ Seminary Seminex: An Adult Educations Series in American Church History.* Final research project, Lutheran Seminary Program in the Southwest, Austin, Texas, December 1995. 75 pages.

Robinson, Jack T. *The Spirit of Triumphalism in The Lutheran Church–Missouri Synod: The Role of the "A Statement* [of the Forty-Four]*" of 1945 in the Missouri Synod.* PhD dissertation, Vanderbilt University, 1972. 361 leaves.

Saatkamp, James. *A New Beginning: The Birth of the* Concordia Journal. Student paper, Wisconsin Lutheran Seminary, Mequon, December 2010. 18 pages.

Schallert, Jeffrey L. *Lights! Camera! Seminex! The Press and the Controversy in Missouri.* Student paper for Church History, Wisconsin Lutheran Seminary, Mequon, April 1984. 19 pages.

Scharlemann, Martin H. (Martin Henry). "The Bible as Record, Witness and Medium." 1959. 31 pages.

Possible conference paper. Written in pen on page 1: "Northern Illinois District, April 1959."

Scharlemann, Martin H. "This Matter of 'Inerrancy' Once Again." 1961. 9 pages.

Possible conference paper. Written on page 1: "To the Pastoral Conference of the Western District, June 14, 1961."

Schuetze, Armin W. *The WELS and the LCMS—Where Are We Today?* Paper read at the Nebraska District Convention, Waco, Nebraska, June 13–15, 1988.

Shaud, James H. *A Study in Idolatry: An Evaluation of the Doctrine of the Word in the Recent Lutheran Church—Missouri Synod Controversy, Based on Owen Barfield's Theory of the Idolatry of a Literal Consciousness.* PhD dissertation, Syracuse University, 1981. 187 leaves.

Wagner, Alvin E. *In Statu Confessionis* (A State of Confessional Protest) Adopted: Conference of Authentic Lutherans at North Hollywood, California, January 19, 1975. essays.wls.wels.net

Westra, Tom. *Missouri's New Direction: 1962 and 1973.* Student paper for Church History, Wisconsin Lutheran Seminary, Mequon, April 1985. 22 pages.

Wilson, Donn. *The Word-of-God Conflict in The Lutheran Church—Missouri Synod in the 20th Century.* MTh thesis, Luther Seminary, Saint Paul, Minnesota, 2018. 132 pages.

Wilson, James E. *The Association of Evangelical Lutheran Churches' Rhetoric of Unity, 1970–1987.* PhD dissertation, Indiana University, Bloomington, 1993. 271 leaves.

Wood, Kathryn Franzen. *Reluctantly American: The Schism in The Lutheran Church—Missouri Synod, 1969–1976.* PhD dissertation, University of Virginia, Charlottesville, 2004. 271+11 leaves.

1.3 Audiovisual Resources

(Including Resources Available Online)

(alphabetical by author / source)

Bode, Gerhard, and Erik Herrmann. *The LCMS: Controversy in the 1960s and 1970s.* Saint Louis: Concordia Seminary Library, March 8–May 16, 2010. Video recording.

scholar.csl.edu/controversylcms

A series of twenty video segments from a ten-week graduate-level course on controversies in the LCMS. See especially video sessions 12–20 (05a–08).

Note: Digitized versions of sound and video recordings held by Concordia Seminary Library / Media Services are available at: **scholar.csl.edu**

Bohlmann, Ralph A., and Robert W. Bertram. *Holy Scripture and the Gospel.* Springfield, Illinois: Concordia Theological Seminary, January 30, 1973. 1 hour, 27 minutes. Sound recording.

scholar.csl.edu/synodhistory/Synodical_History/Year/15

Debate recorded at Concordia Theological Seminary, Springfield, Illinois, spring 1973 regarding *A Statement* and *Faithful to Our Calling, Faithful to Our Lord.* The digitized version of the sound recording held at Concordia Theological Seminary, Fort Wayne, Indiana.

Opening Statements: Bohlmann (00:35–12:23), Bertram (12:23–26:52); Responses to Opening Statements: Bertram (27:02–34:37), Bohlmann (34:56–42:57); Responses to Questions: (43:02–1:27:00).

Evangelical Lutherans in Mission. *Coffee Kit.* Saint Louis: Evangelical Lutherans in Mission, 1974.

Frakes, Tim. *Seminex: Memories of a Church Divided.* [Glen Ellyn, Illinois:] TF Productions, 2015. Video recording.

Documentary video about the "walkout" at Concordia Seminary, February 19, 1974; includes interviews with Seminex students and faculty.

Hoyer, George W. *Student Prayer Assembly, January 20, 1974.* Saint Louis: Concordia Seminary Media Services, 1974. Sound recording.

KFUO. Kirchenkampf *1973–1974: The Lutheran Church—Missouri Synod Controversy at Concordia Seminary*. KFUO, Saint Louis, 1974. Radio.

Sound recording made by Concordia Seminary Media Services, Saint Louis, 1974.

KFUO broadcast from the campus of Concordia Seminary.

Lutheran Church—Missouri Synod, The. *Warrior of God, Man of Peace: The Life and Times of J. A. O. Preus*. Saint Louis: The Lutheran Church—Missouri Synod, 1995. Video recording.

Marty, Martin E., and Robert W. Bertram. *Rally for Seminex at Christ Church Cathedral, February 6, 1974.* Saint Louis: Concordia Seminary Media Services, 1974. Sound recording.

Nafzger, Samuel H. *A Statement* [*on Scriptural and Confessional Principles*]. Saint Louis: Concordia Seminary Media Services, 1974. 1 hour, 29 minutes. Sound recording.

scholar.csl.edu/sem/Recorded_Seminars/Year/76

Recording of a special presentation at Concordia Seminary, April 29, 1974. Since December 1973 Nafzger served as assistant executive secretary of the CTCR. In this presentation, Nafzger chronicles the history, intent, context, and status of *A Statement*—as well as the proper procedures for those who believe *A Statement* is not confessional, scriptural, or Lutheran. Nafzger responds to the charge that *A Statement* was created simply as a tool to conveniently remove faculty of Concordia Seminary, Saint Louis. Nafzger reports that 350 individuals have mailed the CTCR letters of dissent; Nafzger outlines the authority and purpose of the CTCR to respond to letters of dissent. Questions from students begin at 31:28. Nafzger quotes Richard John Neuhaus in believing *A Statement* was necessary because some were being dishonest in using similar vocabulary but with different meanings (1:10:20).

Preus, J. A. O. *The Greatest Challenge Facing the Missouri Synod Today*. Saint Louis: Concordia Seminary Media Services, 1977. Sound recording.

scholar.csl.edu/missions/World_Missions/Schedule/5

Recorded during a convocation at Concordia Seminary on March 23, 1977.

Preus, J. A. O. *Historical Reflections on the Walkout.* Saint Louis: Concordia Seminary Media Services, 1985. Sound and video recordings.

scholar.csl.edu/synodhistory/Synodical_History/Year/2

J. A. O. Preus discussing Seminex in a history class at Concordia Seminary.

Preus, J. A. O. *The State of Affairs in The Lutheran Church—Missouri Synod.* Saint Louis: Concordia Seminary Media Services, 1980. Sound recording.

scholar.csl.edu/sem/Recorded_Seminars/Year/40

Recorded during a convocation at Concordia Seminary on October 1, 1980.

Preus, J. A. O., and Rudolph Ressmeyer. "Interview with J. A. O. Preus and R. Ressmeyer." *Today Show.* NBC, KSD (now KSDK), Saint Louis, 1976. Television.

Video recording made by Concordia Seminary Media Services, Saint Louis.

Preus, Robert D. *Synodical Issues.* Saint Louis: Concordia Seminary Media Services, 1973. Sound recording.

scholar.csl.edu/synodhistory/Synodical_History/Year/19

Recorded during open forum at Concordia Seminary, October 24, 1973.

Rast, Lawrence, Jr. *What Happened to the LCMS during the 1970s?* Saint Louis: Concordia Seminary Library. *CSLScholar* December 2009. Video recording.

scholar.csl.edu/ccchurchhist3/64

Scharlemann, Martin H. *Historical-Critical What?* Saint Louis: Instructional Media Center, Concordia Seminary, 1973. Sound recording.

scholar.csl.edu/synodhistory/Synodical_History/Year/17

Address to Task Force on Seminary and Synod, October 24, 1973.

Scharlemann, Martin H. *Installation Service of Dean John Klotz, Dean Roland Hopmann, Daniel Moriarity, Arthur Graudin, Louis Brighton, and H. Paul Esala.* Saint Louis: Concordia Seminary Media Services, 1975. Sound recording.

Martin Scharlemann, preacher, July 26, 1974; rebuilding Concordia Seminary faculty.

Scharlemann, Martin H. *Radical Orthodoxy: Answer to Missouri's Problems.* Saint Louis: Instructional Media Center, Concordia Seminary, 1972. Sound recording.

scholar.csl.edu/synodhistory/Synodical_History/Year/32

Lecture at Concordia Seminary, May 18, 1972.

Scharlemann, Martin H., and Robert W. Bertram. *Conflict at Concordia.* KTVI, Saint Louis, 1975. Television.

Video recording made by Concordia Seminary Media Services, Saint Louis, 1975.

Theological Convocation, Concordia Seminary, Saint Louis. *Theological Convocation, Saint Louis, April 14–18, 1975.* Saint Louis: Concordia Publishing House, 1975. Sound recording.

Participants include Howard Tepker, Ralph Bohlmann, Martin Franzmann, Herbert J. A. Bouman, and Fred Kramer.

Tietjen, John H. *Update of Latest Board of Control Actions of November 19, 1973.* Saint Louis: Concordia Seminary Media Services, 1973. Sound recording.

scholar.csl.edu/synodhistory/Synodical_History/Year/1

Tietjen, John H., and Ralph A. Bohlmann. *Lutherans in Dispute.* KSD (now KSDK), Saint Louis, 1975. Television.

Video recording made by Concordia Seminary Media Services, Saint Louis, 1975.

Volz, Carl A. *The Content of* 'A Statement [on Scriptural and Confessional Principles].' Saint Louis: Concordia Seminary Media Services, January 1, 1974. 56 minutes. Sound recording.

scholar.csl.edu/synodhistory/Synodical_History/Year/27

A point-by-point critique of *A Statement of Scriptural and Confessional Principles.* Questions from students at 40:22.

Photograph by Paul Ockrassa

Concordia Seminary students gather in the gymnasium to discuss their response to the suspension of seminary president John Tietjen.

2.0 ARTICLES IN LUTHERAN PERIODICALS HELD IN THE CHI COLLECTION

2.1 Official LCMS Periodicals

2.1.1 *The Lutheran Witness* (signed articles)

(chronological order)

1972

Feucht, Oscar E. "The Bible, Its Nature and Form." 91:14 (November 5, 1972), pages 12–13, 24–25; "The Bible, Understanding It." 91:15 (November 26, 1972), pages 6–7, 26–27; "The Bible, Interpreting It." 91:16 (December 17, 1972), pages 8–9, 26–27.

A series of three articles reprinted from *Learning to Use Your Bible* (London: Concordia Press, 1970) as a "contribution to one of the livest [liveliest ?] issues being discussed in the church today" (12).

1973

Lutheran Church—Missouri Synod, The, Commission on Theology and Church Relations (prepared by Ralph A. Bohlmann). "Gospel and Scripture: A Synopsis." 92:1 (January 7, 1973), pages 18–19.

A point of contention concerning the position of the Concordia Seminary faculty majority.

Preus, Jacob A. O. "From the President: Biblical or Biblicistic?" 92:2 (January 28, 1973), page 29.

Preus, Jacob A. O. "From the President: Two Kinds of Biblical Authority." 92:6 (April 22, 1973), page 29.

Melde, Gus, Lois Dankenberg, and Jay Pfotenhauer. "Three Laymen View the Role of the Convention in Attaining Unity within the Church." 92:8 (June 3, 1973), pages 10–12.

Huth, Harry A., and Arthur C. Repp. "Synodically Adopted Doctrinal Resolutions: Are They Binding?" 92:9 (June 24, 1973), pages 10–13.

From the pre-convention audiocassette series *New Orleans '73* (Saint Louis: Concordia Publishing House).

Preus, J. A. O. "The New Orleans Convention: Report of the President of the Synod: [Part] I." 93:2 (December 16, 1973), pages 18, 26.

1974

Preus, J. A. O. "The New Orleans Convention: Report of the President of the Synod: II—Doctrinal Resolutions." 93:2 (January 27, 1974), page 18.

Preus, J. A. O. "The New Orleans Convention: Report of the President of the Synod: III—Doctrinal Resolutions." 93:2 (January 27, 1974), pages 18–20, 30–31.

Preus, J. A. O. "The New Orleans Convention: Report of the President: IV—Seminary Issues." 93:3 (February 17, 1974), pages 2, 12–15.

Preus, J. A. O. "The New Orleans Convention: Report of the President: V—The Future." 93:4 (March 17, 1974), page 19.

Lutheran Church—Missouri Synod, The, Board of Directors. "Letter from the Board of Directors [dated March 29, 1974]." 93:5 (April 7, 1974), pages 30–31.

"Resolved, That the Board of Directors give first priority and devote most of its time, prayers, and energy to these problems (of the Synod) until they are resolved" (30).

Lutheran Church—Missouri Synod, The, Commission on Constitutional Matters. "On Doctrinal Resolutions, Placement of Seminex Candidates, Parishes Calling Men to Serve as Seminex Instructors, Authority of District Presidents to Place Candidates and Vicars." 93:5 (June 16, 1974), pages 24–25.

Preus, J. A. O. "From the President: With One Voice [concerning biblical inspiration and inerrancy]." 93:13 (August 25, 1974), pages 18, 26.

Preus, J. A. O. "From the President: With One Voice [concerning the historical-critical method]." 93:14 (September 15, 1974), pages 18, 26.

Preus, J. A. O. "From the President: With One Voice [concerning the historical-critical method]." 93:15 (October 6, 1974), pages 19, 28.

Preus, J. A. O. "From the President: With One Voice [concerning the historical-critical method]." 93:17 (November 3, 1974), page 18.

Lutheran Church—Missouri Synod, The, Commission on Constitutional Matters. "An Analysis of Assertions in the Present Controversy [concerning the Gospel and the autonomy of LCMS congregations; document dated October 11, 1974]." 93:17 (November 3, 1974), pages 26–27.

Preus, J. A. O. "From the President: With One Voice [concerning church fellowship and consensus within the church]." 93:18 (November 24, 1974), page 19.

Preus, J. A. O. "From the President: With One Voice [concerning 'Gospel reductionism,' and church fellowship]." 93:19 (December 15, 1974), page 18.

1975

Preus, J. A. O. "From the President: With One Voice [on approving doctrinal statements]." 94:1 (January 5, 1975), page 20.

Huth, Harry A. "Commission on Theology Issues Report on Dissent to '*A Statement* . . . .'" 94:2 (January 26, 1975), page 19.

Faur, Peter. "[Theological] Convocation Concludes with a Hopeful Note." 94:7 (April 27, 1975), pages 3, 20.

Lutheran Church—Missouri Synod, The, Commission on Theology and Church Relations. "The Inspiration of Scripture: Excerpts from a Document Issued by the Commission on Theology and Church Relations." 94:10 (June 15, 1975), pages 28–31.

Preus, J. A. O. "From the President [concerning resolutions approved at Anaheim convention, including the resolution regarding LCMS position on ELIM]." 94:18 (November 30, 1975), page 17.

1976

Preus, J. A. O. "Excerpts from a Report to the Synod [from J. A. O. Preus to pastors, teachers, and congregational officers concerning District actions on controverted issues, dated February 23, 1974]." 95:4 (March 14, 1976), pages 18–19, 25.

Preus, J. A. O. "From the President [concerning LCMS congregations calling pastors not endorsed by Synod]." 95:6 (April 25, 1976), page 19.

Starr, Frank. "Leaving the Synod." 95:7 (May 16, 1976), page 20.

Lutheran Church—Missouri Synod, The, Department of Public Relations. "Special Report: Walking Together: A Simple Question and Answer Look at the Controversy Confronting The Lutheran Church—Missouri Synod." 95:8 (June 6, 1976), pages 10–16.

Lutheran Church—Missouri Synod, The, Commission on Constitutional Matters. "Official Notice: Report of Commission on Constitutional Matters [concerning Anaheim Resolution 5-02A]." 95:9 (July 4, 1976), pages 26–28.

Starr, Frank. "From the Editor's Desk: Achieving Peace . . . And Returning to Work." 95:10 (August 1, 1976), page 20.

Lutheran Church—Missouri Synod, The, Commission on Constitutional Matters. "Official Notice: Report on Constitutional Matters: Opinion Re Association of Evangelical Lutheran Churches [AELC], Opinion Re Legality of District Conventions and Circuit Meetings Involving Ineligible Participants." 95:11 (August 29, 1976), page 24.

1977

Preus, J. A. O. "From the President [concerning possible relations between the LCMS and the AELC]." 96:5 (April 10, 1977), page 19.

Starr, Frank. "From the Editor's Desk [concerning the bodily resurrection of Christ, the AELC, and convention election lists]." 96:5 (April 10, 1977), page 20.

2.1.2 *The Lutheran Witness* (news articles)

(chronological order)

1971

"News/Scan." 90:8 (August 1971) [re 1971 LCMS convention action on binding force of doctrinal statements], pages 3, 7; [re president's Fact Finding Committee regarding Concordia Seminary], page 5.

"St. Louis Sem[inary]'s Board Will Interview Faculty [re complaints about theological teachings and positions of faculty members]." 90:10A (October 1971), page 19.

"Third Parish in Wisconsin Severs Ties with Synod [re St. John's Lutheran, Watertown: 1971 convention actions 'tolerating' false doctrine and maintaining 'unscriptural fellowship' with ALC]." 90:10 (October 1971), page 23.

1972

"St. Louis Sem[inary] Board [of Control] Reengages Professor [Arlis Ehlen, whose contract had not been renewed]." 91:3 (February 27, 1972), page 20.

"Special Report: Preus, Tietjen Issue Statements [pursuant to 1971 LCMS convention Resolution 2-28 on results of FFC]." 91:4 (March 19, 1972), pages 23–24.

"Prof. Ehlen Asked to Appear before St. Louis Sem[inary] Board [re methods of teaching Old Testament]." 91:5 (April 9, 1972), page 22.

"Special Report." 91:6 (April 30, 1972). "[Concordia Seminary] Faculty Replies to Preus Statement [*A Statement of Scriptural and Confessional Principles*]," page 24; "*A Statement of Scriptural and Confessional Principles*," pages 24–28; "Response of the Faculty of Concordia Seminary, St. Louis," pages 28–31; "Synod, Seminary Presidents Agree on Prof's Teaching Assignments [re Arlis Ehlen]," page 31.

"Dr. Preus Discusses Concerns in Meeting with [Concordia] Sem[inary] Faculty [along with five LCMS vice presidents and President H. Scherer of Missouri District]." 91:8 (June 11, 1972), page 21.

"[Concordia] Seminary Placed on Probation [by AATS]." 91:8 (June 11, 1972), page 25.

"Prof's Appointment Unconfirmed [re Arlis Ehlen]." 91:8 (June 11, 1972), page 25.

"St. Louis Sem[inary] Board of Control Responds to [AATS] Probation Ruling." 91:9 (July 2, 1972), page 20.

"Extracts from Report of the Synodical President to The Lutheran Church—Missouri Synod in Compliance with Resolution 2-28 of the 49th Regular Convention [re Concordia Seminary Fact Finding Committee]." 91:11 (September 3, 1972), pages 19–26.

"Sem[inary] President, Faculty, Readers Respond [to report of the synodical president]": "Extracts from 'Fact Finding or Fault Finding?' [Concordia Seminary faculty response]"; "Letters [from readers]"; "A Declaration by the Faculty of Concordia Seminary in Response to the 'Report of the Synodical President.'" 91:12 (September 24, 1972), pages 24–30.

Mueller, Martin W. (*The Lutheran Witness* editor). "Special Report": "They Came to Heal the Hurts [meeting of CoP on Concordia Seminary campus]"; "A Joint Statement [of Presidents Preus and Tietjen]." 91:12 (September 24, 1972), page 31.

"Council of Presidents' Proposal Accepted by St. Louis Faculty." 91:13 (October 15, 1972), page 23.

"Fact Finding Committee, Others Respond." 91:13 (October 15, 1972), pages 25–27, 31.

> "The Fact Finding Committee Replies"; "Letters" (13) [from, e.g., Paul Bretscher, Ralph Bohlmann, Richard Klann, Robert Preus, Martin Scharlemann, Lorenz Wunderlich, Karl Barth, Paul Zimmerman, Harry Coiner, A. C. Mueller, Luther Meinzen, Gary Mehl].

"Bible Interpretation Issues Explored in Conferences [hosted by CTCR]." 91:15 (November 26, 1972), page 19.

"CTCR Finds '*A Statement* [*of Scriptural and Confessional Principles*]' in Accord with Scriptures." 91:16 (December 17, 1972), page 21.

1973

"[Concordia Seminary] Faculty Issues Stance Papers [re *Faithful to Our Calling, Faithful to Our Lord*]." 92:2 (January 28, 1973), page 19.

"[Concordia Seminary] Board [of Control] Favors '*A Statement* [*of Scriptural and Confessional Principles*].'" 92:3 (February 18, 1973), page 19.

"[Concordia Seminary] Board [of Control] Vote 'Commends' Faculty [on basis of the report of the FFC]." 92:4 (March 11, 1973), page 19.

"Muted Hallelujahs [convention votes on *A Statement of Scriptural and Confessional Principles* and charge of false teaching by majority of Concordia Seminary faculty]." 92:10 (August 5, 1973), page 6.

1974

"St. Louis [seminary] Board [of Control] Suspends Tietjen for False Doctrine." 93:2 (January 27, 1974), page 25.

"Scenes from a Troubled Campus [re Concordia Seminary]." 93:3 (February 17, 1974), page 3.

"Charges, Counter Charges Swirl about the Seminary." 93:3 (February 17, 1974), pages 8–11.

"Most Unusual [initiation of Joint Project for Theological Education]." 93:4 (March 17, 1974), page 4.

"[Concordia] Seminary Begins Quarter as 82 Students Enroll." 93:4 (March 17, 1974), page 23.

"Special [Atlantic] District Convention Backs 'Seminary in Exile.' " 93:4 (March 17, 1974), page 23.

"20 New Faculty Appointments in Process [at Concordia Seminary]." 93:5 (April 7, 1974), page 19.

"[Council of] Presidents Include Students from 'Seminex' in Placement of Vicars at Congregations." 93:5 (April 7, 1974), page 20.

"Vicars at Seminex Accept Appointments but Keep Ties [to Seminex]." 93:5 (April 7, 1974), page 21.

"Seminex Grads Not Eligible for Placement." 93:5 (April 7, 1974), page 21.

"President Preus Reiterates Conciliation Group's Role." 93:5 (April 7, 1974), page 22.

"St. Louis Sem[inary] Board [of Control] Thanks Scharlemann." 93:6 (April 28, 1974), page 20.

"[LCMS] Board for Higher Education Adopts Statement on Academic Freedom." 93:6 (April 28, 1974), page 21.

"ALC President Addresses Missouri in 'Open Letter.' " 93:6 (April 28, 1974), page 22.

"LCA President Marshall Eyes Dispute in Missouri Synod." 93:6 (April 28, 1974), page 23.

"Seminex Assignments Pending: 86 Ministerial Candidates Placed by [LCMS] Council [of Presidents]." 93:7 (May 19, 1974), page 20.

---

*See 2.1.3 *The Lutheran Witness Reporter Edition* 93:8 for articles covering the period between May 19 and June 16, 1974.

"ELIM Activities Viewed as Divisive by [LCMS Board of Directors]." 93:9 (June 16, 1974), page 18.

"California-Nevada District Questions Synod Actions." 93:9 (June 16, 1974), page 20.

"[Concordia] Seminary Board [of Control] Hears Estimate of 135 Students for Fall Term [six Seminex grads endorsed for ordination; thirty-nine accepted into ministerial position without endorsement]." 93:10 (July 7, 1974), page 19.

"Atlantic District Convention Welcomes Bishop, Senator [actions on Seminex]." 93:10 (July 7, 1974), page 20.

"Inter-Lutheran Cooperation Urged by New Englanders [actions on Seminex]." 93:10 (July 7, 1974), page 20.

"Colorado Convention Urges Understanding, Repentance [actions on Seminex]." 93:10 (July 7, 1974), page 21.

"Mid-South District Makes Its Presidency Full-Time [actions on Seminex]." 93:10 (July 7, 1974), page 21.

"Florida-Georgia Convention Elects [L. Lloyd] Behnken President [actions on Seminex]." 93:10 (July 7, 1974), page 22.

"Rev. Harold Hecht Elected English District President [actions on Seminex]." 93:10 (July 7, 1974), page 22.

"Indiana Delegates Plead for Reconciling Attitude [re controversy in LCMS]." 93:10 (July 7, 1974), page 23.

"Missouri District Delegates Urge Efforts to Seek Unity [actions on Seminex]." 93:10 (July 7, 1974), page 24.

"Minnesota South District Reelects President Lieske [actions on Seminex]." 93:10 (July 7, 1974), page 24.

"LCA Delegates Adopt 'Statement of Concern' [concerning 'schism' in LCMS]." 93:11 (July 28, 1974), page 20.

"President [J. A. O.] Preus Responds [to LCA concerns]." 93:11 (July 28, 1974), page 20.

"'Resume Dialogue,' Pleads Ohio District's Convention [actions on Seminex]." 93:11 (July 28, 1974), page 21.

"Central Illinois Convention Elects New District Head [actions on ELIM and *A Statement*]." 93:11 (July 28, 1974), page 22.

"Eastern [District] Convention Favors Ordaining Seminex Grads." 93:11 (July 28, 1974), page 22.

"Northwest [District] Delegates Urge Resubmitting '*A Statement* . . . .'" 93:11 (July 28, 1974), page 23.

"Texas [District] Delegates Propose Calling Special Convention [of the Synod]." 93:11 (July 28, 1974), page 23.

"Trouble God's Chastening, Michigan Delegates Hear [actions on doctrinal statements, ELIM]." 93:11 (July 28, 1974), page 24.

"Northern Illinois Delegates Debate Seminex Question." 93:11 (July 28, 1974), page 24.

"Southern District Requests 'Council for Reconciliation' [actions on Seminex, *A Statement*]." 93:11 (July 28, 1974), page 24.

---

*See 2.1.3 *The Lutheran Witness Reporter Edition* 93:12 for articles covering the period between July 28 and August 25, 1974.

"Dr. Tietjen Reaffirms His Decision to 'Remain Silent' in Proceedings." 93:13 (August 25, 1974), page 20.

"442 Students at Seminex." 93:14 (September 15, 1974), page 21.

"578 Students Are Listed at St. Louis, [and] Springfield [seminaries]." 93:14 (September 15, 1974), page 21.

"ELIM's Direction Set by 1400 at Meeting [in Chicago; ready to ordain Seminex graduates]." 93:14 (September 15, 1974), page 22.

"[LCMS] Council [of Presidents] Plan Would Certify Seminex Grads." 93:15 (October 6, 1974), pages 20–21.

"[LCMS Board of] Directors Report Progress in Reconciliation Efforts." 93:15 (October 6, 1974), page 21.

"[Concordia] Seminary, Seminex Begin Discussion of Key Issues." 93:15 (October 6, 1974), page 22.

"[Concordia] Seminary Board [of Control] Receives Findings of Committee's Work on Charges [against President Tietjen]." 93:15 (October 6, 1974), page 23.

---

*See 2.1.3 *The Lutheran Witness Reporter Edition* 93:16 for articles covering the period between October 6 and November 3, 1974.

"Impasse Blocks Committee of 20 [re problems related to Seminex]." 93:17 (November 3, 1974), page 19.

"[Concordia Seminary] Board [of Control] Pledges an Accounting on Dismissal [of President Tietjen]." 93:17 (November 3, 1974), page 19.

"[LCMS] Council of Presidents Proposes Convening Special Theological Convocation of Synod." 93:18 (December 15, 1974), pages 20–21.

"[LCMS] Board [of Higher Education] Requests Refraining from ELIM Participation." 93:18 (December 15, 1974), page 21.

1975

"Plans Set for Special Convocation [on 'nature and function of Holy Scripture']." 94:1 (January 5, 1975), page 21.

"Congregations Urged to Call by Procedure [joint resolution of LCMS seminary faculties]." 94:1 (January 5, 1975), page 21.

"Synod, District Leaders, Seminex Faculty Confer." 94:2 (January 26, 1975), page 4.

"Convocation Plans Presented [on inspiration, inerrancy, historical-critical method, Gospel-Scripture relationship, Church under the Scriptures]." 94:2 (January 26, 1975), page 21.

---

*See 2.1.3 *The Lutheran Witness Reporter Edition* 94:3 for articles covering the period between January 26 and February 23, 1975.

"Seminex Now Accredited [by ATS in the United States and Canada]." 94:4 (February 23, 1975), page 21.

"Tietjen [installed as] Seminex President." 94:4 (February 23, 1975), page 25.

"[LCMS] Commission [on Constitutional Matters] Issues Ruling on Removing [District] Presidents." 94:5 (March 16, 1975), page 3.

"[LCMS Council of] Presidents' Meeting Focus Is on Preparing Pastors." 94:5 (March 16, 1975), pages 3, 22.

"'Moderates' Start Group [Evangelical Lutherans in Mission (ELIM), after Second Assembly in August 1974]." 94:5 (March 16, 1975), page 21.

"New [Concordia Seminary] Library Policy Announced [re Seminex patrons]." 94:5 (March 16, 1975), page 23.

"Missouri District Directed to Rule in Tietjen Case." 94:5 (March 16, 1975), page 24.

"ELIM Requests Further Action on Four Proposals [re doctrinal statements, Seminex, etc.]." 94:6 (April 6, 1975), page 21.

2.1.2.1 Articles on April 1975 Theological Convocation

(names of presenters in brackets)

"Preus: We Hope for Consensus [at theological convocation]." 94:7 (April 27, 1975), pages 3, 19.

"Witness Special Report [on theological convocation]." 94:7 (April 27, 1975), pages 14–20.

"Spirit's Part in Inspiration Noted [Howard Tepker]." 94:7 (April 27, 1975), page 14.

"Inerrancy Said [to be the] Major Issue [J. A. O. Preus]." 94:7 (April 27, 1975), page 15.

"Inerrancy Not 'Useful' Term [James Childs]." 94:7 (April 27, 1975), page 15.

"Scripture Study: 'Historical and Critical' [Martin Franzmann]." 94:7 (April 27, 1975), pages 15, 16.

"Hits [historical-critical] Method as a Threat [Harold H. Buls]." 94:7 (April 27, 1975), page 16.

"Defends Use of [the historical-critical] Method [Ralph Klein]." 94:7 (April 27, 1975), page 16.

"Unity [a] 'Given' and a 'Goal' [Ralph Bohlmann]." 94:7 (April 27, 1975), page 17.

"Scripture 'a Tool to Use' [Herbert J. A. Bouman]." 94:7 (April 27, 1975), page 17.

"Gospel, Scripture Is Presentation Topic [Fred Kramer]." 94:7 (April 27, 1975), page 18.

"[Acts 15] Passage [on circumcision conflict] Seen as Guideline [Robert Bertram]." 94:7 (April 27, 1975), pages 18–19.

"Gospel Came before Bible [Harry Huth]." 94:7 (April 27, 1975), page 19.

"[Concordia Seminary] Board [of Control], Faculty Object to Service [at theological convocation]." 94:6 (April 6, 1975), page 22.

"[Seminex] Vicars Placed Outside Synod." 94:7 (April 27, 1975), page 22.

"[LCMS Council of] Presidents Attempt to Curb Ordaining Uncertified Grads." 94:8 (May 18, 1975), page 3.

"Acting Seminary President [Bohlmann] Is Elevated to Presidency." 94:8 (May 18, 1975), page 3.

---

*See 2.1.3 *The Lutheran Witness Reporter Edition* 94:9 for articles covering the period between May 18 and June 15, 1975.

"Resolution Drawn Up for Synod Convention [Seminex, English District, etc.]." 94:10 (June 15, 1975), pages 3, 20.

"[Missouri] District Exec[utive] Removes Self from Hearing [on case against Tietjen]." 94:10 (June 15, 1975), page 20.

"Can't Support Resolution 8 District Presidents Say [on Seminex problems]." 94:10 (June 15, 1975), page 21.

"[Concordia] Seminary under Censure [of AAUP]." 94:11 (July 6, 1975), page 22.

---

*See 2.1.3 *The Lutheran Witness Reporter Edition* 94:12 for articles covering the period between July 6 and August 3, 1975.

"Anaheim [LCMS convention] Wrap-Up: 'No-win Convention.' " 94:13 (August 3, 1975), pages 4–7.

"ELIM Will Form Clusters, Steps Taken to Leave [Synod]." 94:14 (August 24, 1975), page 3.

"Seminex Grad Is Ordained, the First Since Convention [at Calvary Lutheran Church, Ferguson, Missouri]." 94:14 (August 24, 1975), page 18.

"Congregation Reverses Itself, Declines Seminex Graduate [Trinity Lutheran Church, Anna, Illinois]." 94:14 (August 24, 1975), page 18.

*See relevant Sturz letter (October 5, page 21); Neunaber letter (November 9, page 15).

"[Dissident] District Heads under Fire Reported Feeling 'Secure.'" 94:14 (August 24, 1975), page 22.

*See relevant letter by Colorado District's Duane M. Reetz (November 9, 1975, page 15).

"Group of [Concordia Senior College, Fort Wayne, Indiana] Profs Reaffirms Stand [on ELIM]." 94:15 (September 15, 1975), page 20.

"Synodical President Urges Steps to Ease Tensions." 94:15 (September 15, 1975), page 21.

"[Concordia Seminary] Board [of Control] Asks Study of Role." 94:15 (September 15, 1975), page 21.

"English District Directs [President Harold] Hecht to Ordain Seminex Grads." 94:16 (October 5, 1975), page 23.

"Concordia, River Forest Board Adopts ELIM Policy." 94:16 (October 5, 1975), page 24.

"[Concordia Seminary] Faculty Added." 94:16 (October 5, 1975), page 24.

"[District] Presidents Meet [on Synod resolutions, congregational autonomy, Seminex, etc.]." 94:16 (October 5, 1975), page 25.

"Interview Committee Chosen [to interview Concordia Seminary former faculty majority]." 94:17 (November 9, 1975), page 16.

"[LCMS CCM] Decision Stands [that charges against Tietjen are not valid]." 94:17 (November 9, 1975), page 16.

"[Concordia] Seminary Inaugurates Seventh President [Ralph Bohlmann]." 94:17 (November 9, 1975), page 17.

"[LCMS CTCR says] 'Problem Is Doctrine.'" 94:17 (November 9, 1975), page 17.

"Preus Confident Synod Can Move Forward [in October letter to church leaders]." 94:18 (November 30, 1975), page 20.

"[LCMS] President Asked [by Harlan L. Harnapp and Leonard P. Buelow] to Intervene in Tietjen Case." 94:18 (November 30, 1975), page 20.

"[Concordia Teachers College, Seward, Nebraska] Faculty Supports Synodical Doctrine [and LCMS Anaheim convention Resolution 3-06 on ELIM]." 94:18 (November 30, 1975), page 21.

1976

"Preus to Continue Dialogue [with Southern Illinois District President Neunaber]." 95:1 (January 11, 1976), page 22.

"Preus, Neunaber Debate Compliance [with regulations of the Synod]." 95:3 (February 22, 1976), page 22.

"[LCMS] Board of Directors Cautions English District [re severance from the Synod]." 95:3 (February 22, 1976), page 23.

"Concordia Seminary Retains Accreditation [of AATS]." 95:3 (February 22, 1976), page 23.

"Interview Committee [re doctrinal position of former Concordia Seminary faculty] Asks to Be Discharged." 95:3 (February 22, 1976), page 24.

"Preus Makes Report [on dissident District presidents]." 95:4 (March 14, 1976), page 23.

"Convention Wrap-Up [Southern Illinois actions on Neunaber, Seminex]." 95:4 (March 14, 1976), page 23.

"[Texas District] Will Not Suspend [congregation for having a woman Seminex vicar]." 95:5 (April 4, 1976), page 21.

"[Dissenting] Presidents Reply [re complying with Anaheim Resolution 5-02A]." 95:5 (April 4, 1976), page 21.

"[Atlantic] District Forms 'Alternative Association' [within District]." 95:5 (April 4, 1976), page 21.

"Four District Presidents Are Removed from Office [Frincke, Hecht, Ressmeyer, Riedel]." 95:6 (April 25, 1976), page 22.

"'Moderates' Refuse to Accept [District] Presidents' Removal." 95:7 (May 16, 1976), page 22.

"District Convention Resolutions Addressed to Various [controverted] Issues." 95:7 (May 16, 1976), page 22.

"[LCMS seminary] Faculties Urge Synod to 'Stand Firm' in Crisis." 95:7 (May 16, 1976), page 24.

"Peace Effort Fails [meeting of Preus and Tietjen]." 95:8 (June 6, 1976), page 32.

"[LCMS] Council [of Presidents] Tries Reconciliation after Walkout [of eight District presidents]." 95:8 (June 6, 1976), page 32.

"Spring [District] Conventions Generally Restrained on Synodical Issues." 95:9 (July 4, 1976), page 22.

"[District] Conventions Reflect Varying Reactions to Synodical Tensions." 95:10 (August 1, 1976), pages 22–23.

"Tietjen Case Referred [to Third LCMS Vice President Nickel]." 95:11 (August 29, 1976), page 20.

"Southern Illinois [District] Has New Leader [following Neunaber resignation]." 95:12 (September 19, 1976), page 20.

"ELIM to Continue." 95:12 (September 19, 1976), page 20.

"[SELC student] Aid Policy Adopted [dependent on adherence to Synod certification process]." 95:12 (September 19, 1976), page 20.

"Ressmeyer Steps Out [following removal from office]." 95:13 (October 10, 1976), page 21.

"Atlantic [District] to Hold Special Convention [following official resignations]." 95:14 (October 31, 1976), page 22.

"[Former New England District president] Riedel Resigns Synod Membership." 95:14 (October 31, 1976), page 22.

"[Colorado District president Waldemar] Meyer Resigns." 95:14 (i.e., 15) (November 21, 1976), page 34.

1977

"Atlantic [District] Picks Leader [action re certification of Seminex graduates]." 96:1 (January 16, 1977), page 22.

"New Church Body Formed [Association of Evangelical Lutheran Churches (AELC)]." 96:1 (January 16, 1977), page 24.

"Group of [District] Presidents Proposes Position Statements on Issues." 96:2 (February 6, 1977), page 22.

"Theology, Church Relations Discussed [by CoP; re certifying Seminex graduates]." 96:5 (April 10, 1977), page 22.

"Five Presidential Nominees Discuss Directions for Our Synod [Seminex, AELC, etc.]." 96:8 (June 12, 1977), pages 3–8.

"[Concordia Seminary] Board [of Control] Publishes Report on Seminary Walkout [*Exodus from Concordia*]." 96:8 (June 12, 1977), page 23.

"That We May Grow: Higher Education [re endorsement of Seminex graduates]." 96:10 (August 7, 1977), pages 6–7.

"[Fifth] ELIM Assembly Held [Seminex expenditures 'spun off']." 96:12 (September 25, 1977), page 22.

"Tietjen Is Removed [from the Synod's clergy roster]." 96:12 (i.e., 13) (October 16, 1977), page 22.

"Official Notices: Notice Re: Dr. John Tietjen." 96:12 (i.e., 13) (October 16, 1977), page 26.

"Doctrine of the Church Asserted as Key to Concord." 96:15 (November 27, 1977), page 20.

2.1.3 *The Lutheran Witness Reporter / Reporter Edition* (news articles)

(chronological order)

1970

"CTCR Member Cites 'Threats to Authentic Lutheranism' [at testimonial dinner for Rev. Herman Otten]." 6:4 (March 1, 1970), page 2.

"[Concordia Seminary faculty] 'Openness and Trust' Document Said to Draw 'Sympathetic Response.'" 6:4 (March 1, 1970), page 3.

"Synod President Issues Statement on Document ['A Call to Openness and Trust']." 6:4 (March 1, 1970), page 3.

Danker, William J. "On Dividing the Missouri Synod." 6:7 (April 5, 1970), page 8.

Mueller, Martin W. "Theology Commission [CTCR] Evaluates 'Call to Openness and Trust.'" 6:9 (May 3, 1970), page 5.

Hummel, Horace D. "Document Criticized ['A Call to Openness and Trust']." 6:9 (May 3, 1970), page 11.

"St. Louis Sem[inary] 'Good Image,' Survey Shows; 15% are 'Unhappy.'" 6:9 (May 3, 1970), page 20.

"From Private Pipelines—Movements, Developments within Synod [various contentious issues]." 6:13 (July 5, 1970), page 3.

"[J. A. O.] Preus: Ordination of Women beyond Bounds of Scripture." 6:13 (July 5, 1970), page 3.

"From Private Pipelines—Movements, Developments within Synod [various contentious issues]." 6:15 (August 2, 1970), page 3.

Mehl, Carl E., and Edwin Betker. "Michigan [District convention] Hears Reaction to 'Heresy Hunt' Charges [from J. A. O. Preus]." 6:16 (August 16, 1970), page 3.

"Talk of Split Disavowed by Leaders of [Lutheran] Congress [in Chicago]." 6:17 (September 6, 1970), page 2.

Danker, William J. "Wave of Shame [re effect of church controversies in mission field]." 6:19 (October 4, 1970), page 7.

President Preus Announces Plans for St. Louis [seminary] Inquiry." 6:21 (November 1, 1970), pages 2, 11.

"St. Louis [seminary] Faculty Issues Confessional Statement [includes 'Declaration' of faculty members and 'Explanation' of nonsigners]." 6:22 (November 15, 1970), page 2.

Loose, George A. "[Concordia Seminary] Board [of Control] Chairman Objects to Inquiry at Seminary." 6:23 (December 6, 1970), pages 9, 12.

1971

Mueller, Martin W. "[Concordia Seminary] Faculty Interviews Continue 'Under Protest.'" 7:2 (January 17, 1971), pages 1–2.

"Five Profs Protest Resolution [of Concordia Seminary faculty majority re fact-finding inquiry]." 7:2 (January 17, 1971), page 2.

"Reconciliation Asked [by 323 Concordia Seminary students]." 7:2 (January 17, 1971), page 2.

"Synodical [District] Presidents Hear Principals in [Concordia] Sem[inary] Inquiry." 7:5 (March 7, 1971), pages 1, 3.

"Synodically Adopted Doctrinal Statements . . . " 7:10 (May 16, 1971), page 4.

". . . Points of View on Their 'Binding Nature' [in form of eight letters]." 7:10 (May 16, 1971), pages 4–5.

"Controversial Issues Mark 49th Synodical Convention [in Milwaukee]." 7:12 (June 20, 1971), pages 1, 4.

Mueller, Martin W. "[1971 LCMS] Convention [in Milwaukee] Debates Binding Nature of Synodical Statements." 7:14 (July 25, 1971), pages 1, 3.

Preus, J. A. O. "After the Convention: Reconciliation." 7:14 (July 25, 1971), pages 1, 3.

"[Concordia] Sem[inary] Inquiry Report Kept Confidential." 7:14 (July 25, 1971), page 6.

"Close Vote 'Repudiates' Document ['A Call to Openness and Trust']." 7:14 (July 25, 1971), page 13.

---

*See 2.1.1 *The Lutheran Witness* (news articles) for articles in the period between July 25, 1971, and May 14, 1972.

1972

"District Conventions Air Current Issues [North Wisconsin re Concordia Seminary]." 8:2 (May 14, 1972), pages 2, 11.

"False Judgments Made, Synod [District] Presidents Say [re Concordia Seminary faculty]." 8:2 (May 14, 1972), page 5.

Starr, Frank D. "New Jersey, New England Form New Synod Districts [actions re Concordia Seminary by Florida-Georgia, Atlantic, Southeastern, Missouri, South Wisconsin, Iowa West, English, Northwest, Southern, Northern Illinois, Michigan, Colorado Districts]." 8:3 (July 16, 1972), pages 1, 3, 10, 11.

"[Synod] President's Authority Ruled On [by CCM]." 8:5 (October 22, 1972), page 1.

"LCMS Commission on Constitutional Matters: An Opinion on Presidential Authority." 8:5 (October 22, 1972), page 11.

1973

"St. Louis Seminary, Doctrine, Church Relations Top Issues [for 1973 LCMS convention in New Orleans]." 9:2 (May 27, 1973), pages 1, 4.

"[District] Presidents View Convention Issues." 9:2 (May 27, 1973), pages 5, 10.

"[Concordia Seminary] Faculty Majority Positions Declared 'False Doctrine.'" 9:3 (July 22, 1973), pages 1, 13.

"Move to Oust Tietjen Shifted to [Concordia] Sem[inary] Board [of Control]." 9:3 (July 22, 1973), pages 1, 13.

"Majority, Minority Skirmish." 9:3 (July 22, 1973), pages 1, 14.

"Delegates Vote to Elevate Dr. Preus's '*A Statement*.'" 9:3 (July 22, 1973), page 3.

"Missouri at a 'Doctrinal Crossroads.'" 9:3 (July 22, 1973), page 14.

1974

"[Concordia Seminary] Faculty Majority, Staff Contracts Terminated." 10:1 (March 3, 1974), pages 1, 6.

"[Concordia Seminary] Students Continue Studies in 'Exile.'" 10:1 (March 3, 1974), pages 1, 6.

"Conciliation Group Gets Under Way." 10:1 (March 3, 1974), page 2.

Manz, James G. "In His Church: God Can Use Trouble." 10:1 (March 3, 1974), page 7.

"Seminex Question Goes to Parishes." 93:8 (June 2, 1974), page 1.

"[Concordia] Sem[inary] Calls 14 to Fill Positions." 93:8 (June 2, 1974), page 1.

"Advisory Opinion in Tietjen Case." 93:8 (June 2, 1974), page 1.

"District Conventions Express Concern for Synod Tension." 93:8 (June 2, 1974), pages 2–3, 13–14.

"Convention Resolutions Are Upheld [re doctrine by LCMS CCM]." 93:8 (June 2, 1974), page 15.

"[Concordia Seminary] Board [of Control] Names Acting Head of Seminary [Ralph A. Bohlmann]." 93:8 (June 2, 1974), page 16.

"150 Students Expected at Concordia [seminary], St. Louis." 93:12 (August 11, 1974), page 1.

"Seminex: Iowa West Votes 'No.'" 93:12 (August 11, 1974), page 4.

"LCMS Commission on Theology and Church Relations [CTCR]: 'A Comparative Study of Varying Contemporary Approaches to Biblical Interpretation.'" 93:12 (August 11, 1974), pages 5–8.

"Tietjen Ousted from Presidency by St. Louis [seminary] Board of Control [following earlier suspension]." 93:16 (October 20, 1974), pages 1, 5.

[Otto, E. J.] "Official Replies [to Tietjen's public statements on decision]." 93:16 (October 20, 1974), pages 1, 5.

"Special Committee Will Explore Proposed Steps to Reconciliation." 93:16 (October 20, 1974), page 2.

"Theology Commission [CTCR] Suggests Clarifications of '*A Statement* [*on Scriptural and Confessional Principles*].'" 93:16 (October 20, 1974), page 3.

"St. Louis [seminary] Faculty Sets Terms for Certifying Seminex Grads." 93:16 (October 20, 1974), page 5.

1975

"[LCMS] Seminary Boards of Control Hold Combined, Separate Sessions." 94:3 (February 9, 1975), page 3.

Preus, J. A. O. "The State of the Church [excerpts from a report]." 94:3 (February 9, 1975), pages 6–7.

"Letters [to Seminex students] Urge Certification." 94:9 (June 1, 1975), page 1.

"[1975 LCMS Anaheim] Convention Previews: Missourians Examine Issues." 94:9 (June 1, 1975), pages 3–4, 12.

Faur, Peter. "If Congregation Splits, Who Keeps Property?" 94:9 (June 1, 1975), page 11.

"[District] Presidents Face Removal." 94:12 (July 20, 1975), page 1.

"Preus: God Has Helped Us [re Seminex, ELIM]." 94:12 (July 20, 1975), pages 1, 2.

"Dr. Tietjen Declared Not Guilty of Heresy." 94:12 (July 20, 1975), pages 1, 6.

"Seminex Asked [by 1975 LCMS Anaheim convention] to Close Its Doors, to Promote Synodical Peace, Unity." 94:12 (July 20, 1975), page 3.

"[1975 LCMS Anaheim] Convention Calls ELIM 'Schismatic,' Asks Individuals to Cease Activity." 94:12 (July 20, 1975), page 5.

"Doctrinal Statements Declared 'Binding' [by 1975 LCMS Anaheim convention]." 94:12 (July 20, 1975), page 5.

Starr, Frank D. "Editorial: Future Will Require Patience, Caution." 94:12 (July 20, 1975), page 5.

"Eight District Presidents Respond [to charges of violating Synod's Constitution and Bylaws]: Say They Will Consult Constituents." 94:12 (July 20, 1975), page 7.

"Doctrinal Harmony to Be Pursued in Next Two Years." 94:12 (July 20, 1975), page 8.

"Seminary Wants Another Opinion [re censure by AAUP]." 94:12 (July 20, 1975), page 12.

"[1975 LCMS Anaheim convention] Resolution Generates Heated Discussion [re placement of uncertified pastoral candidates]." 94:12 (July 20, 1975), page 13.

2.1.4 *Reporter* (news articles)

(chronological order)

1975 *(continued)*

"[LCMS Synod president says] 'Only Recourse' [in] Tietjen Case." 1:1 (October 6, 1975), page 1.

"Problem Is Doctrine, CTCR Says." 1:1 (October 6, 1975), page 2.

"Dispute Concerns [Texas] Woman [Seminex] Vicar." 1:1 (October 6, 1975), page 7.

"[Stegemoeller] Resignation [at Concordia College, Saint Paul] Prompts Document." 1:1 (October 6, 1975), page 7.

"[Oklahoma City] Congregation Votes to Leave [the Synod]." 1:2 (October 13, 1975), page 2.

"Seminex Profs to Be 'Candidates' [CRM status]." 1:2 (October 13, 1975), page 7.

"Seminex Grads Seek Colloquies." 1:2 (October 13, 1975), page 7.

"[Concordia] Seminary Replies to Librarians [re ATLA censure over access to Concordia Seminary library by Seminex students / faculty]." 1:2 (October 13, 1975), page 8.

"Interview Committee Appointed [re former faculty majority]." 1:3 (October 20, 1975), pages 1–2.

"[Concordia] Seminary Head Inaugurated [Ralph A. Bohlmann]." 1:4 (October 27, 1975), page 1.

"[Atlantic, New England, New Jersey District] Pastors Protest Synod Actions." 1:4 (October 27, 1975), page 2.

"Interview Committee Meets [re former Concordia Seminary faculty majority]." 1:5 (November 3, 1975), page 1.

"LCA Sets Seminex Policy." 1:5 (November 3, 1975), page 2.

"California and Nevada District Holds Convocation." 1:6 (November 10, 1975), page 2.

"3 More Leave [LCMS] Parish Ed Staff [for ELIM, ALC]." 1:6 (November 10, 1975), page 7.

"Stage Is Set for Action against 8 [District] Presidents." 1:7 (November 17, 1975), pages 1, 8.

"[J. A. O.] Preus Asked to Step In [re case against Tietjen]." 1:7 (November 17, 1975), page 2.

"[New Jersey District] Convocation Upholds Seminex." 1:7 (November 17, 1975), page 7.

"[Seminex] Students Say Procedure Is Wrong [re interviews of former Concordia Seminary faculty majority]." 1:7 (November 17, 1975), page 7.

"Neunaber: 'Reporter' Incorrect [re ordaining Seminex graduate]." 1:8 (November 24, 1975), page 1.

"[President Jackayya of IELC seminary in Nagercoil, India] Calls for Rehiring [Concordia] Sem[inary] Profs." 1:8 (November 24, 1975), page 8.

"[District President] Neunaber Explains Ordination [of Seminex graduate by Mount Calvary Lutheran Church, Cahokia, Illinois]." 1:9 (December 1, 1975), pages 7–8.

"8 District Presidents Stand Firm [re ordaining uncertified Seminex graduates]." 1:10 (December 8 1975), pages 1, 8.

"Oklahoma Church's Property Battle Goes to Court [re majority vote to leave the LCMS]." 1:11 (December 15, 1975), page 7.

"District Leaders Counsel Preus [re Anaheim Resolution 5-02A on District presidents who ordain uncertified candidates]." 1:12 (December 22, 1975), pages 1, 2.

"14 Colloquy Applicants Accepted [including four from Seminex]." 1:12 (December 22, 1975), pages 1, 8.

"Pres. Preus Decides to Continue with District Head [Herman Neunaber]." 1:13 (December 29, 1975), pages 1, 8.

"Neunaber Responds to Preus." 1:13 (December 29, 1975), page 8.

1976

"Seminex Faculty Declines Interviews but Will Meet Committee." 2:2 (January 19, 1976), page 2.

"Preus, Neunaber Discuss Issues at Circuit Meeting." 2:3 (January 26, 1976), page 2.

"[Melvin] Kieschnick Resigns Synod Post [citing climate in Synod]." 2:3 (January 26, 1976), page 8.

"[Concordia] Seminary's Probation Is Ended [by AATS]." 2:5 (February 9, 1976), page 1.

"[LCMS] Board [of Directors] Questions English District Proposals [to leave Synod]." 2:5 (February 9, 1976), page 1.

"Interview Committee Says Assignment Completed [in view of former Concordia Seminary faculty majority's position not to meet individually]." 2:5 (February 9, 1976), page 2.

"Southern Illinois Convention Addresses Controversy [supports Neunaber's stance]." 2:8 (March 1, 1976), pages 1, 7.

"Preus Will Not Vacate Offices of [District President] Jacobs, Jaech, Meyer." 2:8 (March 1, 1976), pages 1, 8.

"Reconciliation Plan Given to COP." 2:8 (March 1, 1976), page 2.

"[Samuel] Roth, [C. A.] Swanson React to [Preus's] Decision [not to vacate their offices]." 2:8 (March 1, 1976), page 8.

"ACDC [LCMS Advisory Committee on Doctrine and Conciliation] Report Readied for Release [on divisive issues of Synod]." 2:9 (March 8, 1976), page 1.

"ELIM Meets to Discuss Options." 2:9 (March 8, 1976), page 1.

"'Sharp Censure,' but No Expulsion [of LCMS congregation in Denton, Texas, re woman Seminex vicar]." 2:10 (March 15, 1976), pages 1–2.

"Women, Seminex Grads Get Calls [to ALC, Evangelical Lutheran Church Canada]." 2:10 (March 15, 1976), page 8.

"Atlantic District Forms Alternative Association." 2:11 (March 22, 1976), page 1.

"Preus Letter Prompts Replies from District Leaders: Preus Responds to Jacobs' Letter; Eight District Presidents Prepare Letter [re ordaining uncertified Seminex grads]." 2:11 (March 22, 1976), page 2.

"ELIM Coordinating Council Meets." 2:11 (March 22, 1976), page 2.

"Eight District Presidents Stand Firm, Will Not Comply [re ordination of uncertified Seminex grads]." 2:12 (March 29, 1976), page 1.

"Preus Proposes Moratorium to Four District Leaders [facing removal from office: Eastern, English, Atlantic, New England]." 2:13 (April 5, 1976), page 1.

"[LCMS] Board [of Directors] Pleads with [four District] Presidents: 'Cease being Divisive.'" 2:13 (April 5, 1976), page 7.

"Preus Removes Four District Presidents [Frincke, Hecht, Ressmeyer, Riedel]." 2:14 (April 12, 1976), pages 1–2.

"Districts, ELIM Respond to Oust." 2:14 (April 12, 1976), page 7.

"Synod's Lawyer Issues Statement [on Districts as representatives of the Synod to member congregations]." 2:14 (April 12, 1976), page 7.

"Preus Names Acting Presidents [of four Districts]." 2:15 (April 19, 1976), page 1.

" 'Return the Exiles' President [David Preus of ALC] Asks." 2:15 (April 19, 1976), page 2.

"[J. A. O.] Preus Calls for an End to 'Emotion and Politics' [in letter to congregations of Atlantic, Eastern, English, New England Districts]." 2:16 (April 26, 1976), page 1.

"CTCR Offers Aid to Parishes [re controverted doctrinal issues]." 2:17 (May 3, 1976), page 1.

Bryant, Victor [Public Relations Director of LCMS]. "News Analysis: [ELIM] 'Coordinating Council' Attempts to Split the Synod." 2:17 (May 3, 1976), pages 1, 8.

"Six Districts Report on Convention Action [California-Nevada, Kansas, Montana, North Wisconsin, Southeastern, Southern California]." 2:17 (May 3, 1976), pages 2, 7.

"Four District Presidents Walk Out of COP [Jacobs (California-Nevada), Jaech (Northwest), Meyer (Colorado), Neunaber (Southern Illinois)]." 2:18 (May 10, 1976), page 1.

"Four Districts Report on Convention Action [Manitoba-Saskatchewan, Northwest, Oklahoma, Wyoming]." 2:18 (May 10, 1976), pages 2, 8.

"[LCMS] Council of [Presidents]: 'Keep Lines of Communication Open.' " 2:19 (May 17, 1976), page 1.

"Preus, Tietjen Dialog Fails." 2:19 (May 17, 1976), pages 1–2.

Lutheran Church—Missouri Synod, The, Department of Public Relations. "Walking Together: A Simple Question and Answer Look at the Controversy Confronting The Lutheran Church—Missouri Synod." 2:19 (May 17, 1976), pages 7–14.

"[New Jersey] District Convention Meets [Seminex, Tietjen-Nickel debate]." 2:20 (May 24, 1976), page 2.

"Seminary Notes 50th Year on Campus." 2:20 (May 24, 1976), page 7.

"Preus Sends Letter to Districts [re complying with Synod resolutions]." 2:21 (May 31, 1976), page 1.

"Special COP Meeting Set [re eight dissenting District presidents]." 2:21 (May 31, 1976), page 1.

"[Rev. Walter M.] Schoedel Responds to Dialog [sessions between Preus and Tietjen]." 2:21 (May 31, 1976), pages 1, 8.

"[Concordia] Seminary Will Address Issues [re theological education, Synod controversy]." 2:21 (May 31, 1976), page 8.

"[Northwest District] Board [of Directors] Asks Pres. Jaech to Quit [post on ELIM Coordinating Council]." 2:22 (June 7, 1976), page 1.

"Eastern District Forms New Church." 2:22 (June 7, 1976), page 2.

"LCA Head: 'New Church' Likely [re 'imminent' split in LCMS]." 2:22 (June 7, 1976), page 2.

"Nebraska Convention Wrap-Up [re Seminex graduates]." 2:22 (June 7, 1976), page 7.

"[LCMS] Council of Presidents Holds Special Meeting [re eight removed / dissenting presidents]." 2:23 (June 14, 1976), pages 1–2.

"Committee on Constitutional Matters Clarifies Anaheim [convention] Resolution [5-02A re properly endorsed ministerial candidates]." 2:24 (June 21, 1976), page 1. [See *The Lutheran Witness*, July 4, 1976.]

"Preus Reaffirms Acting [District] Presidents [Atlantic, New England]." 2:24 (June 21, 1976), pages 1, 8.

"Seven Districts Report Convention Action [Atlantic, Colorado, Florida-Georgia, Mid-South, Minnesota South, New England, Ontario]." 2:24 (June 21, 1976), pages 2, 7–8.

"English District Votes to Form New Synod." 2:25 (June 28, 1976), pages 1, 8.

"[District President] Hecht Writes to English District Congregational Leaders." 2:25 (June 28, 1976), pages 1, 8.

"Districts Report on Convention Action [Central Illinois, Indiana, Ohio, Texas]." 2:25 (June 28, 1976), page 8.

"ATS Accredits Seminex." 2:25 (June 28, 1976), page 8.

"[LCMS Past President Oliver] Harms Releases Proposal for Reconciliation Statement [after LCMS CoP does not act on it]." 2:26 (July 5, 1976), page 1.

"Five Districts Report Convention Action [Eastern, Iowa West, Missouri, South Wisconsin, Southern]." 2:26 (July 5, 1976), pages 2, 8.

"Acting [District] Presidents to Sign Changes [on official roster]." 2:27 (July 12, 1976), page 1.

"Preus Comments on [District] Conventions." 2:27 (July 12, 1976), pages 1, 8.

"Three Districts [Iowa East, Michigan, Northern Illinois] Report Convention Action [re Seminex, doctrinal matters]." 2:27 (July 12, 1976), page 2.

"Preus Refers Decision on Tietjen Case to [LCMS Third Vice President] Nickel." 2:28 (July 19, 1976), page 1.

"Bohlmann Repudiates ATLA Censure [re requirement that Seminex students / faculty able to use Concordia Seminary library]." 2:29 (July 26, 1976), page 2.

"Hymnal, Communion Practices Dominate LCA Convention [Spitz (AELC) and Preus (LCMS) address convention]." 2:30 (August 2, 1976), page 2.

" 'Study the Issues,' [Robert] Sauer Urges Congregations." 2:31 (August 9, 1976), page 2.

"CCM Rules on Membership in AELC, Uncertified Pastors at Conventions." 2:33 (August 23, 1976), page 1. [See *The Lutheran Witness*, August 29, 1976.]

"[Fourth] ELIM Assembly Backs Continued Protest in LCMS." 2:34 (August 30, 1976), page 2.

"AELC Membership Ruling by CCM Effective Sept. 30." 2:35 (September 6, 1976), page 1.

"New President in Southern Illinois [following resignation of Neunaber]." 2:35 (September 6, 1976), page 1.

"Five Faculty Resign at [Concordia College] St. Paul [including Paul Manz]." 2:35 (September 6, 1976), page 2.

"Committee on Doctrinal Statements." 2:36 (September 13, 1976), page 7. [See *The Lutheran Witness*, August 1, 1976.]

"Ressmeyer Relinquishes Office [as president of Atlantic District]." 2:37 (September 20, 1976), page 2.

"CTCR Asks ALC to Substantiate Charge [that *A Statement* has narrowed confessional base of LCMS]." 2:38 (September 27, 1976), page 1.

"CCM Sets Rehearing for AELC Ruling." 2:38 (September 27, 1976), page 1.

"Moderates 'More Guilty,' Pastor [Milton Nauss] Says [re rift in LCMS]." 2:38 (September 27, 1976), page 2.

"[Northwest District President] Jaech Is Reaffirmed [re work on ELIM Coordinating Council]." 2:38 (September 27, 1976), page 2.

"[Robert] Riedel Resigns [from LCMS]." 2:39 (October 4, 1976), page 1.

"[LCMS CCM] Ruling [on membership in AELC] Effective Dated Moved to 1977." 2:39 (October 4, 1976), page 1.

"ALC Leader: Inerrancy Overplayed." 2:39 (October 4, 1976), page 2.

"Synodical [Board of Directors] Act on AELC Concerns." 2:40 (October 11, 1976), page 1.

"[Atlantic] District Plans Special Convention." 2:40 (October 11, 1976), page 2.

"[LCMS] Synod President Suggests Dissidents Transfer to ALC." 2:41 (October 18, 1976), page 1.

"ALC Vice-President [Fred W. Meuser] Responds." 2:41 (October 18, 1976), page 1.

"[LCMS Board of] Directors Express Concern over Benefits of Those Who Leave [the LCMS]." 2:41 (October 18, 1976), pages 1, 7.

"Inter-Lutheran Matters Occupy ALC General Convention." 2:41 (October 18, 1976), page 2.

"[Waldemar] Meyer Steps Down from [Colorado] District Post." 2:43 (November 1, 1976), page 1.

"[Northwest] District Studies Constitutional Issues." 2:43 (November 1, 1976), page 1.

[Lutheran Church—Missouri Synod, The, Department of Public Relations]. "Questions to Consider regarding the AELC." 2:43 (November 1, 1976), pages 3–4.

"[LCMS] Administrator [Earl Haake] Refutes AELC Claims [that its pension and welfare plans are comparable to the Synod's]." 2:45 (November 15, 1976), pages 1, 4.

"[LCMS Council of] Presidents: 'Leave Door Open' [to congregations joining the AELC]." 2:46 (November 22, 1976), pages 1, 8.

"AELC Synods Hold Constituting Conventions." 2:47 (November 29, 1976), page 4.

"Atlantic District Elects Officers [and recognizes uncertified ordained Seminex graduates]." 2:49 (December 13, 1976), page 1.

"[LCMS Board of] Directors Amend [Concordia Worker Benefit] Plans, Clarify Property Rights [of congregations]." 2:49 (December 13, 1976), pages 1, 7.

"AELC Founded." 2:49 (December 13, 1976), page 2.

"[ALC-LCMS] Fellowship Meeting Found Disappointing." 2:51 (December 27, 1976), pages 1, 8.

1977

"[LCMS] Board [of Directors] Adopts Statement concerning Withdrawals of Synod Congregations." 3:5 (February 7, 1977), pages 6–7.

"Walkout Report to Be Released [*Exodus from Concordia*]." 3:20 (May 23, 1977), page 8.

"Tietjen Letter [to Third Vice President Nickel re charges filed by Harlan L. Harnapp and Leonard P. Buelow] Draws Response." 3:21 (May 30, 1977), page 2.

"[Third Vice President] Nickel Releases Correspondence with Tietjen." 3:24 (June 20, 1977), page 1.

"Delegates [to LCMS Dallas convention] Address Eastern District Problems [placement of Seminex graduates]." 3:30 (July 25, 1977), page 2.

"Certification Route for Seminex Graduates Is Extended." 3:31 (August 1, 1977), page 7.

"ELIM to Remain 'Voice of Conscience.'" 3:35 (August 29, 1977), page 1.

"[Concordia] Seminary Enrollment Continues to Climb." 3:38 (September 19, 1977), page 1.

"Tietjen Removed from Clergy Roster." 3:40 (October 3, 1977), pages 1–2.

Bryant, Victor. "Record Set Straight [on Tietjen case]." 3:40 (October 3, 1977), pages 1, 3.

"Official Notice re Dr. John H. Tietjen." 3:40 (October 3, 1977), page 2.

"AELC Accepts Synod's Offer to Talk ['all but two members of the Seminex faculty remain as members of the LCMS']." 3:50 (December 19, 1977), page 4.

1978

"AELC Becomes Lutheran Council Member ['only 21 Seminex students have entered Synod's ministry through colloquy']." 4:11 (March 20, 1978), pages 1–2.

"Oswald Elected [president of California-Nevada-Hawaii District], District Ministries Affirmed [vote not to seat 'uncertified pastors']." 4:15 (April 17, 1978), page 3.

"Kansas District Elects Bruening as President [votes not to seat uncertified pastor]." 4:15 (April 17, 1978), page 3.

"New Jersey Reelects [Walter L.] Zeile President [requests new colloquy procedure for Seminex graduates]." 4:21 (May 29, 1978), pages 1, 4.

"Atlantic [District] Presidency Becomes Full-Time Office [vote urging Seminex grads to seek certification]." 4:24 (June 19, 1978), page 4.

"North Wisconsin Reelects Simon, Reaffirms Commitment [concern: uncertified Seminex grads invite 'ecclesiastical chaos']." 4:25 (June 26, 1978), page 4.

"[Arnold E.] Kromphardt Elected [to presidency of Eastern District], Christ Seminary[—Seminex] Graduates Endorsed." 4:26 (July 3, 1978), page 2.

"Bornemann Urges Goal for Church, Bible Class Attendance [urges seating nine Seminex graduates serving in District congregations]." 4:26 (July 3, 1978), page 3.

"[Concordia] Seminary Receives Joint [ATS, NCA] Accreditation, an Historic First." 4:31 (August 7, 1978), page 2.

1980

"Retreats Held for Seminex Grads Seeking Certification by Synod." 6:8 (March 3, 1980), pages 1, 3.

"Nine Seminex Grads Certified; Remainder Could Be after Study." 6:10 (March 17, 1980), pages 1, 4.

"70 Percent of Seminex Grads Now Certified after February Retreats." 6:23 (June 16, 1980), pages 1–2.

"Seminex Considers Invite from Chicago Seminary [LSTC]." 6:37 (September 22, 1980), page 2.

1981

"Pastor's Manuscripts on Moderate Movement Go to Library Archives [Henry L. Lieske papers to Oberlin College library]." 7:3 (January 26, 1981), page 3.

1982

"Lutheran Seminary Plan to Move Seminex Staff [to LSTC]." 8:17 (May 3, 1982), page 4.

"Seminex to Relocate Faculty in Fall 1983." 8:22 (June 7, 1982), page 3.

"Dr. M[artin] Scharlemann Dies, Was Theologian, Teacher." 8:34 (August 30, 1982), page 1.

"Association of Evangelical Lutheran Churches (AELC) [endorsed plan to deploy Seminex resources to LCA and ALC seminaries in Chicago; Berkeley, California; and Austin, Texas, beginning in 1983]." 8:36 (i.e., 37) (September 20, 1982), page 4.

2.2 *Official Periodicals of Other Lutheran Entities*

2.2.1 *The Lutheran Standard* (American Lutheran Church)

(chronological order)

1972

"Newsfront: A House Divided [re 'guidelines' for use by Concordia Seminary, Board of Control]." 12:8 (April 18, 1972), page 18.

"Newsfront: 'Guidelines' Rejected at Concordia [Seminary]." 12:9 (May 2, 1972), page 23.

"Newsfront: Reach Accord [re agreement that Arlis Ehlen not teach course on the Pentateuch at Concordia Seminary]." 12:10 (May 16, 1972), page 26.

"Newsfront: [Arlis Ehlen] Given Walking Papers [at Concordia Seminary]." 12:12 (June 20, 1972), page 18.

"Who's News? Faculty [of Concordia Seminary] Asks Synod for Help [re AATS probation ruling]." 12:13 (July 4, 1972), page 29.

"Newsfront: Revised [AATS] Standards [affirm two-year probation of Concordia Seminary]." 12:14 (July 18, 1972), page 29.

Muedeking, George. "Newsfront: Who's Really Lutheran [Tietjen rebuttal of FFC interview findings]." 12:19 (October 3, 1972), pages 16–17.

1973

"Newsfront: LCMS Unit [CTCR] Urges Fellowship Delay [states that faculty document *Faithful to Our Calling* shows 'substantive' differences on doctrinal issues in the Synod]." 13:8 (April 17, 1973), page 19.

Muedeking, George. "Newsfront: A Juggernaut Rolls at Rivergate [1973 LCMS convention in New Orleans]." 13:15 (August 7, 1973), pages 20–22.

"Newsfront: Concordia [Seminary] Professors Protest Convention Action." 13:16 (August 21, 1973), page 20.

"Newsfront: [LCMS] Campus Ministers Support Moderates [among Concordia Seminary faculty]." 13:17 (September 4, 1973), page 19.

"Newsfront: Suspension [of Tietjen] Delayed." 13:18 (September 18, 1973), page 10.

"Newsfront: 800 Attend LCMS 'Protest' Meeting [of New Orleans convention actions, August 28–29, Des Plaines, Illinois]." 13:19 (October 2, 1973), page 22.

"Newsfront: LCMS Moderates' Meeting Called 'Rebellion.'" 13:20 (October 16, 1973), page 15.

"Newsfront: [Concordia] Seminary Board [of Control] to Review All Courses." 13:24 (December 18, 1973), page 20.

1974

"Newsfront: Action on Suspension [of Tietjen] Delayed." 14:1 (January 1, 1974), page 18.

"Newsfront: Arthur Carl Piepkorn [obituary]." 14:2 (January 15, 1974), page 19.

"Newsfront: [Concordia Seminary president] Tietjen Suspended." 14:3 (February 5, 1974), page 18.

"Newsfront: 'Fraternal Concern' Extended to LCMS [by LCA, ALC seminary presidents and deans]." 14:3 (February 5, 1974), page 22.

"Newsfront: [Concordia Seminary] Students Back Faculty; Mission Exec[utive] [James Mayer] Dropped." 14:3 (February 5, 1974), page 22.

"Newsfront: 'On One Condition' [ELIM representatives agree to serve on reconciliation committee]." 14:3 (February 5, 1974), page 22.

"Newsfront: Stalemate [between Concordia Seminary faculty majority and President J. A. O. Preus]." 14:4 (February 19, 1974), page 19.

"Newsfront: A House Divided." 14:5 (March 5, 1974), page 19.

"Newsfront: Support for Seminex [by Atlantic District]." 14:6 (March 19, 1974), page 16.

Preus, David W. "A Letter to Missouri." 14:8 (April 16, 1974), page 13.

"Newsfront: Seminex Grads 'Ineligible' [for placement as pastors]." 14:8 (April 16, 1974), page 18.

"Newsfront: LCMS leaders Devise Seminex Ordination Plan." 14:10 (May 21, 1974), page 19.

"Newsfront: The Gospel Is Enough [Tietjen commencement speech at Wartburg Seminary]." 14:11 (June 4, 1974), page 18.

"Newsfront: New Warning Issued [by President J. A. O. Preus re placement of Seminex graduates]." 14:13 (July 2, 1974), page 22.

"Newsfront: Seminex Grads Ordained [five of thirty-eight LCMS Districts accept Seminex graduates]." 14:14 (July 16, 1974), page 26.

"Newsfront: Concordia Seminary Retains [ATS] Accreditation." 14:15 (August 6, 1974), page 19.

"Newsfront: Seminex Teacher [William Danker] Gets Synod Post." 14:16 (August 20, 1974), page 18.

"Newsfront: 1300 at ELIM Meeting [Second Assembly]: Should They Restore Old Missouri?" 14:18 (September 17, 1974), page 25.

"Newsfront: Seminex Reports Fall Enrollment of 442." 14:19 (October 1, 1974), page 22.

"Newsfront: LCMS District Heads Censured [re invalid ordinations of Seminex graduates]." 14:20 (October 15, 1974), page 19.

"Newsfront: LCMS [Concordia Seminary] Board [of Control] Fires Tietjen." 14:21 (November 1, 1974), page 26.

"Newsfront: Ordinations [of Seminex graduates] Spur Charges." 14:22 (November 19, 1974), page 18.

"Newsfront: Cease and Desist [re LCMS faculties joining ELIM and similar movements]." 14:24 (December 17, 1974), page 19.

1975

"Newsfront: Dr. John H. Tietjen [to serve as theological consultant to nongeographic district of the LCMS]." 15:2 (January 21, 1975), page 21.

"Newsfront: The Year in Religion—1974 [picture of Concordia Seminary 'walkout']." 15:2 (January 21, 1975), pages 22–23.

"Newsfront: Charges [against Rudolph Ressmeyer, Atlantic District] Dismissed." 15:4 (February 18, 1975), page 20.

"Newsfront: Tietjen Named Seminary in Exile Head." 15:4 (February 18, 1975), page 20.

"Newsfront: Dr. Edgar Krentz [resigns from the Concordia Seminary faculty]." 15:4 (February 18, 1975), page 26.

"Newsfront: LCMS Head Offers Anaheim [convention] Preview." 15:5 (March 4, 1975), page 23.

"Newsfront: Largest Seminary [Seminex: 414 students; Concordia Seminary: 174 students]." 15:5 (March 4, 1975), page 26.

"Newsfront: Board [ALC Division for Theological Education and Ministry] Acts on Seminex Intern Request." 15:11 (June 3, 1975), page 20.

"Newsfront: Tietjen Absolved of Heresy." 15:15 (August 5, 1975), page 14.

"Newsfront: AAUP Censures [Concordia] Seminary." 15:15 (August 5, 1975), page 14.

"Newsfront: LCMS [convention] at Anaheim: Missouri in 'Fantasyland' [re actions on ELIM, Seminex]." 15:15 (August 5, 1975), pages 18–19.

"Newsfront: 'To Leave or Not to Leave' Debated by LCMS Moderates [LCM, ELIM]." 15:17 (September 2, 1975), page 16.

"Newsfront: LCMS Educator Resigns [Harvey Stegemoeller, Concordia, Saint Paul]." 15:18 (September 16, 1975), page 14.

"Newsfront: [St. Paul Lutheran Church, Denton, Texas, calls female Seminex vicar]." 15:19 (October 7, 1975), page 16.

"Newsfront: [English] District Repudiates LCMS [Anaheim] Convention." 15:20 (October 21, 1975), page 21.

"Newsfront: Tietjen Case Closed." 15:21 (November 4, 1975), page 23.

"Newsfront: Ouster Moves Begin [of LCMS District presidents who ordain uncertified Seminex graduates]." 15:23 (December 2, 1975), page 14.

"Newsfront: Eight LCMS District Presidents Refuse to Promise Ban [on ordaining uncertified Seminex graduates]." 15:24 (December 16, 1975), page 13.

1976

"Newsfront: Seminex Faculty Declines Synod Interviews." 16:3 (February 3, 1976), page 18.

"Newsfront: Separation [of English District] from LCMS Recommended." 16:3 (February 3, 1976), page 19.

"Newsfront: ALC President Deplores Missouri Synod Firings [of District presidents]." 16:8 (April 20, 1976), pages 12–13.

"Newsfront: Leaders Replaced [re removal of four LCMS District presidents]." 16:9 (May 4, 1976), page 14.

"Newsfront: Moderates Organize [AELC]." 16:10 (May 18, 1976), page 14.

"Newsfront: [Missouri] Synod Peace Elusive [re doctrinal issues, Seminex]." 16:11 (June 1, 1976), page 12.

"Newsfront: Northern Minnesota District Responds to LCMS 'Anguish' [re *A Statement*]." 16:11 (June 1, 1976), page 16.

"Newsfront: The Rev. Richard E. Koenig . . . Left The Lutheran Church—Missouri Synod." 16:13 (July 6, 1976), page 21.

"Newsfront: Ousted by Human Bylaws [re LCMS District president Herman Neunaber]." 16:16 (September 21, 1976), page 14.

"Newsfront: Quits Post and Synod [re LCMS District president Robert Riedel]." 16:18 (October 19, 1976), page 14.

"Newsfront: Back Charges, ALC Asked [re action on *A Statement*]." 16:18 (October 19, 1976), page 16.

"Newsfront: 5th LCMS Leader Quits [District president Waldemar Meyer]." 16:20 (November 16, 1976), page 14.

"Newsfront: AELC Synods Organize." 16:21 (December 7, 1976), page 14.

"Newsfront: New Church Launched [AELC]." 16:22 (December 21, 1976), page 14.

1977

"Newsfront: 'Dallas Nine' Express Concern: New Directions Sought for Missouri Synod." 17:6 (March 15, 1977), page 22.

"Newsfront: At Convention in Dallas: [Missouri] Synod Delays Hymnal Action, Protests ALC Fellowship; ALC President Cautions LCMS on 'Tyranny.'" 17:14 (August 9, 1977), pages 22–23.

"Newsfront: ELIM Votes Continuance as 'Voice of Conscience' [for moderates in the LCMS]." 17:16 (September 20, 1977), page 15.

"Newsfront: New Lutheran Church Body [AELC] Third to Ordain Women." 17:17 (October 4, 1977), page 16.

"Newsfront: Tietjen Expelled [from LCMS]." 17:18 (October 18, 1977), page 18.

"Newsfront: Tietjen Ouster from LCMS Called Slanderous [by ELIM board]." 17:20 (November 15, 1977), page 14.

1978

"Newsfront: Southwest Pastors Ask End to [Missouri] Synod Factionalism." 18:4 (February 21, 1978), page 15.

"Newsfront: Luther Seminary Largest [Concordia Seminary: 432 students; Seminex: 283 students]." 18:6 (March 21, 1978), page 14.

"Newsfront: [AELC] Joins: Lutheran Council Acts on Disputed Membership [joint AELC / LCMS]." 18:7 (April 4, 1978), pages 22–23.

1979

"Newsfront: Plea for Understanding Voiced by LCMS Leaders [ALC and LCMS District presidents meet in Minneapolis]." 19:7 (April 3, 1979), page 14.

1980

Almen, Lowell G. "News in These Times: Tietjen: Can We Be Signs of God's Unity and Peace? [ALC Illinois District convention]." 20:9 (May 6, 1980), page 21.

1981

"Newsfront: Unity within Synod Goal of New LCMS Leader [Ralph Bohlmann]." 21:14 (August 7, 1981), page 17.

"Newsfront: LCMS Will End Dual Memberships [with AELC]." 21:14 (August 7, 1981), page 18.

1982

Almen, Lowell G. "News in These Times: [ALC] Theology Board Hears of Possible Shift of Seminex Resources [to LSTC, etc.]." 22:8 (April 16, 1982), page 25.

"Newsfront: Kohn Reelected President [of AELC]." 22:17 (October 1, 1982), page 23.

1983

"News Quick Look: Christ Seminary—Seminex [closes campus in Saint Louis]." 23:12 (July 8, 1983), page 25.

2.2.2 *The Lutheran* (Lutheran Church in America)

(chronological order)

1972

"News: Concordia Seminary Ordered to Teach Bible Literally [Arlis Ehlen center of controversy]." 10:7 (April 5, 1972), page 26.

"News: Concordia [Seminary] Faculty Rejects Bible Teaching 'Guidelines' [of President J. A. O. Preus]." 10:9 (May 3, 1972), page 29.

"News: Compromise Reached in Concordia Seminary Professor [Arlis Ehlen] Dispute." 10:10 (May 17, 1972), page 28.

"News: Firing of Professor [Arlis Ehlen] Widens Rift in Missouri Synod." 10:13 (July 5, 1972), page 25.

"News: Stop Teaching False Doctrine, [J. A. O.] Preus Warns [Concordia] Seminary." 10:18 (October 4, 1972), page 25.

"News: Missouri [Synod] District Leaders Seek to End Controversy." 10:19 (October 18, 1972), pages 25, 28.

Marty, Martin E. "Missouri's Inner Struggle [analysis of the issues]." 10:21 (November 15, 1972), pages 8–11.

1973

"News: Concordia [seminary] Faculty Affirms Stand on Faith and Doctrine [forty-four of forty-seven faculty members sign *Faithful to Our Calling, Faithful to Our Lord*]." 11:4 (February 21, 1973), pages 28–29.

"News: Missouri Synod Leaders Ask a Halt in 'Politicking' [Concordia Seminary Board of Control 'commends entire faculty']." 11:7 (April 4, 1973), pages 28–29.

"News: Missouri Synod Commission [CTCR] Chides [Concordia] Seminary Faculty [re *Faithful to Our Calling, Faithful to Our Lord*]." 11:9 (May 2, 1973), pages 32, 34.

"News: Missouri Synod Leader [J. A. O. Preus] Asks Synod to Resolve Seminary Dispute [at New Orleans convention]." 11:11 (June 6, 1973), pages 26–27.

"News: Election [of LCMS president] Is Major Issue as Missouri Synod Meets." 11:12 (June 20, 1973), page 24.

"News: Missouri Synod Censures [Concordia] Seminary Faculty [at 1973 LCMS convention]." 12:12 (i.e., 11:14) (August 8, 1973), pages 28–29.

Stauderman, Albert P. "News: Concordia [Seminary] Faculty Protests Synod Rule." 12:13 (i.e., 11:15) (September 5, 1973), page 20.

"News: [Concordia] Seminary Head [Tietjen] Is 'Suspended'—Maybe." 11:16 (September 19, 1973), page 20.

"News: Missouri's Moderates Set Up New 'Movement' [two-day meeting in Chicago in late August]." 11:17 (October 3, 1973), page 20.

"News: [J. A. O.] Preus Calls Opponents Insurgents and Rebels." 11:18 (October 17, 1973), page 20.

"News: Tietjen 'Suspension' Rescinded by [Concordia Seminary] Board [of Control]." 11:19 (November 7, 1973), pages 17–18.

"News: Missouri Moderates Name Director and Cite Goals." 11:20 (November 21, 1973), pages 19–20.

"News: Missouri [English] District Says Synod Acted Illegally." 11:21 (December 5, 1973), page 20.

"News: One Missouri Seminary Prexy Quits [Schultz], but the Other Gets a New Reprieve [Tietjen]." 11:22 (December 19, 1973), page 20.

1974

"News: Seminary Leaders [from ALC and LCA] Decry Purge at Concordia [Seminary]." 12:3 (February 6, 1974), pages 19–20.

"News: Strike Shuts Down Concordia [Seminary] after Board [of Control] Suspends Tietjen." 12:4 (February 20, 1974), page 18.

"News: New Group Named to 'Conciliate' Controversy in Missouri Synod." 12:5 (March 6, 1974), page 18.

"News: Concordia 'Seminary-in-Exile' Set Up as Missouri Synod Seeks Conciliation." 12:6 (March 20, 1974), page 19.

"News: Exiled Seminary Enrolls 384 students, 40 profs." 12:7 (April 3, 1974), pages 18–19.

"News: LCMS Districts Accept 'Exiles' as Vicars." 12:8 (April 17, 1974), page 20.

"News: Tensions within the Missouri Synod May Affect LCA, Dr. Marshall Notes." 12:9 (May 1, 1974), pages 18–19.

"News: Missouri Synod to Place All Seminary Seniors [including Seminex]." 12:11 (June 5, 1974), page 17.

"News: Seminex Seniors Reject Plans for Placement." 12:12 (June 19, 1974), pages 20–21.

"News: Noted Theologians [including George W. Forell, Krister Stendahl] Aid Seminex Program." 12:13 (July 10, 1974), page 16.

"News: Dr. [J. A. O.] Preus Rejects LCA Statement of Concern." 12:14 (August 14, 1974), page 21.

"News: 56 Seminex Graduates Called to Parishes." 12:14 (August 14, 1974), page 22.

"News: Asian Lutheran [church] Bodies Chide Missouri Synod." 12:15 (September 4, 1974), page 20.

"News: ELIM Votes to Remain within Missouri Synod." 12:16 (September 18, 1974), page 18.

"News: Missouri's Seminex Has Largest Fall Enrollment [442 students]." 12:17 (October 2, 1974), page 17.

"News: [J. A. O.] Preus Challenges [LCMS District] Presidents on Seminex Ordinations." 12:18 (October 16, 1974), page 19.

"News: LCMS Seminary Ousts Tietjen as President." 12:19 (November 6, 1974), page 17.

"News: Missouri Synod Dispute Enters New Phase [re ordaining uncertified Seminex graduates]." 12:21 (December 4, 1974), page 18.

1975

"News: Tietjen Elected Seminex President as Missouri Synod Rift Deepens." 13:5 (March 5, 1975), page 18.

"News: 'Standby' Church Body Formed by Missouri Synod Moderates [Lutheran Church in Mission (LCM)]." 13:6 (March 19, 1975), page 18.

"News: Missouri's Cutoff of Funds Creates 'Desperate Crisis' for LCUSA [Lutheran Council in the United States of America]." 13:6 (March 19, 1975), page 18.

"News: Missouri Leaders Feel Schism May Be Avoided." 13:10 (May 21, 1975), page 20.

"News: Missouri's Stewardship Chief Quits in Protest." 13:11 (June 4, 1975), page 19.

"News: Missouri Synod Convention Acts to Silence or Oust Dissenters." 13:14 (August 13, 1975), pages 17–19.

Stauderman, Albert P. "Editor's Opinion: Missouri after Anaheim." 13:14 (August 13, 1975), page 34.

"News: Missouri Synod Moderates [ELIM, LCM] Endorse Plans for Separate Organization." 13:16 (September 17, 1975), page 16.

"News: 'Extremists on Both Sides' Chided by Missouri Synod's President." 13:17 (October 1, 1975), page 18.

"News: Dr. Marshall Urges Fellowship with All Missouri Members." 13:18 (October 15, 1975), page 19.

"News: Missouri Synod Head Starts Action against Eight District Presidents." 13:21 (December 3, 1975), page 19.

1976

"News: Congregation Leaving Missouri Synod [Grace Lutheran Church, Oklahoma City] Faces Court Battle for Property." 14:1 (January 7, 1976), page 19.

"News: District Presidents Reject Plea [re ordaining uncertified Seminex graduates]." 14:1 (January 7, 1976), page 19.

"News: [J. A. O.] Preus Decides against Ousting District Head [Neunaber]." 14:3 (February 4, 1976), pages 18–19.

"News: LCMS District [Southern Illinois] Votes Support for Its Leader [Neunaber]." 14:6 (March 17, 1976), page 20.

"News: Eight District Presidents Defy [J. A. O.] Preus; Four Are Dismissed." 14:8 (April 21, 1976), page 18.

"News: Missouri Synod Districts Defy Effort to Oust Their Presidents." 14:9 (May 5, 1976), page 18.

"News: Missouri Synod Moderates Plan 'Interim Church' if Schism Occurs." 14:11 (June 2, 1976), page 19.

"News: New Church Body Seen Emerging from Missouri Synod Conflict [AELC]." 14:12 (June 16, 1976), page 17.

"News: Missouri [Synod] Districts Reject Ouster of Presidents; One Votes to Leave [English District]." 14:13 (July 14, 1976), page 19.

"News: Missouri Moderates [AELC] to Meet in December." 14:14 (August 11, 1976), page 18.

"News: ELIM to Remain 'Voice of Protest' in Missouri." 14:16 (September 15, 1976), page 20.

"News: Two More District Presidents [Hecht, Neunaber] Resign in Missouri Conflict." 14:17 (October 6, 1976), page 20.

"News: Fourth Missouri Synod District Chief [Riedel] Resigns." 14:19 (November 3, 1976), page 17.

"News: New Lutheran Body [AELC] Slates Synod Meetings." 14:20 (November 17, 1976), pages 18–19.

"News: Fifth Missouri Synod Leader [Waldemar Meyer] Quits." 14:21 (December 1, 1976), page 15.

"News: New England [Synod, LCA] Welcomes Former LCMS Church [Immanuel Lutheran Church, Amherst, Massachusetts]." 14:21 (December 1, 1976), page 20.

"News: Former Missourians Form Five Synods [of AELC]." 14:22 (December 15, 1976), pages 18–19.

1977

"News: Missouri Synod Moderates Form New Church [AELC] with 150 Congregations." 15:1 (January 5, 1977), page 18.

"News: Sixth LCMS District President [Paul E. Jacobs] Resigns." 15:4 (February 16, 1977), page 19.

"News: Quiet Convention [in Dallas] Seen for Missouri Synod." 15:13 (July 13, 1977), page 17.

"News: Missouri Synod Reelects Preus, Continues ALC Tie, Delays Hymnal [re District President Frincke and Seminex, dual membership in LCMS and AELC]." 15:14 (August 1977), page 17.

"News: ELIM to Be Missouri's 'Voice of Conscience.'" 15:16 (September 21, 1977), pages 18–19.

"News: Missouri Synod Offshoot [AELC] to Ordain First Woman." 15:17 (October 5, 1977), page 18.

"News: Former LCMS Executive to Direct LCA Foundation [Seminex graduate Victor O. Mennicke]." 15:20 (November 16, 1977), page 26.

"News: Unity Efforts Falter as Disputes Lead to Rifts in Several [LCMS] Churches." 15:21 (December 1977), page 22.

1978

"News: Missouri District [Southern Illinois] Expels Congregation, 4 Pastors [holding AELC membership]." 16:4 (March 1, 1978), pages 20–21.

"News: Lutheran Council Adds AELC as Fourth Member." 16:6 (April 5, 1978), page 21.

"News: Missouri Reports Loss of 111 Congregations [mostly to AELC]." 16:9 (May 17, 1978), page 18.

"News: Missouri Synod, ALC Drop Dissident Congregations [two LCMS parishes in Canada that called Seminex graduates]." 16:12 (July 1978), page 18.

"News: Some Lutherans Sign [biblical] Inerrancy Statement [Robert and J. A. O. Preus, re *Chicago Statement on Biblical Inerrancy*]." 16:21 (December 20, 1978), page 21.

1979

"News: Influx from Other Lutheran Bodies [including graduates from Seminex] Increases Oversupply of LCA Clergy." 16:3 (i.e., 17:3) (February 21, 1979), page 18.

Trexler, Edgar R. "Steady Hand for an Interim Church [William H. Kohn and the AELC]." 17:16 (September 19, 1979), pages 10–12.

1980

"News: LCMS Certifies Some Seminex Graduates." 18:9 (May 7, 1980), page 18.

"News: LCMS President Preus to Decline Re-election." 18:18 (October 15, 1980), page 17.

"News: LSTC Invites Seminex to Relocate in Chicago [enrollment down to 200]." 18:18 (October 15, 1980), page 22.

1981

"News: Seminary Presidents [including AELC Seminex] Call for Lutheran Union." 19:5 (March 4, 1981), page 17.

"News: 3 Seminaries Discuss Closer Ties [Seminex, Wartburg, LSTC]." 19:10 (May 20, 1981), page 21.

"News: LCMS Elects Bohlmann, Ends ALC Ties." 19:14 (August 1981), page 17.

1983

Lyles, Jean Caffey. "John Tietjen: A Thoroughly Orthodox Maverick." 21:8 (April 20, 1983), pages 8–10.

"News: Division Seeks 3-way Seminary Ownership [ALC, LCA, AELC]." 21:11 (June 1, 1983), page 23.

"News: AELC's Seminex Holds Final Commencement [faculty, students to go to LSTC, Chicago; Pacific Lutheran, Berkeley, California; and the Lutheran Seminary Program in the Southwest, Austin, Texas]." 21:12 (June 15, 1983), page 17.

1984

"News: Enrollment Increases at LCA Seminaries [LSTC: from 186 to 243]." 22:2 (January 18, 1984), page 23.

Anderson, H. George. "Roads to Union: The Seminary Ownership Question [post-Seminex]." 22:3 (February 1, 1984), page 7.

"News: LCA Anticipates Surplus of Clergy." 22:7 (April 4, 1984), page 18.

2.2.3 *St. Louis Lutheran*

(Lutheran Publicity Organization of Greater Saint Louis)

(chronological order)

1972

"Synod Scene [LCMS President Preus orders restriction on courses to be taught by Concordia Seminary professor Arlis Ehlen]." 27:12 (March 11, 1972), page 12.

"Synod Scene [controversy begins re CTCR document *A Statement of Scriptural and Confessional Principles*]." 27:13 (April 8, 1972), page 12.

"Synod Scene [Concordia Seminary faculty protests 'theological guidelines put forward in *A Statement*']." 27:15 (April 22, 1972), page 8.

"Synod Scene [LCMS CoP urges resolution of controversy; Preus and Tietjen agree that Ehlen will not teach course on the Pentateuch]." 27:16 (May 13, 1972), page 12.

"Synod Scene [J. A. O. Preus, Synod vice presidents meet with Concordia Seminary faculty re *A Statement*; establish time line for discussion and responses]." 27:17 (May 27, 1972), page 12.

"[Seminary] Faculty Sends Special Message to Students [on theological issues]." 27:18 (June 10, 1972), page 1.

"Synod Scene [LCMS Board for Higher Education terminates services of Arlis Ehlen]." 27:18 (June 10, 1972), page 12.

"English District Supports Ordination of Women, Sem[inary faculty at Concordia, Saint Louis]." 27:20 (July 8, 1972), page 1.

"Synod Scene [Concordia Seminary Board of Control responds to AATS probation of accreditation]." 27:20 (July 8, 1972), page 8.

"Synod Scene [re Concordia Seminary Board of Control study of FFC report]." 27:22 (August 12, 1972), page 8.

"Synod Scene [re J. A. O. Preus report charges false doctrine at Concordia Seminary, at odds with Board of Control findings]." 27:24 (September 9, 1972), page 12.

"Synod Scene [re Tietjen and Concordia Seminary faculty responses to Preus's report]." 28:1 (September 23, 1972), page 12.

"[Concordia Seminary] Professors Lead Studies on Teaching, Interpreting Bible [for those in Saint Louis area]." 28:2 (October 14, 1972), page 1.

"Editorial: [Encouraging attendance at] Bible Study Seminars [to 'see firsthand how our seminary professors are actually dealing with Scripture']." 28:2 (October 14, 1972), page 4.

"Synod Scene: Seminary Controversy [re joint statement from Preus and Tietjen]." 28:2 (October 14, 1972), page 16.

"Synod Scene: Seminary Faculty Accepts Offer [to issue individual / corporate statements]." 28:3 (October 28, 1972), page 12.

"Synod Scene: Biblical Interpretation [CTCR conducts workshops re historical-critical approach]." 28:4 (November 11, 1972), page 12.

"Synod Scene: [CTCR] Vote on Statement [*A Statement of Scriptural and Confessional Principles*]." 28:6 (December 9, 1972), page 12.

1973

"[Concordia Seminary] Faculty Statement: '*Faithful to Our Calling, Faithful to Our Lord*' [is issued]." 28:8 (January 13, 1973), page 5.

"AD ONE: Is All of the Bible God's Truth?" [Advertisement by Lutherans United for Bible Truth, Saint Louis.] 28:9 (January 27, 1973), page 7.

"Synod Scene: Concordia [Seminary] Faculty Statement [published]." 28:9 (January 27, 1973), page 12.

"AD TWO: Is God the Only Author of the Bible?" [Advertisement by Lutherans United for Bible Truth, Saint Louis.] 28:10 (February 10, 1973), page 13.

"Synod Scene: Springfield [Illinois, Concordia Theological] Seminary Board [of Control resolves to employ *A Statement*]." 28:10 (February 10, 1973), page 16.

Feucht, Oscar E. "Letter to the Editor: Is All of the Bible God's Truth?" 28:11 (February 24, 1973), pages 4, 12.

Labels January 27 advertisement "unscholarly, sectarian biblicism." See also March 24 response by John C. Baur and Feucht's response in the same issue.

"AD THREE: Are Both Old and New Testaments Important?" [Advertisement by Lutherans United for Bible Truth, Saint Louis.] 28:11 (February 24, 1973), page 7.

"AD FOUR: Does the Bible Explain Itself?" [Advertisement by Lutherans United for Bible Truth, Saint Louis.] 28:12 (March 10, 1973), page 9.

Baur, John C. "Editorial: What Is Meant?" 28:13 (March 24, 1973), page 4.

Feucht, Oscar E. "Editorial: Sectarian Biblicism." 28:13 (March 24, 1973), page 4.

"A First [Concordia Seminary faculty wives retreat announced; a response to the then-current controversy at the seminary?]." 28:13 (March 24, 1973), page 8.

"AD FIVE: What about Gospel Reductionism?" [Advertisement by Lutherans United for Bible Truth, Saint Louis.] 28:14 (April 14, 1973), page 13.

"Synod Scene: CTCR vs. [Concordia] Seminary [identifies serious deficiencies in part 1 of *Faithful to Our Calling*; asks Synod to reject historical-critical method]." 28:14 (April 14, 1973), page 16.

"AD SIX: What about the Historical-Critical Method? Part One." [Advertisement by Lutherans United for Bible Truth, Saint Louis.] 28:15 (April 28, 1973), page 9.

"AD SEVEN: What about the Historical-Critical Method? Part Two." [Advertisement by Lutherans United for Bible Truth, Saint Louis.] 28:16 (May 12, 1973), page 9.

"AD EIGHT: What Rights Do All of Us Have as Priests?" [Advertisement by Lutherans United for Bible Truth, Saint Louis.] 28:17 (May 26, 1973), page 9.

"AD NINE: What about the Lutheran Confessions?" [Advertisement by Lutherans United for Bible Truth, Saint Louis.] 28:18 (June 9, 1973), page 11.

"AD TEN: What about Authority in Synod?" [Advertisement by Lutherans United for Bible Truth, Saint Louis.] 28:19 (June 23, 1973), page 11.

"[J. A. O.] Preus Reelected; Sees LCMS at 'Doctrinal Crossroads.'" 28:20 (July 14, 1973), pages 1, 4.

"Domination by Conservatives Marks Synod Convention [in New Orleans]." 28:21 (July 28, 1973), pages 1, 5.

"[Concordia Seminary] Faculty Issues Declaration of Protest and Confession." 28:21 (July 28, 1973), page 3.

"[LCMS] Council of [District] Presidents Stress Desire for Unity." 28:22 (August 11, 1973), page 1.

"Tietjen Still Prexy, Sem[inary] Opens Sept. 7." 28:23 (August 25, 1973), page 1.

"85 Pastors [in the Saint Louis area] Appeal to [Concordia Seminary] Board of Control [to deal 'evangelically' with faculty]." 28:23 (August 25, 1973), page 7.

"Seminary Opens with 700 Students." 28:24 (September 8, 1973), page 1.

"LCMS Moderates Organize CEL [Conference of Evangelical Lutherans at O'Hare Inn, Chicago; First ELIM Assembly]." 28:24 (September 8, 1973), page 1.

"[Concordia Seminary faculty and students] Mark Tietjen's 20th Anniversary [of ordination; evening Communion service; Jaroslav Pelikan, preacher; Paul Manz, organist]." 28:2 (October 13, 1973), page 12.

"[Arthur C.] Piepkorn Dies, Noted Lutheran Theologian." 29:7 (December 22, 1973), pages 1, 6.

1974

"Concordia Seminary Board Suspends President Tietjen." 29:9 (January 26, 1974), pages 1, 7.

"Television Specials Feature Crisis in Missouri Synod." 29:10 (February 9, 1974), page 7.

KTVI: *Conflict at Concordia* (see under 1.3 ***Audiovisual Resources***); KMOX: *Conflict in The Lutheran Church—Missouri Synod: Theology or Politics?*

"Steps to End Controversy Taken by Synod [Board of] Directors." 29:10 (February 9, 1974), pages 8–9.

"[Concordia] Seminary Board [of Control] Plans Full Operation for Spring." 29:11 (February 23, 1974), pages 1, 12.

"A Syllabus on Why the '*A Statement*' (Article I) Is Non-Lutheran." [Advertisement by Herbert P. Fritze, executive chaplain, Oklahoma District Conference on *A Statement*, February 3–4, 1974.] 29:11 (February 23, 1974), page 9.

"[Concordia Seminary] Students to Resume Education in Exile." 29:11 (February 23, 1974), page 12.

"Concerned Area Lutherans Organize, Support Seminex." 29:12 (March 9, 1974), page 12.

"Rally [of more than 1,500 people] Welcomes Concordia's New Administration." [J. A. O. Preus, E. J. Otto, Martin Scharlemann, Walter A. Maier II speak.] 29:13 (March 23, 1974), page 6.

"385 Students Enrolled at Exile Seminary." 29:13 (March 23, 1974), page 12.

"Teachers [at LCMS schools] Must Honor [synodically adopted] Statements." 29:14 (April 13, 1974), page 1.

"Seminex Chorus to Give Benefit Concert Apr. 21 [at Second Presbyterian Church]." 29:14 (April 13, 1974), page 1.

"ELIM Assures Future Needs of Seminex." 29:14 (April 13, 1974), page 3.

"A Syllabus on Why the '*A Statement*' (Article II) Is Non-Lutheran." [Advertisement by Herbert P. Fritze, executive chaplain, Oklahoma District Conference on *A Statement*, February 3–4, 1974.] 29:14 (April 13, 1974), page 11.

"Seminex Faculty Document [on congregational autonomy re calling Seminex graduates] Challenges [LCMS] CCM Rulings." 29:15 (April 27, 1974), page 1.

"Scharlemann Resigns [Concordia Seminary presidency for health reasons]." 29:15 (April 27, 1974), page 1.

"[LCMS] Council [of Presidents] Acts on Placement of Ministerial Candidates [including procedure for Seminex graduates]." 29:16 (May 11, 1974), page 1.

"Set Dialogues on Issues in Synod [at local LCMS churches]." 29:16 (May 11, 1974), page 1.

"[Seminary physician Charles G.] Obermeyer Quits after 28 Years at Concordia [to go with friends who left]." 29:16 (May 11, 1974), page 6.

"[Concordia Seminary Board of Control] Name [Ralph A.] Bohlmann Acting President of Seminary." 29:17 (May 25, 1974), page 4.

"[LCMS] Council [of Presidents] Fills 147 Calls for Ministerial Candidates [placement of Seminex graduates at 'impasse']." 29:17 (May 25, 1974), page 5.

"[Seminex] Candidates Appeal to Congregations [declined to be interviewed by Concordia Seminary faculty]." 29:17 (May 25, 1974), page 7.

"Vital Issues in Synod, District Face Delegates [to LCMS Missouri District convention]." 29:18 (June 8, 1974), page 1.

"ELIM Pledges $40,000 for Seminex Grads [until such time as ordained]." 29:18 (June 8, 1974), page 5.

"[LCMS] Board [of Directors] Views Activities of ELIM Divisive." 29:18 (June 8, 1974), page 8.

"Ecumenical Theological Festival [connected with Seminex summer program]." 29:18 (June 8, 1974), page 9.

"Call for Gathering of Church Leaders by [LCMS] English District [to deal with issues agitating the Synod]." 29:19 (June 22, 1974), page 1.

"[Rev. Samuel] Roth Answers Charges of 'Being Divisive' [re joining ELIM]." 29:19 (June 22, 1974), page 4.

"Faculty of Seminex Declines Job Interviews at Concordia." 29:19 (June 22, 1974), page 7.

"New Posts [elsewhere] for Seminex Prof, Staff Members [Robert Bergt, Donald Hinchey, Carl Sachtleben]." 29:19 (June 22, 1974), page 8.

"[President J. A. O.] Preus 'Grieved' over [LCA] 'Judgment' upon LCMS [re adoption of doctrinal statements]." 29:21 (July 27, 1974), page 1.

"[Concordia Seminary Board of Control] Install Professors at Concordia [faculty numbers seventeen with three on leave]." 29:21 (July 27, 1974), page 4.

[Photograph of Seminex graduates painting a house, waiting for placement]. 29:21 (July 27, 1974), page 5.

"Seminex Faculty Seeks Fraternal Discussions Soon [appeal to LCMS Missouri District President Scherer]." 29:22 (August 10, 1974), page 1.

"Tietjen Hearing Date Set for Aug. 30 by [Concordia Seminary] Faculty Committee." 29:22 (August 10, 1974), page 1.

"Tietjen Declines Faculty Hearing." 29:23 (August 24, 1974), page 1.

"ELIM Assembly [1,000 delegates registered for Second Assembly in Chicago, August 26–28, 1974]." 29:23 (August 24, 1974), page 2.

"Concordia [Seminary] Opens." 29:23 (August 24, 1974), page 4.

"ELIM 'In State of Protest' but Rejects LCMS 'Schism' [at Second Assembly in Chicago]." 29:24 (September 14, 1974), page 1.

"Krentz Speaks to Pastors [presentation at Saint Louis Pastors Conference titled 'From Allegory to Event: Bible Interpretation in the History of the Church'; Ralph Bohlmann and John Damm also speak]." 30:1 (September 28, 1974), page 3.

"Install Prof. Bergt at Carbondale [as Minister of Music, Lutheran Student Center at Southern Illinois University]." 30:1 (September 28, 1974), page 7.

"CTCR Approve New Reports on '*A Statement*' and '[*Mission*] *Affirmations*.'" 30:2 (October 12, 1974), page 16.

"Dr. Tietjen Responds to Dismissal." 30:3 (October 26, 1974), page 1.

"[LCMS English District President] Hecht to Speak [at circuit meeting held at Chapel of the Cross, Saint Louis]." 30:3 (October 26, 1974), page 1.

"ELIM Leaders Pledge Support for Dr. Tietjen." 30:3 (October 26, 1974), page 4.

"Exiled Concordia Plan [Reformation Day] Service. [Luther's German Mass celebrated at Second Presbyterian Church; F. Dean Lueking, preacher; John Tietjen, celebrant]." 30:3 (October 26, 1974), page 8.

"Dissension Mars Second 'Committee of 20' Meeting [on 1973 LCMS convention Resolution 3-09, dismissal of Tietjen, etc.]." 30:4 (November 9, 1974), pages 1, 8.

"[Concordia] Seminary Board [of Control] Pledges Report on Dr. Tietjen." 30:4 (November 9, 1974), page 2.

"[Concordia Seminary] Board [of Control] Acts on Certification, Library Services to Seminex." 30:5 (November 23, 1974), pages 1, 3.

"[LCMS] Council of Presidents Set Theological Convocation [and acts on Seminex matters]." 30:6 (December 14, 1974), page 1.

"Seminex Synodwide Outreach [students travel to communicate directly with congregations]." 30:6 (December 14, 1974), page 3.

"Seminex Board Meets, Elects New Officers." 30:6 (December 14, 1974), page 11.

"[Bohlmann, Wunderlich] Interview Seminex Graduates [for certification]." 30:7 (December 28, 1974), page 1.

"ELIM Urges Moratorium on Dismissals [of church workers]." 30:7 (December 28, 1974), page 7.

1975

"[Agenda Committee members] Set Further Plans for [Theological] Convocation [on the 'nature and function of Holy Scripture']." 30:8 (January 11, 1975), page 2.

"St. Louis-ELIM to Meet [at Concordia Lutheran Church, Kirkwood, Missouri]." 30:10 (February 8, 1975), page 3.

"5 Theologians to Give Topics at [theological] Convocation [Ralph Bohlmann, Howard Tepker, Fred Kramer, Martin Franzmann, Herbert Bouman]." 30:10 (February 8, 1975), page 6.

"Dr. [Edgar] Krentz Resigns [from Concordia Seminary faculty]." 30:10 (February 8, 1975), page 7.

"Seminex Board Elects Tietjen President." 30:10 (February 8, 1975), page 12.

"'5-and-5' Meeting [five representatives from ELIM and five from LCMS] Ends, ELIM Repeats Concerns." 30:11 (February 22, 1975), page 5.

"[Concordia Seminary] Board [of Control] Makes Exception to Seminex Library Policy." 30:12 (March 8, 1975), page 4.

"[LCMS] Commission [on Constitutional Matters] Rules on Tietjen Case." 30:12 (March 8, 1975), page 4.

"Plan Seven [LCMS Missouri District] Conferences to Dialogue Issues in Synod." 30:13 (March 22, 1975), pages 1, 13.

"101 Vicar Candidate Requests Not Filled." 30:13 (March 22, 1975), page 6.

"LCMS Dominate News Says [LCA] Lutheran Editor [Albert Stauderman]." 30:13 (March 22, 1975), page 12.

"[Concordia Seminary faculty and Board of Control] Object to Communion Service at [theological] Convocation." 30:13 (March 22, 1975), page 16.

"Analysis of [theological] Convocation [at Saint Louis Pastoral Conference, April 21]." 30:14 (April 12, 1975), page 1.

"90 [Seminex] Student Interns [i.e., vicars] Placed." 30:14 (April 12, 1975), page 5.

"Understanding Emerges at Theological Convocation." 30:15 (April 26, 1975), page 1.

"[Families] Give Libraries to Seminex [of sainted Paul Bretscher, A. C. Piepkorn, Carl S. Meyer]." 30:15 (April 26, 1975), page 9.

"[Concordia Seminary Board of Control] Elect Bohlmann 7th President of [Concordia] Seminary." 30:16 (May 10, 1975), page 3.

"[J. A. O.] Preus at Conference [speaking on 'Issues at Anaheim']." 30:16 (May 10, 1975), page 3.

"119 Graduate at Seminex." 30:16 (May 10, 1975), page 6.

[Photographs of Seminex graduates at May 16 commencement.] 30:17 (May 24, 1975), page 7.

"Resolutions for Anaheim [convention] Deal with Split, Doctrine." 30:19 (June 28, 1975), pages 1, 4.

"Tietjen Case to [LCMS Missouri] District Vice President [Oscar Gerken]." 30:19 (June 28, 1975), page 8.

"[LCMS Anaheim] Convention Opens with Patriotic Observance, Communion Service [overview of Seminex issues]." 30:20 (July 12, 1975), pages 1, 8.

"Dr. John Tietjen Absolved of False Doctrine Charges [by LCMS Missouri District Vice President Oscar Gerken]." 30:20 (July 12, 1975), page 12.

"[LCMS Anaheim] Convention Votes to Deal with Activities of ELIM [re Seminex, *A Statement*, English District, etc.]." 30:21 (July 26, 1975), pages 1, 5.

"Cannot Afford to Maintain Political Battle [in LCMS], ELIM Says." 30:23 (August 23, 1975), page 3.

"Concordia [Seminary] Board [of Control] Requests Study of Synod's Seminaries." 30:23 (August 23, 1975), page 4.

"Seminex Moves to Building in Mid-Town [University Club Building in Saint Louis]." 30:23 (August 23, 1975), page 4.

"Begin[ning of] 137th Academic Year at Concordia [Seminary]." 30:24 (September 13, 1975), page 6.

"English District Adopts Confessional Statement [including authorizing ordaining of uncertified Seminex graduates]." 31:1 (September 27, 1975), page 12.

"Enrollment at Concordia [Seminary] Up 47 Percent." 31:1 (September 27, 1975), page 12.

"Thielicke at Seminex [for October 11–12 event]." 31:2 (October 11, 1975), page 1.

"Inauguration Set for Bohlmann [as seventh president of Concordia Seminary]." 31:2 (October 11, 1975), page 1.

"LCMS Higher Education Board; School Changes, Changes in Synodical Schools; Dr. [J. A. O.] Preus Names Committee to Interview Former [Concordia Seminary] Faculty Members; LCMS Officials Express Regret after Congregation [Grace Lutheran Church, Oklahoma City] Votes to Leave Synod." 31:3 (October 25, 1975), pages 2, 7.

"Seminex Hosts Festival Worship [commemorating Reformation Day; Robert Bergt, celebrant; James Childs of Concordia Senior College, Fort Wayne, Indiana, preacher]." 31:3 (October 25, 1975), page 3.

"Bohlmann Inaugurated at Concordia Seminary." 31:4 (November 8, 1975), pages 1, 6.

[Photographs of Seminex students presenting Reformation drama.] 31:4 (November 8, 1975), pages 1, 6.

"[B. H.] Jackayya [president of Concordia Theological Seminary in Nagercoil, India] Speaks at Seminex." 31:4 (November 8, 1975), page 7.

"'Interview' Committee Holds First Meeting [develops guidelines for interviewing former Concordia Seminary faculty majority]." 31:4 (November 8, 1975), page 8.

"[J. A. O.] Preus Reports Progress to Congregations." 31:4 (November 8, 1975), page 8.

"India Churchman [B. H. Jackayya] Presents Views on Synod Controversy." 31:5 (November 22, 1975), page 1.

"Seminex Advent Service, Dec. 18 [John Tietjen, preacher]." 31:6 (December 13, 1975), page 1.

"Pastor [Richard Koenig] Discusses Religious Upsurge at Seminex." 31:6 (December 13, 1975), page 4.

"Synod Problems Force [J. A. O.] Preus Early Return from Africa." 31:7 (December 27, 1975), page 6.

1976

"Local ELIM Chapter Meets Tomorrow [at Bethel Lutheran Church, University City, Missouri]." 31:8 (January 10, 1976), page 1.

"Seminex Professor [Duane Mehl] Writes Book on Struggles with Drug Addiction." 31:8 (January 10, 1976), page 5.

"English District Membership Is Sought [by congregations sympathetic with theological stance]." 31:8 (January 10, 1976), page 8.

"Preus, Neunaber [Southern Illinois District president] Talk about Issues [re ordaining uncertified Seminex graduates]." 31:9 (January 24, 1976), page 1.

"ELIM: [Missouri District] Clergy Is Split Evenly." 31:9 (January 24, 1976), page 2.

"[Concordia] Sem[inary] Probation [by AAUP] Is Lifted, Censure Stands." 31:10 (February 14, 1976), page 2.

"[Southern Illinois District] Convention Backs Neunaber [re Seminex support]." 31:11 (February 28, 1976), page 1.

"Group Breaks from [Village Lutheran] Church [Ladue, Missouri]." 31:11 (February 28, 1976), page 1.

Andrew Weyermann serving as "pastoral leader" forms Living Word Lutheran Church under Pastor Arden Mead.

"'Moderates' Form Council [of ELIM and LCM]." 31:12 (March 13, 1976), page 4.

"ALC Takes Seminex Grads." 31:13 (March 27, 1976), page 3.

"[LCMS] District Presidents Removed [Frincke (Eastern), Ressmeyer (Atlantic), Riedel (New England), Hecht (English)]." 31:14 (April 10, 1976), page 1.

"Seminex Vicars Are Placed [approximately thirty-eight to LCMS congregations]." 31:14 (April 10, 1976), page 2.

"Editorial: Missouri: Past and Future." 31:14 (April 10, 1976), page 4.

"Seminex Tours [for Lutheran women in area]." 31:14 (April 10, 1976), page 11.

"Action [re removal of four LCMS District presidents] Brings Widespread Response." 31:15 (April 24, 1976), pages 1, 12.

"ELIM Protests Removal [of four District presidents]." 31:15 (April 24, 1976), page 12.

"[Concordia fourth-year] Seminarians Sign Petition to [J. A. O.] Preus [twenty-nine of fifty-three ask that additional year of study for Seminex students be waived]." 31:16 (May 8, 1976), page 1.

"Seminex [commencement] Ceremony Is Set [Harvey Stegemoeller, speaker]." 31:16 (May 8, 1976), page 2.

"'Liberal Leanings' of [local Lutheran high] Schools Discussed at Ad Hoc Meeting." 31:17 (May 22, 1976), page 1.

"[52] Concordia Seminarians Receive Calls." 31:17 (May 22, 1976), page 4.

"Seminex Graduates over 100 Students." 31:17 (May 22, 1976), page 6.

"Church [Luther Memorial, Richmond Heights, Missouri] Votes Out of Synod." 31:17 (May 22, 1976), page 11.

"[Missouri District] Convention Delegates to Face Issues [re Seminex, etc.]." 31:18 (June 12, 1976), page 1.

"Membership Rule Discussed [effect of controversy on local Lutheran high schools]." 31:18 (June 12, 1976), page 1.

"Sem[inary] President [Ralph Bohlmann] Outlines Programs for Future [responds to accusations of injustice]." 31:18 (June 12, 1976), page 4.

"205 Seminex Grads Placed since School Was Founded." 31:18 (June 12, 1976), page 6.

"[J. A. O.] Preus Writes [to] Four Districts [addresses church workers in LCMS Districts where presidents have been removed]." 31:18 (June 12, 1976), page 7

"Seminex-Service Missions to Be Cut [mission congregations supporting uncertified Seminex graduates]." 31:19 (June 26, 1976), page 1.

"Seminex Announces Changes [in faculty]." 31:19 (June 26, 1976), page 9.

"ELIM Meeting [at Luther Memorial, Richmond Heights, Missouri; Elwyn Ewald to answer questions]." 31:19 (June 26, 1976), page 9.

"Luther Memorial [Richmond Heights, Missouri] Leaves [first Saint Louis congregation to leave the Missouri Synod]." 31:20 (July 10, 1976), page 3.

"Great Rivers Synod [of the AELC] Meets [at Concordia Lutheran Church, Kirkwood, Missouri]." 31:21 (July 24, 1976), page 3.

"Editorial: The Upcoming Meeting [re effect of LCMS controversy on local Lutheran high schools]." 31:21 (July 24, 1976), page 4.

"Preus Sends Tietjen Case to Synodical Vice-President [Theodore Nickel]." 31:21 (July 24, 1976), page 8.

"Vote Suspends Membership Article [re allowing local LCMS congregations that leave Synod to remain in high school association]." 31:23 (August 28, 1976), page 1.

"[Fourth ELIM] Assembly Keeps ELIM Alive." 31:23 (August 28, 1976), page 1.

"Editorial [re suspending Lutheran high school association membership rules and ELIM assembly]." 31:23 (August 28, 1976), page 4.

"[Southern Illinois District] President [Neunaber] Resigns in Protest." 31:24 (September 11, 1976), page 1.

"[Concordia] Sem[inary] Enrollment at 354; Seminex Has 335 Students." 32:1 (September 25, 1976), page 1.

"Ressmeyer Resigns as Head of Synod's Atlantic District." 32:1 (September 25, 1976), page 3.

"[New England District President] Riedel Is Fourth to Resign." 32:2 (October 9, 1976), page 8.

"Three More Churches [in Saint Louis area] Go [New Life in Christ Lutheran Church, Our Master Lutheran Church, and Christ Lutheran Church]." 32:3 (October 23, 1976), page 1.

"Lutheran Journalist [Erik Modean] Believes Lutheran Unity Is Doubtful." 32:3 (October 23, 1976), page 4.

"Theologians Will Speak [Seminex and Eden Seminary]." 32:3 (October 23, 1976), page 9.

"Synod and AELC Reps Meet [re worker benefit plans]." 32:3 (October 23, 1976), page 11.

"Funding Procedure Changed [Seminex, Partners in Mission, ELIM, AELC]." 32:4 (November 13, 1976), page 2.

"AELC Plans Are Readied [at Bethel Lutheran Church, University City; five synods and 128 congregations]." 32:4 (November 13, 1976), page 6.

"District Acts on [Sterling] Belcher [Seminex graduate; re mission subsidy]." 32:5 (November 27, 1976), pages 1, 12.

"Association [AELC] Synods Convene." 32:5 (November 27, 1976), page 5.

"Benefits Dispute Is Brewing [re AELC and LCMS worker benefit plans]." 32:5 (November 27, 1976), page 7.

"AELC Convenes, Adopts Constitution and Bylaws." 32:6 (December 11, 1976), page 9.

"Seminex Chorus to Perform [at Frontenac Plaza shopping mall]." 32:6 (December 11, 1976), page 16.

1977

"Seminex Gets Grant for $36,960 [from Lilly Endowment]." 32:7 (January 22, 1977), page 2.

"Seminex Candlemas Feb. 2 [to present seventy-six candidates to the church (AELC)]." 32:7 (January 22, 1977), page 11.

"Seminex Declared Eligible to Receive AAL [Aid Association for Lutherans] funds." 32:8 (February 15, 1977), page 1.

"Seminex Issues Faculty Calls [under authority of AELC]." 32:8 (February 15, 1977), page 2.

"President [W. T. Janzow] of [Concordia] College [Seward, Nebraska] Resigns [related to LCMS controversy]." 32:8 (February 15, 1977), page 2.

"Another President Resigns [California-Nevada District President Paul Jacobs]." 32:8 (February 15, 1977), page 3.

"Dallas Convention Will Be Discussed at Sem[inary] Lectures [focus on controverted issues]." 32:9 (March 15, 1977), page 4.

"Formation of AELC Is Termed Top News Story [by Lutheran Editors' and Managers' Association]." 32:9 (March 15, 1977), page 4.

"Seminex Plans Festival Week in March [Paul Manz, Richard Caemmerer Jr.; T. S. Eliot's *Murder in the Cathedral*]." 32:9 (March 15, 1977), page 7.

"Seminex Guild Tea Readied ['Seminex in Bloom'—tours of renovated areas]." 32:10 (April 15, 1977), page 2.

"Seminex Graduation May 13 [ninety-one earned degrees; Richard John Neuhaus, speaker; honorary degrees to Fr. William J. Sullivan, S.J., Siegfried Reinhardt, and Arnold Bringewatt]." 32:10 (April 15, 1977), page 3.

"[Robert] Preus, [Ralph] Bohlmann to Talk on Formula of Concord [with application to the present synodical situation]." 32:10 (April 15, 1977), page 12.

"A Witness to One-ness [joint worship between English Synod and English District congregations; Bible class led by Dr. Krentz of Christ Seminary—Seminex]." 32:11 (May 15, 1977), page 3.

"[Seminex professor Arthur] Vincent Speaks on Spiritual Renewal [at Concordia Lutheran Church, Kirkwood, Missouri]." 32:11 (May 15, 1977), page 12.

"Rev. Dr. Ralph Klein of Seminex Receives $11,000 Scholarship for Research." 32:11 (May 15, 1977), page 12.

"Seminex Board Reduces Staff [and faculty], Adopts Budget." 32:12 (June 15, 1977), page 10.

"[Concordia] Seminary Board [of Control] Issues Report on Walkout [*Exodus from Concordia*]." 32:12 (June 15, 1977), page 11.

"[Frederick] Danker's Book Chronicles Synod Fracture [*No Room in the Brotherhood*]." 32:12 (June 15, 1977), page 13.

"AELC Enthusiastic over Fellowship [with ALC and LCA]." 32:12 (June 15, 1977), page 13.

"300th Seminex Grad Placed" [ninety-eight candidates in 1977]. 32:13 (July 15, 1977), page 16.

"LCMS Actions [at Dallas convention] in Line with Conservative Tradition [possibility of flexibility in dealing with Seminex graduates]." 32:14 (August 15, 1977), page 3.

"Installation of Dr. [Walter] Wegner [of Seminex] Set at [Grace Lutheran Church] Pagedale [Missouri]." 32:14 (August 15, 1977), page 4.

"Charge LCMS of 'Ecclesiastical Tyranny' [by President David Preus of the ALC]." 32:14 (August 15, 1977), page 6.

"Festival of Theology at Seminex [Norman Gottwald of Graduate Theological Union, Berkeley, California; Nils Dahl of Yale]." 32:14 (August 15, 1977), page 16.

"Seminex Opens [academic year] with Worship [John Tietjen, preacher; Paul Manz, organist]." 32:14 (August 15, 1977), page 16.

"ELIM Sees Role as Voice of Protest in Missouri Synod." 32:15 [i.e., 33:1] (September 15, 1977), page 4.

"Seminex Achieves 76–77 Goal of $1,000,000 [8,000 direct gifts; 500 congregations]." 32:15 [i.e., 33:1] (September 15, 1977), page 9.

"[Lutheran Student Movement] Students Oppose Fellowship 'Protest' [LCMS / ALC]." 32:15 [i.e., 33:1] (September 15, 1977), page 10.

"Tietjen Removed from Missouri Synod's Clergy Roster." 32:16 [i.e., 33:2] (October 15, 1977), pages 1, 3.

"Seminex to Participate in Biblical Festival [with Eden and Kenrick Seminaries, Saint Louis University; featuring Norman Gottwald and Nils Dahl]." 32:16 [i.e., 33:2] (October 15, 1977), page 13.

"Seminex Development Committee Meets [goal for 1977–78: $1,210,000]." 32:16 [i.e., 33:2] (October 15, 1977), page 16.

"Christ Seminary New Name for Seminex." 32:17 [i.e., 33:3] (November 15, 1977), page 1.

" 'Ignore Tietjen Removal' [Seminex] Faculty Urges [in letter to LCMS pastors]." 32:17 [i.e., 33:3] (November 15, 1977), page 5.

"ELIM Offices Relocate [to Seminex building]." 32:17 [i.e., 33:3] (November 15, 1977), page 6.

"Vicaring in St. Louis: A Great Experience [seven Seminex vicars (one female)]." 32:17 [i.e., 33:3] (November 15, 1977), page 7.

"Oldest Book in St. Louis Displayed at Seminex [incunabula from the library of A. C. Piepkorn, gift of Miriam Piepkorn]." 32:18 [i.e., 33:4] (December 15, 1977), page 3.

"English Synod Congregations May Ordain Women." 32:18 [i.e., 33:4] (December 15, 1977), page 7.

"Vicaring in St. Louis: A Great Experience [four Seminex vicars]." 32:18 [i.e., 33:4] (December 15, 1977), page 13.

"Seminex Prepares Intermester [special workshops]." 32:18 [i.e., 33:4] (December 15, 1977), page 17.

"AELC Joins LWM [Lutheran World Ministries; AELC also a member of Lutheran World Federation]." 32:18 [i.e., 33:4] (December 15, 1977), page 17.

1978

"AELC Convention to Focus on Lutheran Unity." 33:5 (January 15, 1978), page 3.

"[Helmut] Thielicke to Lecture at Seminex [February 9, 1978]." 33:5 (January 15, 1978), page 5.

"Seminex Sponsors Candlemas Service [at Christ Church Cathedral]." 33:5 (January 15, 1978), page 6.

"[Lutheran] High School Association [LAHE] to Vote on Associate Membership [for AELC congregations]." 33:6 (February 15, 1978), page 1.

"Parish, Four Pastors [in Southern Illinois District] Dropped from LCMS." 33:6 (February 15, 1978), page 3.

"Seminex Sunday Opens Fifth Year [Tietjen appointed to second four-year term]." 33:6 (February 15, 1978), page 4.

"Seminex Plans Art Fest [Carl Schalk, Gracia Grindahl, Siegfried Reinhardt, Brother Mel]." 33:6 (February 15, 1978), page 6.

"Southern Illinois Convention Delegates Elect Officers [District 'on road back to solid service in our Lord's kingdom']." 33:7 (March 15, 1978), page 1.

"Associate Membership Granted [in LAHE for AELC congregations]." 33:7 (March 15, 1978), page 1.

"Seminex Will Host Workshop [on social and Christian issues]." 33:7 (March 15, 1978), page 4.

"Benefits Dispute Is Brewing [re AELC and LCMS worker benefit plans]." 33:7 (March 15, 1978), page 5.

"Seminex Friends Sponsor Show [on Bach on KWMU-FM]." 33:7 (March 15, 1978), page 13.

"Seminex to Give [honorary] Doctorates [recipients include Harold Hecht and Paul Manz]." 33:8 (April 15, 1978), page 4.

"LCUSA Delegates Elect Officers, Accept AELC." 33:8 (April 15, 1978), page 5.

"[German theologian Dorothee] Soelle to Speak at Christ Seminary in May." 33:8 (April 15, 1978), page 15.

"Pastors and Congregations to Be Removed from the LCMS [three Missouri District congregations, twenty-four pastors, four teachers re AELC membership]." 33:9 (May 15, 1978), page 1.

"Seminex Summer School to Open." 33:9 (May 15, 1978), page 6.

"Seminex Graduation Set for May 19 [fifty-eight MDiv, two MAR, eight STM, one ThD; Norman Habel, commencement speaker]." 33:9 (May 15, 1978), page 8.

"Seminex Sets 78–79 budget [$65,000 less than previous year's budget; Tietjen accepts four-year extension of appointment]." 33:10 (June 15, 1978), page 13.

"LCMS-English District [convention; District President Bornemann urged seating of nine Seminex graduates; English District lost 70 of 220 congregations to AELC]." 33:11 (July 15, 1978), page 3.

"Sem[inex] Reports Summer Success [10 percent increase in enrollment]." 33:11 (July 15, 1978), page 6.

"Opening Scheduled at Seminex [Tietjen, preacher; Paul Manz, organist]." 33:12 (August 15, 1978), page 10.

"ELIM Rally Is Scheduled [presenters: August Bernthal, Paul Bretscher]." 34:1 (September 15, 1978), page 2.

"Seminex Ends Year in Black [reported income of $1,361,760]." 34:1 (September 15, 1978), page 11.

"Concordia Seminary Enrollment Increases [561, 30 percent more than previous year]." 34:2 (October 15, 1978), page 3.

"Combined Session Has Positive Results [re LCMS-AELC fellowship]." 34:2 (October 15, 1978), page 7.

"[Christ] Seminary Is Beneficiary [of $37,560 estate of Florence Tempelmeier]." 34:3 (November 15, 1978), page 11.

1979

"Revised Greek-English Lexicon Makes Debut [Frederick Danker of Seminex, co-editor]." 34:6 (February 15, 1979), page 4.

"Education Session Set [Christ Seminary summer school]." 34:6 (February 15, 1979), page 5.

"Concert / Worship Set at Atonement Church [Florissant, Missouri] [Seminex Chorus returns from five-state tour]." 34:7 (March 15, 1979), page 5.

"Dr. Otto to Preach May 18 [at Concordia Seminary commencement; ninety-nine MDiv, two MAR, seven STM, and two ThD]." 34:9 (May 15, 1979), page 7.

"Dr. [Martin] Marty, Seminex Speaker [for Institute on the Shape of the Church]." 34:10 (June 15, 1979), page 6.

"Seminex Contracts Are Renewed [twenty-five faculty and executive staff; 1979–80 budget: $1,333,541; Martin Marty, commencement speaker]." 34:10 (June 15, 1979), page 10.

"Seminex Begins Classes [202 students (146 full-time, 56 part-time), 42 fewer than 1978–79]." 35:1 (September 15, 1979), page 2.

"At Seminex [eleven intermester courses; DMin program to begin in 1980]." 35:4 (December 15, 1979), page 9.

1980

"Ecumenical Service at Christ [Episcopal Cathedral; Christ Seminary—Seminex a sponsoring school]." 35:5 (January 15, 1980), page 14.

"Seminex on Stage [two dramas: *Endgame* and *Gallows Humor*]." 35:6 (February 15, 1980), page 10.

"Dr. Paul Harms Is Speaker for Seminex Commencement [fifty-two MDiv and one MAR]." 35:9 (May 15, 1980), page 15.

"Eighth Academic Year [of Christ Seminary—Seminex] Begins with Awards [held at Christ Church Cathedral; DD to Elwyn Ewald of ELIM and AELC]." 35:12 (August 15, 1980), page 7.

[Kurt Hendel of Christ Seminary—Seminex Awarded Fulbright Scholarship.] 35:12 (August 15, 1980), page 11.

"Seminex Classes Open [193 students, nine fewer than 1979–80, but smallest drop since school began]." 36:1 (September 15, 1980), page 6.

"Pipe Organ Is Dedicated at Seminex [eleven-rank organ built by Martin Ott, $34,000; Paul Manz, dedicatory recital organist]." 36:1 (September 15, 1980), page 12.

"Dr. [Robert] Conrad to Speak [elected pastoral advisor: National Lutheran Association of Scouters]." 36:2 (October 15, 1980), page 7.

[Dr. Wolfhart Pannenberg lectures at Seminex: "Christian Piety and Guilt Consciousness."] 36:2 (October 15, 1980), page 7.

"Rev. [Samuel] Roth, Chairperson for Christ Seminary [Board of Directors]." 36:2 (October 15, 1980), page 8.

"[Paul] Simon to Receive Degree [Doctor of Laws, Christ Seminary—Seminex]." 36:2 (October 15, 1980), page 11.

1981

"Seminex Scope [re intermester courses, guest lecturers, organ recital, presentation of thirty-four candidates at Christ Church Cathedral on Candlemas, February 1]." 36:5 (January 15, 1981), page 4.

"Seminex Statement Adopted [re union of LCA, ALC, and AELC]." 36:8 (April 15, 1981), page 9.

"Seminex Graduation [forty-three MDiv, two ThD, six STM, two MAR; Walter Wangerin Jr., speaker; held at Third Baptist Church, Saint Louis]." 36:9 (May 15, 1981), page 8.

"[Missouri Conference of] English Synod [AELC] Meets [at Ladue Chapel]." 36:9 (May 15, 1981), page 9.

"Gift to Seminex [$29,000 from AAL branches, presented at Atonement hymn festival; Paul Manz, organist]." 36:11 (July 15, 1981), page 5.

"[Robert H.] Smith Named [Academic] Dean [at Christ Seminary—Seminex]." 36:12 (August 15, 1981), page 7.

"Seminex Begins Ninth Year [with enrollment of two hundred]." 36:12 (August 15, 1981), page 11.

"Era of Optimism Dawns for LCMS—Headed by Bohlmann." 37:2 (October 15, 1981), page 1.

"Archbishop [John May of Saint Louis] Guest at Seminex [preacher at Reformation service at Christ Church Cathedral; John Tietjen, liturgist]." 37:3 (November 15, 1981), page 11.

"[Robert] Bertram [of Seminex] in Russia [at ecumenical consultation in Odessa]." 37:3 (November 15, 1981), page 11.

"[Herbert J. A.] Bouman Dies [taught one year at Seminex]." 37:4 (December 15, 1981), page 2.

"Hans Kung at Seminex [spoke of his clash with Roman Catholic hierarchy]." 37:4 (December 15, 1981), page 9.

"Dr. [William] Danker [Professor of Missions, Seminex] Receives Honor [*Festschrift*]." 37:4 (December 15, 1981), page 12.

1982

"Seminex Intermester Jan. 18–22 to Highlight Third World Theologians." 37:5 (January 15, 1982), page 7.

"Seminex Is Relocated [to the Humbolt Building at 539 N. Grand Blvd.; move from 607 N. Grand Blvd. because of building infrastructure failure]." 37:6 (February 15, 1982), page 8.

"Seminex Chorus Has Concert [at The Lutheran Church of the Atonement, Florissant, Missouri; chorus plans twelve concerts in six states]." 37:7 (March 15, 1982), page 11.

"Christ Seminary—Seminex to Relocate in 1983 [to LSTC (Chicago), Pacific Lutheran (Berkeley, California), Lutheran Seminary Program in the Southwest (Austin, Texas) with 30,000-volume library moved to the Wartburg House of Studies in Austin]." 37:10 (June 15, 1982), page 4.

"Seminex Starts 10th Academic Year [Rev. Mary Konopka installed as instructor in practical theology]." 37:12 (August 15, 1982), page 7.

"ALC, AELC, LCA to Unite." 38:1 (September 15, 1982), page 1.

"Dr. Martin Scharlemann, Was Noted Theologian [and acting president of Concordia Seminary in 1974 after 'walkout']." 38:1 (September 15, 1982), page 2.

"It Was 'a Matter of Merger' [re LCA, ALC, AELC intent to form new Lutheran church]." 38:1 (September 15, 1982), pages 6–7.

"Christ Seminary—Seminex Looks to Positive Future [re plan to deploy faculty to three Lutheran seminaries (Chicago; Berkeley, California; and Austin, Texas); 1981–82 enrollment of 225]." 38:1 (September 15, 1982), page 9.

1983

[Photograph: Tietjen conducts closing worship service at Rabbi Isserman Interfaith Memorial Seminar for clergy and lay leaders at Congregation Temple Israel, Saint Louis.] 38:8 (April 15, 1983), page 8.

"Handel Work on May 18 Concert Bill [event leading to tenth Seminex commencement; Robert Bergt, concertmaster; Paul Manz, guest organist; $200,000 thankoffering set to assist in moving Seminex faculty, etc.]." 38:8 (April 15, 1983), page 11.

"Seminex Graduates 44, Honors Four May 21." 38:9 (May 15, 1983), page 6.

"AELC Missouri Conference Convenes in Webster Groves [Tietjen, Herbert Mayer, Mark Bangert of Seminex participating]." 38:11 (June 15, 1983), page 6.

"Convention of AELC [Missouri Conference] Is June 17, 18 [Tietjen to report on 'new 5.6 million member Lutheran Church' (AELC, LCA, ALC)]." 38:10 (June 15, 1983), page 9.

"June 25 Auction to Aid Seminex." 38:10 (June 15, 1983), page 12.

"Seminex, ELIM in New Locations [ELIM to St. Mark's Lutheran Church, Clayton, Missouri]." 39:1 (September 15, 1983), page 3.

1984

"Noted Area Theologian Dies [retired Seminex Professor Richard R. Caemmerer; funeral at Bethel Lutheran Church, University City, Missouri; John Tietjen, preacher]." 39:9 (May 15, 1984), page 9.

"Pilgrim Installs New Pastor, St. Louisan Herbert Mayer [formerly of Seminex]." 39:10 (June 15, 1984), page 9.

"AELC Delegates Elect Tietjen as V.P.; Review CNLC Report." 39:15 (November 15, 1984), page 5.

1985

"LSTC Celebrates 125 years [including Christ Seminary—Seminex]." 39:21 (May 15, 1985), page 1.

"Rev. [Richard] Mueller Leaves Position at *Lutheran Perspective* [formerly *Missouri in Perspective*, which 'grew out of the doctrinal controversy at Concordia Seminary']." 39:28 (December 15, 1985), page 4.

2.2.4 *The Lutheran Layman* (Lutheran Laymen's League [LCMS])

(chronological order)

1972

"False Doctrine Not Evident at [Concordia] Seminary [according to Board of Control member Charles Burmeister]." 43:2 (February 1972), page 1. [*Major article.]

"[Concordia] Seminary Board [of Control] Gives [Professor Arlis] Ehlen One Year Pact." 43:3 (March 1972), page 3.

"Preus Says He Has Support of Clergy, Laity for Doctrinal Guidelines [directs Tietjen to suspend Arlis Ehlen from teaching biblical interpretation courses]." 43:4 (April 1972), page 5.

"Preus and Tietjen Take First Steps toward Agreement [re Arlis Ehlen action]." 43:5 (May 1972), page 7.

"Synod President [J. A. O. Preus] Meets with [Concordia] Seminary Faculty [re response to *A Statement* and other statements adopted by the LCMS, e.g., Milwaukee Resolutions 2-21, 5-24]." 43:6 (June 1972), page 5.

"Preus Picks AATS Rules Study Unit [re suspension of Concordia Seminary's accreditation by AATS] 43:7 (July 1972), page 1.

"[Concordia] Sem[inary] Board [of Control] Takes Action on [AATS] Probation." 43:7 (July 1972), page 10.

"[LCMS] Council of Presidents Action Is Aimed at Solving Church's Doctrinal Controversy." 43:10 (October 1972), page 10.

"Dr. Preus '*Statement* [*of Scriptural and Confessional Principles*]' Gets CTCR Approval." 43:12 (December 1972), page 2.

1973

"Seminary Faculty Gives Statement on Beliefs [*Faithful to Our Calling, Faithful to Our Lord*]." 44:2 (February 1973), page 6.

Preus, J. A. O. "President's Desk: The Bible's History and Bible History." 44:2 (February 1973), page 9.

"[Concordia Theological Seminary] Springfield [Illinois] Will Make Use of '*A Statement.*'" 44:3 (March 1973), page 6.

"[1973 LCMS] Convention Workbook Is Handful [including Concordia Seminary issues]." 44:6 (June 1973), page 3.

"Synod [convention at New Orleans] Acts on Doctrinal Stance [including action re Concordia Seminary faculty]." 44:8 (August 1973), pages 1, 3.

Scharlemann, Martin H. "Letters from Readers [re Scharlemann's position on historical-critical method of biblical interpretation]." 44:9 (September 1973), page 4.

"[Concordia Seminary] Board of Control Votes to Suspend Tietjen." 44:9 (September 1973), page 10.

[Photograph: John Tietjen Receives Honorary Degree (DD) from Eden Seminary.] 44:10 (October 1973), page 7.

"[J. A. O.] Preus Urges Lay Example for Church [at LLL Board of Governors meeting]." 44:12 (December 1973), page 1.

"Action Is Taken by Concordia Seminary's Board of Control [plan to review syllabi, require faculty to respond to 1973 LCMS convention resolutions]." 44:12 (December 1973), page 9.

"Theological Consensus Is Discussed by CTCR [re dealing with dissent, principles for use of *A Statement.*]." 44:12 (December 1973), page 9.

1974

"Synod President [J. A. O. Preus] Names Doctrine Advisory Group [ACDC]." 45:2 (February 1974), page 11.

"Early Solution Hoped For, but Not Seen in Seminary Dispute." 45:2 (February 1974), pages 11, 12.

"Tietjen Charges 'Deal' [to avoid suspension by accepting call]: Plans Defense Action." 45:2 (February 1974), pages 11, 12.

"Bulletin [re Preus 'Message to the Church': information on Concordia Seminary dispute and call for prayer and unity]." 45:2 (February 1974), page 12.

"[Concordia Seminary] Faculty Statement Supports Tietjen [issued by thirty-six faculty members]." 45:2 (February 1974), page 12.

"[Concordia] Seminary Gets New [interim] President [Martin H. Scharlemann]." 45:2 (February 1974), page 12.

"Dr. Preus Urges Faculty to Return to Classroom [following suspension of Concordia Seminary president Tietjen]." 45:2 (February 1974), page 12.

"[LCMS] PR Director [Victor Bryant] Describes His Role in Controversy." 45:2 (February 1974), page 12.

"ALC President [David Preus] Distressed at [Missouri] Synod Turmoil." 45:3 (March 1974), page 5.

"[Seminex] Seminarians' Future in Doubt [re eligibility for placement as vicars and pastors]." 45:4 (April 1974), page 9.

Note: Three different articles are presented under one title, including one from the Religious News Service in Chicago.

"Concordia [Seminary] Board Seeks 11 Additions to Faculty." 45:5 (May 1974), page 9.

"All Positions on Synod Advisory Board Are Filled [i.e., ACDC]." 45:5 (May 1974), page 9.

"[Martin] Scharlemann Resigns [as interim president of Concordia Seminary] Due to Exhaustion." 45:5 (May 1974), page 9.

"[William] Kohn Resigns LCMS Mission Board Post [protesting 'legalism' in Synod]." 45:5 (May 1974), page 9.

"Board [of Control] Calls 14 to Serve [Concordia] Seminary." 45:6 (June 1974), page 1.

"[Ralph] Bohlmann Named to Sem[inary] Post [of president of Concordia Seminary]." 45:6 (June 1974), page 10.

"[Concordia] Seminary Rebuilding; 135 Students Expected in Fall." 45:7 (July 1974), page 7.

"[LCMS Council of] Presidents Recommend Plan [to place Seminex graduates]." 45:10 (October 1974), page 6.

"Concordia [Seminary] Board [of Control] to Participate in Meeting on Synod Issues." 45:10 (October 1974), page 7.

"[Doctrinal] Dispute Is 'Family Feud,' [J. A. O.] Preus Says." 45:10 (October 1974), page 10.

"[J. A. O.] Preus Says Laity Majority Backs Synod [re official doctrinal position]." 45:11 (November 1974), page 3.

"ALC Convention Adopts LCMS Dispute Stance [opposes *A Statement*]." 45:11 (November 1974), page 5.

"[J. A. O.] Preus Predicts Seminex Grads 'Will Be Properly Certified.'" 45:11 (November 1974), page 9.

"Participation in ELIM by LCMS Faculty Members [LCMS Board for Higher Education requests faculties to refrain from participation in ELIM]." 45:12 (December 1974), page 2.

"[Concordia] Sem[inary] Board [of Control] Action Seeks 4th Year Seminex Group [to enroll at Concordia Seminary to qualify for certification]." 45:12 (December 1974), page 9.

1975

"Tietjen Takes Call to Synod English District [as theological consultant]." 46:1 (January 1975), page 6.

"Synod District Presidents Seek to Ease Dispute [by planning theological convocation at Concordia Seminary, April 14–18]." 46:1 (January 1975), page 7.

"[Concordia] Sem[inary] Officials Interview 'Seminex' Graduates." 46:1 (January 1975), page 10.

"[Theological] Convocation Speakers Are Listed." 46:2 (February 1975), page 1.

"Ruling Asked on Release of Tietjen Case Materials [Concordia Seminary Board of Control decides not to release materials; Tietjen case still 'undecided'; Board of Control accepts resignation of Edgar Krentz]." 46:2 (February 1975), page 3.

"LCMS Board [of Directors] Calls for End to 'Splinter Groups' [e.g., ELIM]." 46:3 (March 1975), page 5.

"Date Set for [Concordia] Sem[inary] Election [of president]." 46:3 (March 1975), page 10.

"Concordia [Seminary] Will Host LCMS Issues Lectures." 46:4 (April 1975), page 10.

"[Theological] Convocation Ends, Problems Not Solved." 46:5 (May 1975), page 5.

"Missouri Synod Places 457 Pastors, Teachers, Lay Workers [including twenty certified Seminex graduates]." 46:6 (June 1975), page 3.

"Bohlmann Sees Life, Growth at Concordia [Seminary]." 46:6 (June 1975), page 5.

"[Seminex] Grads Urged to Apply for Certification [Rev. Herman Otten also urged to apply]." 46:6 (June 1975), page 9.

"LCMS Acts [during 1975 convention in Anaheim, California] to Resolve Seminex, ELIM, Ordination Problems." 46:8 (August 1975), pages 1, 3. [*Major article.]

"Tietjen Ruling Explained [charges of false doctrine dismissed]." 46:8 (August 1975), page 6.

"[Concordia Seminary] Board [of Control] Requests [theological] Education Study." 46:9 (September 1975), page 12.

"Concordia Seminary Begins 137th Year [with 277 students enrolled]." 46:10 (October 1975), pages 1–2.

"LCMS Church in Texas Calls Woman [Seminex student] as Vicar." 46:10 (October 1975), page 2.

"Dr. Stegemoeller Resigns Concordia–St. Paul Post [cannot comply with Synod convention actions]." 46:10 (October 1975), page 6.

"Concordia Faculty Members [Martin Scharlemann, H. Richard Klann] Named Top Teachers [Outstanding Educators of America]." 46:11 (November 1975), page 1.

"[Concordia Seminary faculty majority] Interview Committee Is Named." 46:11 (November 1975), page 2.

"[J. A. O.] Preus Urges [LCMS] Board [of Directors] to Forget Past, Go Ahead." 46:11 (November 1975), page 2.

"'Concordia [Seminary] Exists to Train Pastors,' Bohlmann Says in Inaugural Address." 46:11 (November 1975), page 10.

"[LCMS] District Presidents Reject Ordination Plea [refuse to promise in writing not to ordain uncertified Seminex graduates]." 46:12 (December 1975), page 7.

1976

"LCMS President [J. A. O. Preus] Declines to Remove [Southern Illinois] District Head [Herman Neunaber]." 47:1 (January 1976), pages 1–2.

"Courts Will Decide Who Gets Lutheran Property [after Grace Lutheran Church, Oklahoma City, joins LCM]." 47:1 (January 1976), page 7.

"[LCMS CCM] Sets Guidelines in Tietjen Case." 47:1 (January 1976), page 7.

"Dr. [Melvin] Kieschnick Quits Parish Education Post [cites politics, broken promises]." 47:2 (February 1976), page 5.

"LCMS [Southern Illinois] District Is Asked to Uphold Missouri Synod's Constitution." 47:2 (February 1976), page 10.

"CTCR Adopts Program to Promote Synod Unity." 47:3 (March 1976), page 3.

"Preus Will Not Vacate Three District Offices [California-Nevada, Northwest, Colorado]." 47:3 (March 1976), page 5.

"Majority Supports [Southern Illinois District president] Neunaber [re congregational rights]." 47:3 (March 1976), page 10.

"Library Group [ATLA] Concerned with Politics [re restrictions on Seminex use of Concordia Seminary Library]." 47:8 (August 1976), page 2.

"Concordia [Seminary] Has [audio] Cassettes [available] on Synod Issues." 47:8 (August 1976), page 8.

"Bohlmann Responds to ATLA [re Concordia Seminary library restrictions]." 47:9 (September 1976), page 12.

"[LCMS] Commission [on Constitutional Matters] Bans Dual [LCMS-AELC] Membership." 47:9 (September 1976), page 12.

"ALC Is Questioned [by CTCR] on '*A Statement*' Charges." 47:10 (October 1976), page 3.

"[LCMS CCM] Ruling on AELC Effective September '77 [re dual membership]." 47:10 (October 1976), page 6.

"St. Louis Seminary Growth Continues [22 faculty, 354 students (160 more than 1974–75 enrollment)]." 47:10 (October 1976), page 10.

"Synod Offers Two Study Brochures [re AELC charges against LCMS]." 47:11 (November 1976), page 7.

1977

"Formula [of Concord] Still Relevant Lutheran Editors Told [Dr. Lewis Spitz Jr. affirms *A Statement*]." 48:4 (April 1977), page 3.

Preus, J. A. O. "President's Desk: AELC Is Major Synod Concern." 48:4 (April 1977), page 4.

"Concordia [Seminary] Board [of Control] Publishes Report on 1974 Walkout [*Exodus from Concordia*]." 48:8 (August 1977), page 9.

2.2.5 *The Northwestern Lutheran*

(Wisconsin Evangelical Lutheran Synod)

(chronological order)

1973

Toppe, Carleton. "Reversing Time and Tide [LCMS New Orleans convention]." 60:17 (August 26, 1973), page 263.

Fredrich, Edward C. "Neuhaus and New Orleans [LCMS convention]." 60:18 (September 9, 1973), page 290.

1974

Gerlach, Joel C. "Politics of Polarization [re Concordia Seminary faculty]." 61:3 (February 10, 1974), page 44.

Gerlach, Joel C. "Phoenix in St. Louis [re Board of Control action on Concordia Seminary faculty and President Tietjen]." 61:7 (April 7, 1974), pages 106–7.

Toppe, Carleton. "The Grace That Has Spared Us [re Concordia Seminary troubles]." 61:9 (May 5, 1974), page 131.

Gerlach, Joel C. "Missouri Stalemate [between Concordia Seminary Board of Control and faculty / administration]." 61:13 (July 14, 1974), pages 215, 222.

1975

Fredrich, Edward C. "A Month to Anaheim [LCMS convention issues: Seminex, doctrinal differences]." 63:11 (i.e., 62:11) (June 1, 1975), page 173.

Gerlach, Joel C. "Missouri's Freedom Struggle [uncertain sounds re tolerating false doctrine]." 62:13 (June 29, 1975), page 203.

Gerlach, Joel C. "[English] District Prepares to Leave the Missouri Synod." 62:22 (November 2, 1975), page 358.

Fredrich, Edward C. "Memo to Missouri [re doctrinal disagreements]." 62:24 (November 30, 1975), page 390.

1976

Toppe, Carleton. "Why Not a Frank Admission [re doctrinal position of ELIM]?" 63:2 (January 25, 1976), page 19.

Gerlach, Joel C. "Missouri Meanderings [re placement of Seminex graduates]." 63:7 (April 4, 1976), page 108.

Gerlach, Joel C. "Seminex Rebuffs Synod [faculty refuses to meet with committee]." 63:7 (April 4, 1976), page 108.

Gerlach, Joel C. "Missouri Realignment Continues [re ELIM, AELC, Tietjen case]." 63:19 (September 19, 1976), page 304.

1977

Fredrich, Edward C. "For $60,000 [re LCMS expense for public relations for Dallas convention]." 64:7 (April 3, 1977), pages 108–9.

Fredrich, Edward C. "Developments in Lutheran Relations [re AELC, ALC, LCMS, LCUSA]." 64:11 (May 29, 1977), page 171.

Fredrich, Edward C. "Dallas Fellowship Action—and Reaction [re 1977 LCMS convention actions]." 64:20 (October 2, 1977), pages 318, 326.

Gerlach, Joel C. "Missouri Miscellany [re doctrinal actions at 1977 LCMS convention]." 64:21 (October 16, 1977), page 339.

Toppe, Carleton. "Dreadful Unawareness [re LCMS and confessional heritage]." 64:22 (October 30, 1977), pages 351, 361.

1978

Fredrich, Edward C. "Missouri and Dual Membership [re dropping Seminex professors in AELC from LCMS roster]." 66:15 (i.e., 65:15) (July 23, 1978), page 240.

Gerlach, Joel C. "Missouri Moderates Challenge Synod on Biblical Inerrancy [Sixth ELIM Assembly in Saint Louis]." 65:26 (December 24, 1978), page 419.

1979

Gerlach, Joel C. "LCA Declines Request to Ordain Seminex Graduates." 66:17 (August 19, 1979), page 270.

Gerlach, Joel C. "Missouri's Mission Emphasis [LCMS convention, Seminex, and related matters]." 66:22 (October 28, 1979), pages 349–50.

Janke, M., and H[arold E.] Wicke. "The LCMS 1979 Convention [re Seminex graduates at Valparaiso, some districts]." 66:23 (November 11, 1979), pages 369–70.

1980

Gerlach, Joel C. "*Quo Vadis*, Missouri [re ELIM 'white paper' on LCMS future]?" 67:23 (November 9, 1980), pages 366–67.

1981

Wicke, Harold E. "Comments by the Editor: LCMS Breaks with ALC." 68:16 (August 2, 1981), page 242.

Frey, Immanuel. "A Divided House Must First Be Set in Order [re break in fellowship between LCMS and ALC]." 68:17 (August 16, 1981), page 259.

2.2.6 *Lutherans Alert National*

(Protest Group of the American Lutheran Church)

(chronological order)

1973

"Missouri Synod Conservatives Gain Control [at the New Orleans convention]." 8:8 (August 1973), page 23.

"LC/MS Liberals Protest [Concordia Seminary faculty 'Declaration of Protest']." 8:9 (September 1973), page 19.

1974

"*A Statement of Scriptural and Confessional Principles* [1 of 3]." 9:2 (February 1974), pages 17–20.

"Editorial [on Tietjen response to his suspension]." 9:3 (March 1974), pages 8–9.

"St. Louis Seminary Board [of Control] Suspends President [Tietjen]." 9:3 (March 1974), pages 10–11.

Tietjen, John H. "Statement to The Lutheran Church—Missouri Synod [re suspension from office]." 9:3 (March 1974), pages 11–12.

"*A Statement of Scriptural and Confessional Principles* [2 of 3]." 9:3 (March 1974), pages 18–20.

"*A Statement of Scriptural and Confessional Principles* [3 of 3]." 9:4 (April 1974), pages 12–15.

"LCMS President Preus Urges Seminex Students Not Be Placed." 9:7 (July 1974), page 20.

1975

"LCMS Higher Education Board Commends Senior College [Fort Wayne, Indiana] for Resisting Seminex [recruitment efforts]." 10:5 (May 1975), page 19.

"Notes from the Anaheim Convention of the LC-MS." 10:8 (August 1975), page [24].

"President's Page [re support for Seminex in the ALC]." 10:10 (October 1975), page 2.

"New Lutheran Church in the Making [re ELIM and LCM]." 10:10 (October 1975), page 11.

"Did You Know [re ELIM matters]?" 10:12 (December 1975), page 22.

1976

"[LCMS Colorado District] Board of Directors Stonewalls Preus." 11:5 (May 1976), page 15.

Pederson, Carl O. "Moral Ground to Stand On [re *Colorado Laymen's Newsletter* (May 1976) on deposition of four LCMS District presidents]." 11:7 (July 1976), pages 13–14.

Redal, R. H. "President's Address [re ALC support for Seminex, call to support President David Preus]." 11:9 (September 1976), pages 4–7.

Vigness, Paul G. "The Coming Donnybrook [re conflict between LCMS Districts and LCMS administration]." 11:9 (September 1976), page 23.

"Missouri Synod Members Can't Affiliate with AELC without Forfeiting Membership [ruling of LCMS CCM]." 11:11 (November 1976), page 3.

"LCMS Commission [CTCR] Asks ALC to Substantiate Charges [that LCMS has narrowed its confessional base]." 11:11 (November 1976), pages 6–7.

"Dr. [J. A. O.] Preus Tells LCA 'Missouri Controversy Drawing to Close.' " 11:11 (November 1976), pages 7–8.

1977

"The AELC's Constitution [preamble]." 12:4 (April 1977), page 7.

"[J. A. O.] Preus Sees Dual Membership Not Feasible [in LCMS and AELC]." 12:5 (May 1977), page 6.

2.2.7 *The Lutheran* (Lutheran Church of Australia)

(chronological order)

1973

Wiebusch, E. W. "Convention Jottings: New Orleans, Louisiana, U.S.A. [re LCMS action on Concordia Seminary faculty]." 7:16 (August 13, 1973), pages 10–11.

Grope, L. B. "President's Column: Future of Concordia Seminary." 7:17 (August 27, 1973), page 5.

1974

Wiebusch, E. W. "At Home and Abroad [re 'crisis' at Concordia Seminary]." 8:5 (March 11, 1974), page 5.

Grope, L. B. "President's Column: Visit to St. Louis; Concordia Seminary." 8:18 (September 9, 1974), page 2.

1975

Wiebusch, E. W. "At Home and Abroad [re Seminex, issues dividing the LCMS]." 9:2 (January 27, 1975), page 6.

Wiebusch, E. W. "At Home and Abroad: From the American Scene [re Seminex, Tietjen, etc.]." 9:7 (April 7, 1975), page 6.

Wiebusch, E. W. "At Home and Abroad: Theological Convocation at St. Louis [April 14–18]." 9:8 (April 21, 1975), page 8.

Wiebusch, E. W. "At Home and Abroad: [Ralph Bohlmann elected president of Concordia Seminary]." 9:11 (June 2, 1975), page 3.

Wiebusch, E. W. "At Home and Abroad: From the American Scene [re LCMS convention, Seminex, etc.]." 9:12 (June 16, 1975), page 5.

Wiebusch, E. W. "At Home and Abroad: False Doctrine Charges [against Tietjen] Dismissed." 9:15 (July 28, 1975), page 10.

Marquart, Kurt E. "Dateline Anaheim: Part 1 [report on LCMS convention, July 4–11]." 9:16 (August 11, 1975), pages 12–13.

Marquart, Kurt E. "Dateline Anaheim: Part 2 [report on LCMS convention, July 4–11]." 9:17 (August 25, 1975), pages 10–11.

Wiebusch, E. W. "At Home and Abroad: Two Seminary in Exile Female Interns [one at St. Paul Lutheran Church, Denton, Texas]." 9:22 (November 17, 1975), page 7.

2.2.8 *The Lutheran Spokesman*

(Church of the Lutheran Confession)

(chronological order)

1973

Sydow, G. "It Bears Watching [re actions at LCMS New Orleans convention]." 16:3 (September 1973), pages 3–5.

1974

Eibs, M. H. "Lutherans in Turmoil [re events at Concordia Seminary]." 16:9 (March 1974), pages 6–9.

Sydow, G. "There Is a Way [re Seminex, LCMS controversy]." 16:11 (May 1974), pages 3–6.

1975

Sydow, G. "Still a Question [re LCMS Anaheim convention, Seminex, ELIM]." 18:2 (August 1975), pages 2–3.

1976

Eibs, M. H. "The Highest Priority [re LCMS politics, placement of Seminex graduates]." 18:10 (April 1976), pages 2–3.

Sydow, G. "Right Move, Wrong Reason [re formation of AELC, Seminex as seminary of AELC]." 19:6 (December 1976), pages 3–4.

1977

Sydow, G. "What Missouri Did [re LCMS Dallas convention, LCMS and AELC, doctrine vs. politics]." 20:2 (August 1977), pages 12–13.

Photograph by Paul Ockrassa

The chapel at Seminex. The shoot growing from a dead stump became the symbol of the new school, a reference to Isaiah 11:1.

3.0 Articles in Assorted Periodicals

3.1 Signed Articles and Editorials

(alphabetical order by author, then chronological within author)

Adams, James E. "Lutheran Church—Missouri Synod: Dynamic Tensions of Sect and Church." *The Christian Century* 88:36 (September 8, 1971), pages 1058, 1060, 1062.

Adams, James E. "Missourian Dilemma: What Price Preus?" *The Christian Century* 90:21 (May 23, 1973), pages 591–92.

Adams, James E. "Missouri Synod Lutherans: Conservative Takeover [1973 LCMS convention]." *The Christian Century* 90:28 (August 1–8, 1973), pages 772–73.

Adams, J. [James E.?] "How Conservatives Took Over a Church." *National Catholic Reporter* 10 (October 26, 1973), page 1+.

Adams, James E. "Seed of Schism: A Seminary in Exile." *The Christian Century* 91:9 (March 6, 1974), pages 252–54. [See also response by Virginia Berry: "Portrait of Tietjen."]

Adams, James E. "Missouri's 'Compromise' [1977 LCMS Dallas convention]." *The Christian Century* 94:26 (August 17–24, 1977), pages 709–10.

Adams, Robert Lynn. "Conflict over Charges of Heresy in American Protestant Seminaries." *Social Compass* 17:2 (1970), pages 243–60.

Aleshire, Daniel O. "Watching Hope Grow: Distant Reflections on Seminex: June 2009." *Currents in Theology and Mission* 38:2 (April 2011), pages 84–89. [Aleshire with ATS]

Anderson, Bernhard W. "Unity and Diversity in God's Creation: A Study of the Babel Story [J-E-D-P]." *Currents in Theology and Mission* 5:2 (April 1978), pages 69–81.

Arndt, William. "The Seminary and the Church." *Concordia Journal* 1:3 (June 1975), pages 140–43.

A reprint of Arndt's article in *Concordia Theological Monthly* 14:8 (August 1943), pages 556–69. "Paper read at the free conference of Lutheran seminary professors, held at Augustana Seminary, Rock Island, Illinois, June 9–11, 1943."

Bachmann, E. Theodore, ed. "Lutheran Church—Missouri Synod [includes comments on Seminex]." *Lutheran World* 24:2 and 3 (1977), pages 340–41.

Bachmann, E. Theodore, ed. "Association of Evangelical Lutheran Churches [includes comments on Seminex]." *Lutheran World* 24:2 and 3 (1977), page 342.

Bangert, Mark P. "How My Mind Has Changed." *Currents in Theology and Mission* 38:2 (April 2011), pages 90–92.

Barr, James. "The Problem of Fundamentalism Today." *Old Testament Society of South Africa* 23/22 (1979–80), pages 1–25.

Barth, Karl L. "Together in Christ—To Gather for Christ [Gospel, Scripture, doctrine in the Lutheran Confessions]." *Concordia Journal* 1:2 (March 1975), pages 62–68.

Bauer, Walter E. "Some Observations on History, Historicity, and the Historical-Critical Method." *The Cresset* 40:9–10 (September / October 1977), pages 24–29.

Bauermeister, Jeannette H. "To John [Tietjen]: With Appreciation for Your Shared Ministry." *Currents in Theology and Mission* 15:1 (February 1988), pages 18–20.

Bauermeister, Paul. "Seminex: A Spiritual Journey." *Currents in Theology and Mission* 38:2 (April 2011), pages 128–32.

Beck, Joan L., and Donna Herzfeldt-Kamprath. "Camelot [a sermon by two Seminex alumnae on the thirty-fifth anniversary of Seminex]." *Currents in Theology and Mission* 38:2 (April 2011), pages 136–39.

Benne, Robert. "The Trials of American Lutheranism: The Torments that the Two Major American Lutheran Churches Have Visited on Themselves." *First Things* 213 (May 2011), pages 21–23.

Berry, Virginia, B.V.M. "Portrait of Tietjen." *The Christian Century* 91:12 (March 27, 1974), page 350. [Response to James E. Adams's March 1974 article "Seed of Schism."]

Boehme, Armand J. "The Smokescreen Vocabulary [re inerrancy, infallibility, Word of God, the Scriptures]." *The Springfielder* 41:2 (April 1977), pages 25–40.

Bohlmann, Ralph A. " 'Strictly Orthodox': Fifty Years Later." *Concordia Journal* 1:1 (January 1975), page 2.

Bohlmann, Ralph A. "Theological Education, Truth and Freedom at Concordia Seminary Today." *Concordia Journal* 2:1 (January 1976), pages 6–8.

Bohlmann, Ralph A. "Closing the Academic Year [rebuilding of Concordia Seminary]." *Concordia Journal* 2:5 (September 1976), pages 188–90.

Bouman, Herbert J. A. "Some Thoughts on Authentic Lutheranism." *Concordia Theological Monthly* 42:5 (May 1971), pages 283–89.

Bouman, Walter R. "History and Dogma in Christology." *Concordia Theological Monthly,* 42:4 (April 1971), pages 203–21. [See *III. Concluding Postscript,* re LCMS convention resolutions, page 220.]

Braaten, Carl E. "Grand Inquisitor of Missouri [J. A. O. Preus]." *Dialog* 10:2 (Spring 1971), pages 84–86.

Braaten, Carl E. "Garbage In, Garbage Out: The Preus Report on the St. Louis Faculty." *Dialog* 11:4 (Autumn 1972), pages 250–51.

Braaten, Carl E. "Current Controversy in the Missouri Synod." *Dialog* 13:2 (Spring 1974), pages 84–90.

Bretscher, Paul G. "The Log in Your Own Eye [re 'Christ vs. Scripture' and 'Gospel reductionism']." *Concordia Theological Monthly* 43:10 (November 1972), pages 645–86.

Bretscher, Paul G. "*A Statement* [*of Scriptural and Confessional Principles*] and Confessional Lutheranism [the doctrine of the Word of God]." *In Touch* (January[?] 1974), pages 1–10.

"This essay is the full development of a lecture presented to the faculty of Concordia Teachers College, River Forest, Illinois, January 28, 1974."

Bretscher, Paul G. "An Inquiry into Article II [of the LCMS Constitution]." *Currents in Theology and Mission* 1:2 (October 1974), pages 38–42.

Bretscher, Paul G. "Missouri's Purifying: A Special Report." *Lutheran World* 21:2 (1974), pages 173–76.

Brueggemann, Walter. "A Cosmic Sigh of Relinquishment." *Currents in Theology and Mission* 11:1 (February 1984), pages 5–20.

Burkee, James C. "Power, Politics, and the Missouri Synod [excerpt from the book of the same name]." *Lutheran Forum* 45:1 (Spring 2011), pages 16–23.

Busch, Edward E. "Another Turning Point [in the Missouri Synod]." *Currents in Theology and Mission* 2:2 (April 1975), pages 75–81.

Caemmerer, Richard R., Sr. "Preserve the Unity of the Spirit." *Concordia Theological Monthly* 41:7 (July–August 1970), pages 387–409.

Caemmerer, Richard R., Sr. "How the Gospel Works." *Concordia Theological Monthly* 44:2 (March 1973), pages 83–88.

Caemmerer, Richard R., Sr. "Parish or Perish." *Currents in Theology and Mission* 1:1 (August 1974), pages 23–26.

Caemmerer, Richard R., Sr. "A Glance at '*A Stance*' [re CTCR document *A Lutheran Stance toward Ecumenism*]." *Currents in Theology and Mission* 2:3 (June 1975), pages 174–75.

Carlan, Margaret M. "Missouri Synod: Still the Church Militant [re LCMS issues leading to Seminex]." *Commonweal* 100 (May 3, 1974), pages 208–12.

Castleman, Jerry. "The Pastoral Role in Times of Parish Conflict." *Currents in Theology and Mission* 3:3 (June 1976), pages 158–62.

Chandler, E. Russell. "Missouri Waltz: Whose Tunes?" *Christianity Today* 15:22 (August 6, 1971), pages 31–32.

Chandler, E. Russell. "Conservative Fallout [on the LCMS and Presbyterian Church in the United States]." *Christianity Today* 15:25 (September 24, 1971), pages 42–43.

Childs, James M., Jr. "The Third Use of the Law and Constructive Ethics." *Currents in Theology and Mission* 2:1 (February 1974), pages 35–40.

Christ Seminary—Seminex. "For the Ordination of Women: A Study Document Prepared by the Faculty." *Currents in Theology and Mission* 6:3 (June 1979), pages 132–43.

Clarke, Erskine. "Relationships: Boards, Faculties, Staffs, Students, and Constituencies." *Theological Education* 32 (Autumn 1995), pages 47–62.

Clarke, Erskine. "Leadership: The Study of the Seminary Presidency in Protestant Theological Seminaries." *Theological Education* 32/Supplement 2 (1995), pages 77–89.

Coiner, Harry G. "A Study of the 'Ordination of Women' Issue." *Currents in Theology and Mission* 2:4 (August 1975), pages 221–27.

Coleman, Richard J. "Biblical Inerrancy: Are We Going Anywhere?" *Theology Today* 31:4 (January 1975), 295–303.

Concordia Seminary Faculty. "Statements Adopted by the Faculty of Concordia Seminary, St. Louis, Mo. [on November 24, 1970]." *Concordia Theological Monthly* 42:1 (January 1971), pages 46–47.

Conrad, Robert L. "Seminex: The Hidden Curriculum." *Currents in Theology and Mission* 15:1 (February 1988), pages 77–83.

Constable, John. "Of Congregational and Synodical Authority." *Concordia Theological Monthly* 43:4 (April 1972), pages 212–31.

Cottrell, Raymond F. "A Church in Crisis." [SDA] *Review and Herald* 154:2 (January 13, 1977), pages 3–5.

Cottrell, Raymond F. "The Authority of Scripture." [SDA] *Review and Herald* 154:3 (January 20, 1977), pages 7–10.

Cottrell, Raymond F. "Decisions that Polarized the Missouri Synod." [SDA] *Review and Herald* 154:4 (January 27, 1977), pages 8–10.

Cottrell, Raymond F. "The Parting of the Ways." [SDA] *Review and Herald* 154:5 (February 3, 1977), pages 6–9.

Cottrell, Raymond F. "Postmortem on the LCMS Conflict." [SDA] *Review and Herald* 154:6 (February 10, 1977), pages 3, 6–7.

Cottrell, Raymond F. "An Ounce of Prevention." [SDA] *Review and Herald* 154:7 (February 17, 1977), pages 3, 10–11.

The six entries above comprise a major series—"A Church in Crisis"—by an elder of the Seventh-Day Adventist denomination in its official periodical. The author explains the issues, interviews some principals, provides a fairly detailed historical background and overview of events, and, in conclusion, comes down on the side of the Concordia Seminary faculty majority. A subsequent publication—"The Concordia Crisis: A Crisis that Affected Our Own [SDA] Church"—takes issue with Cottrell and draws parallels between the LCMS controversy and a theological crisis in the SDA in the early 1980s. See http://www.sdadefend.com/MINDEX-C/Concordia.pdf.

Cowley, S. C., and R. Wade. "Schism in the Synod [re Third ELIM Assembly, 1975 LCMS Anaheim convention]." *Newsweek* 86 (September 1, 1975), page 55.

Cross, William M. "Perceived Influences on Occupational Choice of Seminarians." *Concordia Theological Quarterly* 44:1 (January 1980), pages 3–16.

Damm, John S. "The Trial of John H. Tietjen: Implications for Our Synodical Educational Task." *In Touch* (November 1974), pages 1–2.

Danker, William J. "Editorial: Will the Real Missouri Synod Please Stand Up?" *Concordia Theological Monthly* 42:6 (June 1971), pages 339–44.

Danker, William J. "Who Wrote the Pivotal Quotation in Francis Pieper's *Christian Dogmatics*?" *Currents in Theology and Mission* 4:4 (August 1977), pages 235–39.

Danker, William, James Mayer, and Alfred von Rohr Sauer. "Jonah: Fishin' or Mission?" *Currents in Theology and Mission* 1:2 (October 1974), pages 43–49

Discussion between Danker, Mayer, and von Rohr Sauer on the Book of Jonah in Christ Seminary—Seminex / ELIM context.

Diem, Hermann. "Is Doctrinal Discipline Possible?" *Lutheran Forum* 5:2 (February 1971), pages 11–15.

Dorris, Tom. "Moving from Missouri [re Third ELIM Assembly, post-1975 LCMS Anaheim convention]." *Christianity Today* 19:24 (September 12, 1975), page 66.

Doyle, Barrie. "Missouri Synod's Troubled [Concordia Seminary] Campus." *Christianity Today* 17:4 (November 24, 1972), pages 40–41.

Ebertz, Susan. "Christ Seminary—Seminex Library: From Concordia Seminary in Exile Library to Seminex Legacy Collection." *Currents in Theology and Mission* 38:2 (April 2011), pages 120–25.

Ehlen, Arlis J. "Deliverance at the Sea: Diversity and Unity in a Biblical Theme [re documentary hypothesis; J-E-D-P source of 'Reed Sea' event]." *Concordia Theological Monthly* 44:3 (May 1973), pages 168–91.

Ehlen, Arlis J. "Religious Certainty and the Toleration of Our Theological Knowledge." *Currents in Theology and Mission* 2:2 (April 1975), pages 65–74.

Fiske, E. "Missouri Lutherans: The Story behind the Story." *Christian Herald* (October 1973), pages 20ff.

Franzmann, Martin H. "The Nature of the Unity We Seek." *Religion in Life* (Spring 1957), pages 207–14. [Reprinted in *Concordia Theological Monthly* 28:11 (November 1957), pages 801–9.]

Fredrich, Edward C. "Ehlen, Preus, Tietjen." *Wisconsin Lutheran Quarterly* 69:3 (July 1972), pages 194–95.

Fredrich, Edward C. "From Seminex to Methodism." *Wisconsin Lutheran Quarterly* 75:3 (July 1978), page 229.

Furberg, Ingemar. "Must We Lose Our Love for the Sake of Pure Doctrine?" *Concordia Journal* 1:4 (October 1975), pages 151–52.

Gehrke, Ralph. "Address to Congregation Meeting of Grace Lutheran Church, River Forest, March 11, 1975 [re charges of teaching false doctrine; includes editorial comment by Robert Weinhold of Valparaiso University]." *In Touch* 2:7 (March 1975), pages 5–8.

Goetz, Lloyd H. "Let's Be Lutheran: Theses on a Lutheran Understanding and Use of the Word." *Concordia Theological Monthly* 43:4 (April 1972), pages 258–61.

Goetz, Ronald G. "Missouri Rumble [re genesis of ELIM]." *The Christian Century* 93:9 (March 17, 1976), page 244.

Graf, Arthur E. "Theology of Ordination: With Some Applications to the Church Today." *Concordia Journal* 2:3 (May 1976), pages 121–26.

Granquist, Mark. "A Tale of Two Schisms [LCMS—1970s; ELCA—2000s]." *Lutheran Forum* 52:2 (Summer 2018), pages 25–29.

Groh, John E. "The War, Perceptual Revolution and the Missouri Synod Crisis." *The Christian Century* 90:27 (June 27, 1973), pages 696–98.

Groh, John E. "Keeping the Church Credible [re church as social institution and secularity in the LCMS]." *Currents in Theology and Mission* 2:4 (August 1975), pages 221–27.

Hadden, Jeffrey K. "A Protestant Paradox—Divided They Merge [survey / analysis of beliefs among mainline Protestants]." *Trans-action* 4 (July / August 1967), pages 63–69. [Also reprinted in *Religion in Radical Transition* (Transaction Books, 1971), pages 48–66.]

Hager, H. Lucille, compiler. "Bibliography of John H. Tietjen [includes books authored, books edited, articles, and public addresses listed by year]." *Currents in Theology and Mission* 15:1 (February 1988), pages 10–11.

Hahn, Tom. "Confessionex: Christ Seminary—Seminex (The LCMS confession movement in exile)." *DayStar Journal* (online) (Fall 2014).

Hannah, John R. "The New York Role in the Missouri War." Pages 407–24 in *Eastern Lutheranism and the National Church—Influence and Foil: Containing the Essays and Reports of the 19th Biennial Meeting Held at Wagner College, Staten Island, October 29–31, 1998.* Edited by David J. Wartluft. Vol. 18 of LHC Essays and Reports. Saint Louis: Lutheran Historical Conference.

Harms, Oliver R. "Editorial: Why Missouri? [re doctrinal controversy]." *Concordia Theological Monthly* 42:5 (May 1971), pages 261–64.

Hass, Leroy. "Theological Stance and Personality (a Study of Selected Missouri Synod Pastors)." *Currents in Theology and Mission* 2:3 (June 1975), pages 167–73.

Hein, Steven A. "'A Scrutiny' Scrutinized." *The Cresset* 36:3 (January 1973), pages 21–23. [A critique of Walter E. Keller, "Scrutiny of *A Statement* on Scripture," *The Cresset* 35:8 (June 1972), pages 6–9.]

Hendel, Kurt K. "How My Mind Has Changed." *Currents in Theology and Mission* 38:2 (April 2011), pages 117–19.

Herzfeld, Will Lawrence. "What's Goin' On." *Currents in Theology and Mission* 10:6 (December 1983), pages 346–50.

Huber, C. E. "Editorial: The Gospel Needs Protection [re 'synodical confessional substitutes']." *Concordia Theological Monthly* 42:5 (May 1971), pages 259–60.

Hultgren, Arland J. "Can We Not Afford Seminex?" *Dialog* 18:2 (Spring 1979), page 146.

Hummel, Horace D. "No Other Gospel! Do American Lutherans Need a Confessing Movement?" *Lutheran Forum* 3:9 (October 1969), pages 4–9.

See also responses by David Scaer, David Gustafson, and Richard John Neuhaus, as well as Hummel's rejoinder, in *Lutheran Forum* 3:11 (December 1969), pages 16–20.

Hummel, Horace D. "Is There a Lutheran View of the Bible? [part 1 of 2 on the use of the historical-critical method of biblical interpretation from Christian perspective]." *Lutheran Scholar* 27 (January 1970), pages 29–32.

Hummel, Horace D. "The Debate Continues on the Nature of Gospel and Confession." *Lutheran Forum* 4:3 (March 1970), pages 8–10.

Hummel, Horace D. "Is There a Lutheran View of the Bible? [part 2 of 2 on the use of the historical-critical method]." *Lutheran Scholar* 27 (April 1970), pages 34–45, 63.

Hummel, Horace D. "Open Forum: President Preus: Pro and Con [letter in response to April 1971 editorial "Editor's Ambo: Where Does J. A. O. Preus Stand?" *Lutheran Forum* 5:4 (April 1971), pages 4–5]." *Lutheran Forum* 5:6 (June / July 1971), page 20.

Hummel, Horace D. "Gospel and Bible." *Affirm: Occasional Papers* (Spring 1973), pages 28–30.

Hummel, Horace D. "Church Discipline Now and in the Old Testament." *Concordia Journal* 1:4 (October 1975), pages 166–74.

Huth, Harry A. "*After the Purifying* by Paul G. Bretscher [book review]." *Lutheran Quarterly* 27:3 (August 1975), pages 262–64.

Huth, Harry A. "Confessional Subscription and Theological Pluralism." *The Springfielder* 39:4 (March 1976), pages 194–202.

Jackayya, B. H. "The Relation between Doctrinal Consensus and Church Fellowship." *Currents in Theology and Mission* 2:5 (October 1975), pages 252–60.

Janzow, F. Samuel. "The Layman and the Notion of Bible Myth." *Concordia Journal* 4:1 (January 1978), pages 24–28.

Jenson, Robert W. "Preus' Statement: Its Heresy and Foolishness [re *A Statement of Scriptural and Confessional Principles*]." *Dialog* 11:3 (Summer 1972), pages 164–65.

Jenson, Robert W. "Missouri and the Existential Fear of Change." *Dialog* 14 (Fall 1975), pages 247–50.

Jeske, Richard L. "Salvation as Liberation: The Domestic Church Body." *Currents in Theology and Mission* 1:2 (October 1974), pages 71–72.

Jeske, Richard L. "Salvation as Liberation: The Only Word Is Near." *Currents in Theology and Mission* 1:3 (December 1974), pages 114–16.

Jewett, Robert. "Gospel as Heresy: Concordia Seminary in Exile." *The Christian Century* 91:12 (March 27, 1974), pages 336–40.

Jewett, Robert. "Correspondence [letter dated February 26, 1974, re controversy at Concordia Seminary]." *Bulletin—Council on the Study of Religion* 5:2 (April 1974), page 22.

Jordahl, Leigh D. "Missouri Synod: Dilemma or Trilemma?" *Dialog* 12:2 (Spring 1973), pages 121–26. [Based on comment on Missouri Synod's dilemma by Martin Franzmann in *Lutheran Outlook* (December 1952).]

Jordan, Horst W. "Kyrios Jesus." *Concordia Theological Monthly* 44:3 (May 1973), pages 213–17.

A "perceptive and pastoral analysis of the key issue before the Synod." Distinction between the form and content of Scripture, necessity of using historical-critical method, "Gospel reductionism" a misnomer, etc.

Jordan, Horst W. "Some Concerns about Current Confessional Statements." *Concordia Theological Monthly* 45:1 (January 1974), pages 27–34.

Jungkuntz, Richard. "Crisis of Authority in The Lutheran Church—Missouri Synod." *Review and Expositor* 75:2 (Spring 1978), pages 235–48.

Kalin, Everett R. "Let Me See! Lessons for the Commemoration of Renewers of the Church, Jeremiah 1:4–10; Mark 10:35–45." *Currents in Theology and Mission* 38:2 (April 2011), pages 133–35.

Kalin, Everett R. "Valid, etc. [sermon on thirty-fifth anniversary of Seminex]." *Currents in Theology and Mission* 38:2 (April 2011), pages 140–43.

Keller, Walter E. "Scrutiny of *A Statement* on Scripture [i.e., *A Statement of Scriptural and Confessional Principles*]." *The Cresset* 35:8 (June 1972), pages 6–9.

Keller, Walter E. "Necessary and Relevant to What?" *The Cresset* 36:4 (February 1973), pages 22–23.

Keller's response to Steven A. Hein, "'A Scrutiny' Scrutinized," *The Cresset* 36:3 (January 1973), pages 21–23, itself a critique of Keller, "Scrutiny of *A Statement* on Scripture," *The Cresset* 35:8 (June 1972), pages 6–9.

Keller, Walter [E.] "Reflections on '*A Statement....*'" *In Touch* (January 1974), pages 1–2.

Keller, Walter E., Kenneth Korby, Robert Schultz, and David Truemper. "A Review Essay of *A Statement of Scriptural and Confessional Principles* [part 1 of 2]." *The Cresset* 36:7 (May 1973), pages 6–20.

Keller, Walter E., Kenneth Korby, Robert Schultz, and David Truemper. "A Review Essay (Part II) of *A Statement of Scriptural and Confessional Principles* [part 2 of 2]." *The Cresset* 36:10 (October 1973), pages 21–38. [A reprint of the two Keller et al. articles in one volume was also published.]

Kingsbury, Jack Dean. "The Historical-Critical Method in Perspective." *Currents in Theology and Mission* 2:3 (June 1975), pages 132–41.

Kirchhoff, Henry C. "The Autonomy of a Congregation of the LCMS." *Concordia Journal* 2:4 (July 1976), pages 141–42.

Klann, Richard. "Criticism of the Bible." *Affirm: Occasional Papers* (Spring 1973), pages 1–4, 38.

Klann, Richard. "Sorting Out the Problems." *Affirm: Occasional Papers* (Spring 1973), pages 9–11.

Klann, Richard. "Biblical Motivations for the Constitution of The Lutheran Church—Missouri Synod." *Concordia Journal* 1:2 (March 1975), pages 86–92.

Klann, Richard. "Reflections after [1975 LCMS convention in] Anaheim." *Concordia Journal* 1:4 (October 1975), pages 146–47.

Klann, Richard. "Means and Ends: Amorality and Christian Confession [re varied motives for Seminex]." *Concordia Journal* 1:4 (October 1975), pages 147–48.

Klann, Richard. "Synod [re membership and rejection of doctrinal position]." *Concordia Journal* 2:3 (May 1976), pages 90–91.

Klausler, Alfred P. "Missourian Dissenters: Anguish and Joy." *The Christian Century* 91:32 (September 25, 1974), pages 869–70.

Klausler, Alfred P. "Servant Church with a New Song [re genesis of the English Synod]." *The Christian Century* 93:39 (December 1, 1976), pages 1067–68.

Klein, Leonard R. "J. A. O. Preus." *Lutheran Forum* 28:4 (November 1994), page 7.

Klein, Ralph W. "How My Mind Has Changed." *Currents in Theology and Mission* 38:2 (April 2011), pages 126–27.

Klein, Ralph W. "Tribute [John Damm; Seminex]." *Currents in Theology and Mission* 38:2 (April 2011), pages 144–46.

Klein, Ralph W. "*Currents in Theology and Mission*: A History." *Currents in Theology and Mission* 43:1 (January 2016), pages 3–7.

Klein, Ralph W., and Gloria Weber. "The Ordination of Women in the Lutheran Church." *Currents in Theology and Mission* 4:3 (June 1977), pages 151–57.

Klotz, John W. "Missouri's Constitutional Crisis [re training of church workers]." *Concordia Journal* 1:3 (June 1975), pages 125–31.

Klotz, John W. "Autonomy of the Congregation [vis-à-vis calling of Seminex graduates]." *Concordia Journal* 2:4 (July 1976), pages 149–55.

Klug, Eugene F. "Saving Faith and the Inerrancy of Scripture." *The Springfielder* 39:4 (March 1976), pages 203–11.

Koenig, Richard E. "Fishhooks Aplenty, but What about the Fish? Missouri, A.D. [after Denver], Is Different." *Lutheran Forum* 3:8 (September 1969), pages 4–7.

Koenig, Richard E. "Missouri at Milwaukee [1971 LCMS convention]: The Issue Is Collegiality." *Lutheran Forum* 5:6 (June / July 1971), pages 6–8.

Koenig, Richard E. "Doctrine and Authority: The Missouri Synod at Milwaukee." *Dialog* 10:4 (Autumn 1971), pages 265–71.

Koenig, Richard E. "Lutheran Split: The Missouri Controversy." *Commonweal* 96 (August 1972), pages 444–45.

Koenig, Richard E. "What's behind the Showdown in the LCMS? Church and Tradition in Collision." *Lutheran Forum* 6:4 (November 1972), pages 17–20.

Koenig, Richard E. "What's behind the Showdown in the LCMS? Missouri Turns Moderate: 1938–1965." *Lutheran Forum* 7:1 (February 1973), pages 19–20, 29.

Koenig, Richard E. "What's behind the Showdown in the LCMS? Conservative Reaction: 1965–1969." *Lutheran Forum* 7:2 (May 1973), pages 18–21.

Koenig, Richard E. "What's after the Showdown in the LCMS? Epilogue to New Orleans [1973 LCMS convention]." *Lutheran Forum* 7:4 (November 1973), pages 10–12.

Koenig, Richard E. "Post-Mortem on the Showdown in the LCMS: The Issue Was Conscience." *Lutheran Forum* 10:3 (September 1976), pages 6–11. [*Major editorial on the LCMS controversies, 1969–76.]

Krentz, Edgar. [Letter to Board of Control, Concordia Seminary, January 6, 1975.] *In Touch* (February 1975), pages 3–4.

Krentz, Edgar. [Interview by Ralph Klein regarding Krentz's resignation from Concordia Seminary faculty]. *In Touch* 2:6 (February 1975), pages 4–5.

Krentz, Edgar. "*After the Purifying* by Paul G. Bretscher [book review]." *Lutheran Quarterly* 27:3 (August 1975), pages 260–62.

Krentz, Edgar. "The Egalitarian Church of Matthew." *Currents in Theology and Mission* 4:6 (December 1977), pages 333–41.

An example of the author's higher-critical hermeneutic; an interpretation of Scripture that promotes an ecumenical agenda. "The church is thus not an exclusive community that is concerned about its purity" (338).

Krentz, Edgar. "Historical Criticism and Confessional Commitment." *Currents in Theology and Mission* 15:1 (February 1988), pages 128–36.

Krentz, Edgar. "Building on the One Foundation—Bible Book of Faith: Lutheran School of Theology at Chicago Seminex Reunion, June 24, 2009." *Currents in Theology and Mission* 38:2 (April 2011), pages 103–16.

Kretzmann, A. T. "The *Statement* of the 44, 1945–1979." *Concordia Historical Institute Quarterly* 55:2 (Summer 1982), pages 69–81.

Kucharsky, David E. "[Concordia] Seminary on the Spot." *Christianity Today* 16:25 (September 29, 1972), page 38.

Kuhl, Steven C. "Bibliography of Robert W. Bertram." *Currents in Theology and Mission* 14:2 (April 1987), pages 140–46.

Lanouette, William J. "Hair-Trigger Debate Splits Lutheran Body." *National Observer* 14 (June 28, 1975), page 6.

Larson, Janet K. "Church Out of Order [LCMS Anaheim convention; ELIM]." *The Christian Century* 92 (July 23–30, 1975), pages 675–76.

Lesher, William E. "John Tietjen—Seminary Builder." *Currents in Theology and Mission* 15:1 (February 1988), pages 161–62.

Lieneck, Marjorie. "The Role of Women in the Church." *Currents in Theology and Mission* 2:3 (June 1975), pages 142–51.

Lindsay, Kenneth M. "Open Forum: Who Is Unsettling Missouri?" *Lutheran Forum* 4:3 (March 1970), page 24.

Response by the director, LCMS Department of Public Relations, to editorial "Unsettled Missouri," *Lutheran Forum* 3:11 (December 1969), pages 13–14. See Saffen response to Lindsay, *Lutheran Forum* 4:5 (May 1970), pages 18–20.

Lindsell, Harold. "Who Is Right in the Missouri Synod Dispute?" *Christianity Today* 19:14 (April 11, 1975), pages 10–11.

Lotz, David W. "The Sense of Church History in Representative Missouri Synod Theology." *Concordia Theological Monthly* 42:9 (October 1971), pages 597–619.

Lotz, David W. "The Gospel, Historical Consciousness, and Risk." *Currents in Theology and Mission* 11:1 (February 1984), pages 21–33.

Luecke, Richard H. "That Cool in the Fiery Furnace." *The Cresset* 37:5 (March 1974), pages 19–22.

Luecke, Richard H. "Church Controversy and the Arts of Ministry." *Theology Today* 31:4 (January 1975), pages 303–13.

Lueker, Erwin L. "Doctrinal Emphases in the Missouri Synod." *Concordia Theological Monthly* 43:4 (April 1972), pages 198–211.

Lueking, F. Dean. "Trial by Fire at Concordia [Seminary] [re reaction to Tietjen's suspension from office]." *The Christian Century* 91:5 (February 6, 1974), pages 116–17.

Lyles, Jean Caffey. "Jack Preus's Last Hurrah." *The Christian Century* 98:26 (August 26–September 2, 1981), pages 819–20.

Madson, Juul B. "Some Statements on Law-Gospel Principle as It Pertains to Hermeneutics." *Lutheran Synod Quarterly* 14:3 (Spring 1974), pages 46–50.

Madson, Juul B. "Gospel Reductionism." *Lutheran Synod Quarterly* 14:3 (Spring 1974), pages 51–69.

Maier, Paul L. "The Two Minds of Christendom: Historical Reflections on the Episode of 'The Forty-Four.'" Pages 183–90 in *Let Christ Be Christ: Theology, Ethics and World Religions in the Two Kingdoms: Essays in Honor of the Sixty-Fifth Birthday of Charles L. Manske.* Edited by Daniel N. Harmelink. Huntington Beach, California: Tentatio Press, 1999.

Marquart, Kurt. "The Swing of the Pendulum: An Attempt to Understand the St. Louis [Seminary] 'Affirmations and Discussions' [re *Faithful to Our Calling, Faithful to Our Lord*]." *Affirm: Occasional Papers* (Spring 1973), pages 12–27.

Marty, Martin E. "Showdown in the Missouri Synod [re *Report of the Synodical President* on the Concordia Seminary faculty in preparation for the 1973 LCMS convention]." *The Christian Century* 89:34 (September 27, 1972), pages 943–46.

Marty, Martin E. "Missouri's Exiles: Heartbeat, Ashes—and Victory." *The Christian Century* 91:23 (June 12–19, 1974), pages 630–32.

Marty, Martin E. "Plug for Seminex [promoting Ecumenical Theological Festival at Seminex, June 24–28]." *The Christian Century* 91:23 (June 12–19, 1974), page 655.

Marty, Martin E. "The Lutheran Church—Missouri Synod: A Clash of World-views and Styles." *In Touch* (November 20, 1974), pages 1–4.

Marty, Martin E. "But, of Course, I'm Prejudiced [re English District, English Synod]." *The Christian Century* 93:23 (July 7–14, 1976), page 647.

Marty, Martin E. "Season for Binding Together [re LCMS, AELC, other Lutheran bodies]." *The Christian Century* 94:3 (January 26, 1977), pages 51–53.

Marty, Myron A. "Moving Out and Moving In: Human Consequences of the Purge at Concordia Seminary." *The Christian Century* 91:15 (April 17, 1974), pages 422–25.

Mayer, Herbert T. "Will the Real Missouri Synod Please Stand Up? [re approach to doctrine, exegesis, etc.]." *Concordia Theological Monthly* 42:6 (June 1971), pages 339–41.

Mayer, Herbert T. "Editorial: A Place for Loyal Opposition." *Concordia Theological Monthly* 43:11 (December 1972), pages 707–8.

Mayer, Herbert T. "A Crisis of Freedom and Trust." *Currents in Theology and Mission* 1:2 (October 1974), pages 35–37.

Miesner, Willis. "Open Forum: President Preus: Pro and Con." *Lutheran Forum* 5:6 (June / July 1971), page 21.

Letter critical of March 1971 article by Richard John Neuhaus, "A Voice in the Church: Missouri's Gift," *Lutheran Forum* 5:3 (March 1971), pages 22–23.

Moeller, Elmer. "Meaning of Confessional Subscription [and the LCMS position on historical-critical scholarship]." *The Springfielder* 38 (December 1974), pages 193–211.

Moellering, H. Armin. "A Rejoinder with Repristinating Notes." *Currents in Theology and Mission* 2:1 (February 1975), pages 10–18. [See E. H. Schroeder, "Current Implications of the 'We Condemn' Statements in the Lutheran Confessions."]

Montgomery, John Warwick. "Missouri Compromise [part 1]." *Christianity Today* 13:8 (January 17, 1969), pages 49–50.

Montgomery, John Warwick. "Missouri Compromise [part 2]." *Christianity Today* 13:13 (March 28, 1969), pages 46–47.

Montgomery, John Warwick. "Missouri Compromise [part 3]." *Christianity Today* 13:18 (June 6, 1969), pages 50–51.

A series of articles on the issues revolving around LCMS / ALC fellowship discussions as well as the internal theological agitations in the LCMS.

Montgomery, John Warwick. "The Last Days of the Late Great Synod of Missouri." *Christianity Today* 15:14 (April 9, 1971), pages 56–57.

Neuhaus, Richard John. "A Modest View of Missouri." *Lutheran Forum* 3:6 (June 1969), pages 14–15.

Neuhaus, Richard John. "Jacob Preus: Theologian or Conservative Functionary?" *Una Sancta* 26:3 (October 1969), pages 53–57.

Neuhaus, Richard John. "More on the Travail of Missouri." *Una Sancta* 27:1 (January 1970), pages 15–21.

Neuhaus, Richard John. "A Voice in the Church: Missouri's Gift." *Lutheran Forum* 5:3 (March 1971), pages 22–23.

Neuhaus, Richard John. "Open Forum: More on 'Missouri's Gift.'" *Lutheran Forum* 5:7 (August / September 1971), page 19.

Letter in response to John Tietjen's critique of Neuhaus's article "A Voice in the Church: Missouri's Gift," *Lutheran Forum* 5:3 (March 1971), pages 22–23.

Neuhaus, Richard John. "Schism and Renewal in American Lutheranism." *Theology Today* 30:3 (October 1973), pages 292–95.

Neuhaus, Richard John. "Arthur Carl Piepkorn, 1907–1973." *Lutheran Forum* 8:1 (January 1974), pages 17–18.

Nieting, Lorenz. "Otten-Preus Heresy." *Dialog* 15 (Summer 1976), pages 192–201.

Piepkorn, Arthur Carl. "The Position of the Church and Her Symbols [essay concerning 'the authority, inspiration and inerrancy of the Sacred Scriptures']." *Concordia Theological Monthly* 25:10 (October 1954), pages 738–42.

Piepkorn, Arthur Carl. "What Does 'Inerrancy' Mean?" *Concordia Theological Monthly* 36:8 (September 1965), pages 577–93.

Piepkorn, Arthur Carl. "Possible Courses of Action Involving a Disaffected or Dissident Individual or Group of Individuals in the Church." *Concordia Theological Monthly* 42:11 (December 1971), pages 726–30.

Plowman, Edward E. "The Battle of New Orleans [1973 LCMS convention]." *Christianity Today* 17:22 (August 10, 1973), pages 40–42.

Plowman, Edward E. "Missouri Synod: The Showdown." *Christianity Today* 18:10 (February 15, 1974), page 45.

Plowman, Edward E. "Man without a Church [re Herman Otten of *Christian News*]." *Christianity Today* 18:14 (April 12, 1974), pages 41–42.

Plowman, Edward E. "March in Missouri [Concordia and Seminex spring term registration]." *Christianity Today* 18:14 (April 12, 1974), pages 42–44.

Plowman, Edward E. "Seeds of Schism: The Misery of Missouri." *Christianity Today* 18:16 (May 10, 1974), pages 48–49.

Plowman, Edward E. "Prospecting for Peace in the Missouri Synod." *Christianity Today* 19:13 (March 28, 1975), pages 35–36.

Plowman, Edward E. "Missouri Synod Lutherans: Talk of Schism." *Christianity Today* 19:22 (August 8, 1975), pages 31–32.

Plowman, Edward E. "Missouri Synod Aftermath [following the 1977 LCMS convention in Dallas]." *Christianity Today* 21:22 (August 26, 1977), pages 36–37.

Preus, J. A. O. "Sent to Reconcile [re report to 1971 LCMS convention in Milwaukee]." *Christianity Today* 15:24 (September 10, 1971), pages 16–20.

Preus, J. A. O. "Integrity, Schism, Neither, Both." *Christianity Today* 19:2 (October 25, 1974), pages 11–12ff.

Preus, J. A. O. "Lutheran Identity Is Insistence on Truth." *Dialog* 16:4 (Fall 1977), pages 292–95.

Preus, Robert D. "May the Lutheran Theologian Legitimately Use the Historical-Critical Method?" *Affirm: Occasional Papers* (Spring 1973), pages 31–38.

Preus, Robert D. "Biblical Authority in the Lutheran Confessions." *Concordia Journal* 4:1 (January 1978), pages 16–24.

Rast, Lawrence R., Jr. "Forty Years after Seminex: Reflections on Social and Theological Factors Leading to the Walkout." *Concordia Theological Quarterly* 80:3–4 (July–October 2016), pages 195–215.

Rehwaldt, Traugott H. "The Other Understanding of the Inspiration Texts." *Concordia Theological Monthly* 43:6 (June 1972), pages 355–67.

Rehwaldt, Traugott H. "Is the Law a Guide for Good Works?" *Currents in Theology and Mission* 1:1 (August 1974), pages 3–11.

Reichwald, Glenn E., and A. T. Kretzmann. "Committee of Ten and Ten [an analysis of 'A Statement (of the Forty-Four)'; part 1 of 2]." *Lutheran Synod Quarterly* 19:4 (December 1979), pages 3–23.

Reichwald, Glenn E., and A. T. Kretzmann. "Committee of Ten and Ten [an analysis of 'A Statement (of the Forty-Four)'; part 2 of 2]." *Lutheran Synod Quarterly* 20:3 (September 1980), pages 47–57.

Repp, Arthur C. "Changes in the Missouri Synod." *Concordia Theological Monthly* 38:7 (July / August 1967), pages 458–78.

Repp, Arthur C. "The Binding Nature of Synodical Resolutions for a Pastor or Professor of The Lutheran Church—Missouri Synod." *Concordia Theological Monthly* 42:3 (March 1971), pages 153–62.

Religion News Service. "'Seminex' Will Graduate Its Last Class Next Spring." *Christianity Today* 27:2 (January 21, 1983), pages 27ff.

Reumann, John Henry Paul. "What in Scripture Speaks to the Ordination of Women?" *Concordia Theological Monthly* 44:1 (January 1973), pages 5–30.

Reumann, John Henry Paul. "Exegetes, Honesty, and the Faith: Biblical Scholarship in Church School Theology [re J-E-D-P, Q]." *Currents in Theology and Mission* 5:1 (February 1978), pages 16–32.

Rinker, Craig W. "Toward Ethical, Edifying Speech [re communication during internal controversy]." *Currents in Theology and Mission* 2:5 (October 1975), pages 271–76.

Robinson, Jack T. "The Spirit of Triumphalism in The Lutheran Church—Missouri Synod." *Currents in Theology and Mission* 1:1 (August 1974), pages 13–20. [Also 1972 PhD dissertation, Vanderbilt University.]

Roth, S. John. "Response to Ralph W. Klein." *Trinity Seminary Review* 6 (1984), pages 24–25.

Rudnick, Milton. "Fundamentalism and the Missouri Synod: A Historical Study of Their Interaction and Mutual Influence." *Concordia Theological Monthly* 43:4 (April 1972), pages 252–57.

A review by the author five years after his book of the same name was first published.

Saffen, Wayne. "Who Needs Public Relations?" *Lutheran Forum* 4:5 (May 1970), pages 18–20.

Letter by the campus pastor, University of Chicago, in response to Kenneth Lindsay's critique (*Lutheran Forum* 4:3 [March 1970], page 24) of the editorial "Unsettled Missouri" (*Lutheran Forum* 3:11 [December 1969], pages 13–14).

Saffen, Wayne. "On Casting Out Devils in Missouri." *Lutheran Forum* 5:5 (May 1971), pages 10–12.

Saffen, Wayne. "Is God Trying to Tell Us Something? [re institutional power]." *Concordia Theological Monthly* 42:11 (December 1971), pages 710–25.

Saffen, Wayne. "The Politics of Faith: Another View [re LCMS 'politics']." *Lutheran Forum* 6:1 (February 1972), pages 9–11.

Saffen, Wayne. "The Voice Is Jacob's but the Hands Are Esau's [critique of J. A. O. Preus and controversy in the LCMS]." *Dialog* 11:2 (Spring 1972), pages 144–46.

Sayler, Gwen. "Werner Elert and the Law / Gospel Dialectic." *Currents in Theology and Mission* 2:1 (February 1975), pages 41–43.

Scaer, David P. "The Law-Gospel Debate in the Missouri Synod." *The Springfielder* 36 (December 1972), pages 156–71.

Scaer, David P. "'The Church's One Foundation' [response to ELIM's doctrinal statement]." *The Springfielder* 38 (December 1974), pages 218–25.

Scaer, David P. "A Response to David Lotz' Writings." *The Springfielder* 38:3 (December 1974), pages 226–31. [See also Lotz's publications in **1.2 *Academic Theses, Dissertations, Student and Conference Papers.***]

Scaer, David P. "On the Nature of Confessional Subscription: An Explanation on the Action of the Missouri Synod at New Orleans in July 1973." *Concordia Theological Quarterly* 74:1–2 (January–April 2010), pages 153–58.

Scaer, David P. "Walther, the Third Use of the Law, and Contemporary Issues." *Concordia Theological Quarterly* 75:3–4 (July–October 2011), pages 329–42.

Scharlemann, Martin. "Some Sobering Reflections on the Use of the Historical-Critical Method." *Affirm: Occasional Papers* (Spring 1973), pages 5–6, 11.

Scharlemann, Martin. "Born of Anguish and Travail [re *Concordia Journal*]." *Concordia Journal* 1:1 (January 1975), pages 4–7.

Scharlemann, Martin. "Remnant: Complex or Model? [faculty / student minority left at Concordia Seminary]." *Concordia Journal* 1:2 (March 1975), pages 51–53.

Scharlemann, Martin. "[Johann M.] Reu and the Doctrine of the Holy Scriptures." *Concordia Journal* 5:1 (January 1979), pages 12–20.

Scharlemann, Robert P. "Lessons from Missouri." *Dialog* 13:4 (Autumn 1974), pages 248–49.

Schroeder, Edward H. "The Orders of Creation—Some Reflections on the History and Place of the Term in Systematic Theology [re women in the pastoral office]." *Concordia Theological Monthly* 43:3 (March 1972), pages 165–78.

Schroeder, Edward H. "Law-Gospel Reductionism in the History of The Lutheran Church—Missouri Synod." *Concordia Theological Monthly* 43:4 (April 1972), pages 232–47.

Schroeder, Edward H. "Responsible Theological Education." *In Touch* 2:6 (February 1975), pages 5–8.

Schroeder, Edward H. "Current Implications of the 'We Condemn' Statements in the Lutheran Confessions." *Currents in Theology and Mission* 2:1 (February 1975), pages 5–9. [See H. Armin Moellering, "A Rejoinder with Repristinating Notes."]

Schuetze, Armin W. "The WELS and the LCMS: Where Are We Today? [paper presented at the Nebraska District Convention, Waco, Nebraska, June 13–15, 1988]." *Wisconsin Lutheran Quarterly* 85:4 (Fall 1988), pages 261–86.

Schultz, Robert C. "Reflections on the Current Controversy in The Lutheran Church—Missouri Synod: An Attempt to Express Pastoral Concern." *The Cresset* 35:10 (October 1972), pages 7–12.

Schultz, Robert C. "Missouri Synod History and Doctrine: Variant Readings." *The Cresset* 35:10 (October 1972), pages 29–33.

A critique of J. A. O. Preus's *Report of the Synodical President.*

Shoemaker, D. "Watching Missouri Wage War." *Christian Herald* (August 22, 1975), page 18.

Sommerfeld, Richard. "Historic Character and / or Cultural Relevance (a Sociologist Looks at the Missouri Synod)." *Currents in Theology and Mission* 2:2 (April 1975), pages 82–87.

Stendahl, Krister. "Reconciliation." *Currents in Theology and Mission* 1:3 (December 1974), pages 85–90.

Strietelmeier, John. "Reflections after Rivergate." *The Cresset* 36:9 (September 1973), page 28.

Strieter, Thomas W. "Luther's View of Scripture." *Currents in Theology and Mission* 1:2 (December 1974), pages 91–97.

Stuenkel, Robert. "The Turns in Ministry through Seminex." *DayStar Journal* (online) (September 2014).

Suelflow, August Robert. "Congregational Autonomy." *Concordia Journal* 3:6 (November 1977), pages 261–69.

Surburg, Raymond F. "Paul Bretscher's *After the Purifying*: A Review Article." *The Springfielder* 39:4 (March 1976), pages 212–15.

Tiemann, Edwin G. "Historical-Critical Method Differs from Higher Criticism." *Affirm: Occasional Papers* (Spring 1973), page 8. [Reprinted from *Badger Lutheran* (February 1, 1973), page 1.]

Tietjen, John H. "Open Forum: More on 'Missouri's Gift.'" *Lutheran Forum* 5:7 (August / September 1971), page 19.

Letter in response to Richard John Neuhaus, "A Voice in the Church: Missouri's Gift," *Lutheran Forum* 5:3 (March 1971), pages 22–23.

Tietjen, John H. "Piercing the Smokescreen: Toward an Understanding of the Issues in the Missouri Synod." *Christianity Today* 19:14 (April 11, 1975), pages 8–10.

Tietjen, John H. "Paradigm for Lutheran Union." *Currents in Theology and Mission* 11:1 (February 1984), pages 64ff.

Tietjen, John H. "In Tribute to George W. Hoyer." *Currents in Theology and Mission* 14:4 (August 1987), pages 296–97.

Vinz, Warren L. "The Tale of Two Controversies: 1946–1976." *Foundations* 24:1 (January–March 1981), pages 54–75.

Viviano, B. "The Mess in Missouri: A Theologian's View." *Priest* 31 (September 1975), pages 39–42.

Vogel, H. "Troubled Missouri." *Wisconsin Lutheran Quarterly* 71:2 (April 1974), pages 141–44.

Vogel, H. "Missouri's Troubles Continue." *Wisconsin Lutheran Quarterly* 71:3 (July 1974), pages 227–31.

Vogel, H. "Missouri Controversy Drawing to a Close." *Wisconsin Lutheran Quarterly* 73:4 (October 1976), pages 305–10.

Vogel, H. "Seminex Gets a New Name." *Wisconsin Lutheran Quarterly* 75:1 (January 1978), page 64.

Walther, Carl F. W. "Why Should Our Pastors, Teachers and Professors Subscribe Unconditionally to the Symbolical Writings of Our Church: Essay Delivered at the Western District Convention in 1858." *Concordia Theological Monthly* 18:4 (April 1947), pages 241–53.

Walther, Carl F. W. [transl. H. Fehner et al.]. "Fidelity to the Written Word: The Burden of the Missouri Synod." *Concordia Journal* 1:2 (March 1975), pages 69–85.

Walther, Carl F. W. [transl. A. W. C. Guebert]. "Dr. Walther's Foreword for Vol. XIV of *Lehre und Wehre*, 1868 [treatment of open questions and error in the church]." *Concordia Journal* 1:3 (June 1975), pages 119–24.

Walther, Carl F. W. [transl. A. F. Krugler]. "Loyalty: Confession and Synod." *Concordia Journal* 2:2 (March 1976), pages 42–43.

Warneck, Richard H. "Women Vicars and the Office of Ministry." *Concordia Journal* 2:3 (May 1976), pages 93–95.

Weber, Arthur M. "Open Forum: Who Needs Public Relations?" *Lutheran Forum* 4:5 (May 1970), page 20.

Letter in response to Wayne Lindsay's March 1970, page 24, critique of the *Lutheran Forum* editorial "Unsettled Missouri" (3:11 [December 1969], pages 13–14).

Weber, Arthur M. "Open Forum: President Preus: Pro and Con." *Lutheran Forum* 5:6 (June / July 1971), pages 20–21.

Letter in response to the editorial "Editor's Ambo: Where Does J. A. O. Preus Stand?" *Lutheran Forum* 5:4 (April 1971), pages 4–5.

Wehmeier, Waldermar W. "Missouri and Public Doctrine." *Currents in Theology and Mission* 2:1 (February 1975), pages 23–31.

Wind, James P. "The Afterlife of Exile." *Currents in Theology and Mission* 38:2 (April 2011), pages 93–100.

Wollenburg, George F. "Conscience: A Preliminary Discussion [re ordination of Seminex graduates, etc.]." *Concordia Journal* 2:3 (May 1976), pages 117–21.

Wunderlich, Lorenz. "Scripture, Word of God, and Gospel: Usage in the Book of Concord." *Concordia Journal* 4:4 (July 1978), pages 155–60.

Zuck, L. "Lutheran Students Hold Balance in Theological Warfare." *A.D.* (May 1974), page 46.

3.2 *Unsigned Articles and Editorials*

(chronological order)

"What Is Troubling the Lutherans?" Part I. *News and Views* 24:1 (January 1961).

"What Is Troubling the Lutherans?" Part II. *News and Views* 24:2 (February 1961).

"What Is Troubling the Lutherans?" Part III. *News and Views* 24:7 (June 1961).

"What Is Troubling the Lutherans?" Part IV. *News and Views*, Special Lutheran Edition (May 1962).

Series of special issues devoted to emerging doctrinal controversies in the LCMS, with focus on Concordia Seminary. Published by the National Laymen's Council of the Church League of America, Wheaton, Illinois.

World-view [editorial]. "Lutheran Campuses: Year of Unrest over Internal Problems [re three-day moratorium on classes at Concordia Seminary]." *Lutheran Forum* 3:6 (June 1969), page 22.

"Editor's Ambo: Unsettled Missouri." *Lutheran Forum* 3:11 (December 1969), pages 13–14. [See also Lindsay and Saffen responses to this editorial in section **3.1 *Signed Articles and Editorials***]

"Editor's Ambo: Reconciliation Begins at Home [re Concordia Seminary faculty investigation]." *Lutheran Forum* 4:10 (November 1970), pages 4–5.

"Editor's Ambo: Understanding the Issues [re Concordia Seminary faculty investigation]." *Lutheran Forum* 5:2 (February 1971), page 5.

"Editor's Ambo: Where Does J. A. O. Preus Stand?" *Lutheran Forum* 5:4 (April 1971), pages 4–5.

"Lutheran Showdown: Missouri Synod Furor [higher criticism of Bible; Arlis Ehlen 'fired']." *Christianity Today* 16:14 (April 14, 1972), pages 42ff.

"Editor's Ambo: The Ehlen Disgrace [nonrenewal of professor's contract at Concordia Seminary]." *Lutheran Forum* 6:3 (August 1972), pages 5–6.

"Editor's Ambo: 'A Needed Voice' and Brotherly Advice." *Lutheran Forum* 6:4 (November 1972), pages 6–7.

"Missouri Synod's Troubled Campus [re Concordia Seminary]." *Christianity Today* 17:4 (November 24, 1972), pages 40–41.

"Twenty-Two Questions on the Historical-Critical Methodology." *Affirm: Occasional Papers* (Spring 1973), pages 7, 38.

"Structures, Confessions, and Conventions." *The Cresset* 36:6 (April 1973), pages 3–5.

"Missouri Lutheran Showdown: The Battle of New Orleans [1973 LCMS convention]." *Christianity Today* 17:22 (August 10, 1973), pages 40–42.

[Participant in "Exile" from Concordia Seminary]. "Exile." *Lutheran World* 21:2 (1974), page 176.

"[Concordia] Seminary Board [of Control] Ousts President [suspension of Tietjen]." *National Catholic Reporter* 10 (February 1, 1974), page 2.

"Discord at Concordia [Seminary] [suspension of Tietjen]." *Time* 103 (February 4, 1974), page 54.

"Prexy Is Fired in Lutheran Controversy [re Tietjen]." *Presbyterian Journal* 32:41 (February 6, 1974), page 4.

"Theology in the Headlines [suspension of President Tietjen]." *America* 130 (February 9, 1974), page 82.

"Lutheran Tensions Continue to Mount." *Presbyterian Journal* 32:42 (February 13, 1974), page 4.

"Missouri Synod: The Showdown [suspension of Tietjen]." *Christianity Today* 18:10 (February 15, 1974), page 45.

"Concordia Seminary in Exile Sighted [Sited?] [re Seminex move to Saint Louis University]." *National Catholic Reporter* 10 (February 22, 1974), page 20.

"Missouri Impasse [re suspension of Tietjen; students at Concordia Seminary boycott classes]." *Christianity Today* 18 (March 1, 1974), page 109.

"From Luther to Rome [re 'walkout,' Seminex, threat of schism within LCMS]." *Time* 103 (March 4, 1974), page 55.

"Jesuit Describes Seminary-in-Exile as New, Unusual Form of Ecumenism." *National Catholic Reporter* 10 (March 8, 1974), page 15.

"Synod Faces Split Nobody Wanted." *National Catholic Reporter* 10 (March 8, 1974), page 15.

"March in Missouri [re 'walkout' at Concordia Seminary]." *Christianity Today* 18:14 (April 12, 1974), pages 42–44.

"Missouri Synod: Hardened Lines [on placement of Seminex grads, limits on academic freedom]." *Christianity Today* 18:15 (April 26, 1974), page 43.

"Editor's Ambo: Missouri's Middle." *Lutheran Forum* 8:2 (May 1974), pages 5–6.

" 'Seminex' Seniors Reject Certification." *Presbyterian Journal* 33:6 (June 5, 1974), page 4.

"Seminex Graduates' Ostracization Urged." *National Catholic Reporter* 10 (June 7, 1974), page 20.

"Editor's Ambo: Attack on LC [Lutheran Council] News." *Lutheran Forum* 8:3 (August 1974), pages 4–5.

"Lutherans at War [Chicago meeting of ELIM 'mainly a clergy movement']." *Time* 104 (September 9, 1974), page 66.

"Missouri Synod: Cooling Off." *Christianity Today* 19:15 (May 9, 1975), pages 47–48.

"Armageddon at Disneyland [preview of 1975 LCMS convention at Anaheim]." *The Christian Century* 92 (June 25, 1975), pages 972–73.

"Preus' Purge [re 1975 LCMS convention permission to depose dissident District presidents]." *Time* 106 (July 21, 1975), page 65.

"Possible Split Seen in Missouri Synod." *Presbyterian Journal* 34:12 (July 23, 1975), pages 4–5.

"Reach for the Bible." *Presbyterian Journal* 34:12 (July 23, 1975), page 12.

"Schism in the Synod [re Third ELIM Assembly, 1975 LCMS convention at Anaheim]." *Newsweek* 86 (September 1, 1975), page 55.

"Missouri Rumble [re ELIM, ordination of uncertified Seminex graduates, English Synod]." *The Christian Century* 93 (March 17, 1976), page 244.

"Missouri Synod: Ousting Some of the President's Men [re LCMS District presidents Hecht, Riedel, Ressmeyer, Frincke]." *Christianity Today* 20:15 (April 23, 1976), pages 45–47.

"The Final Days? [re President Preus's appointing of four acting District presidents to replace those 'fired']." *The Christian Century* 93:16 (May 5, 1976), pages 427–28.

"The Lutherans: Fractured Fellowship." *Christianity Today* 21:3 (November 5, 1976), pages 81–84.

"America's Newest Denomination: Association of Evangelical Lutheran Churches." *Christianity Today* 21:7 (January 7, 1977), page 36.

"[Tietjen] Expelled." *Christianity Today* 22:2 (October 21, 1977), pages 40–41.

"Last [Seminex] Commencement." *The Christian Century* 100:17 (May 25, 1983), page 521.

Photograph by Paul Ockrassa

Disregarding the announced moratorium, Prof. Robert Preus continues teaching his classes at Concordia Seminary, January 1974.

Photograph by Paul Ockrassa

Suspended Concordia Seminary president John Tietjen addresses students at the time of the "walkout."

4.0 SEMINEX AND LCMS MISSIONS

(A Sampling of Periodical Articles)

(chronological order)

Kretzmann, Martin L. "The Church Structures Its Life for Mission—Then Mission [re *Mission Affirmations*]." *The Lutheran Witness* 84:7 (March 30, 1965), pages 10–11.

A. W. G. [Albert W. Galen]. "Poised for Mission [re *Mission Affirmations*]." *The Lutheran Witness* 84:13 (August 1965), page 310.

Mayer, James A. "The Church, the Mission, and the World [re *Mission Affirmations*]." *The Lutheran Witness* 85:8 (August 1966), pages 207–8.

"Facing Convention Issues: New Trends in Missions [re *Mission Affirmations*]." *The Lutheran Witness* 86:5 (May 1967), pages 117–21.

O. S. [Omar Stuenkel]. "Give and Take at the Convention: Mission and Youth." *The Lutheran Witness* 88:9 (September 1969), pages 254–55.

Jordan, A. E. "What's Coming Up at Milwaukee? Missions [re *Mission Affirmations*]." *The Lutheran Witness* 90:7 (July 1971), page 169.

"Rev. Mayer's Staff Work Terminated." *Missouri in Perspective* 1:7 (January 28, 1974), pages 1, 3.

"Missions Are Threatened, Says Staff." *Missouri in Perspective* 1:7 (January 28, 1974), pages 1, 3.

"Kohn Resigns; Mission Board, Staff Controversy Continues." *Missouri in Perspective* 1:13 (April 22, 1974), page 1.

"Mission Head, Four Staff Executives Resign in Protest [William Kohn, Walter H. Meyer, W. F. Bulle, Marion Kretschmar, James W. Mayer]." *St. Louis Lutheran* 29:15 (April 27, 1974), page 1.

"Five More Mission Executives Resign [William Kohn, Walter H. Meyer, W. F. Bulle, Marion Kretschmar, James W. Mayer]." *Missouri in Perspective* 1:14 (May 6, 1974), pages 1, 8.

"[LCMS church bodies in] India, New Guinea Churches Reconsider Ties to Synod." *Missouri in Perspective* 1:15 (May 20, 1974), page 8.

"Mission Board Calls New Executive; Seeks Peace." *Missouri in Perspective* 2:5 (January 13, 1975), page 1.

Photograph by Paul Ockrassa

Concordia Seminary students plant crosses with names of seminary faculty members in the Main Quadrangle of the campus.

5.0 Reviews of Major Books on the Controversy

(alphabetical by author of book, then by author of review)

James E. Adams. *Preus of Missouri and the Great Lutheran Civil War.* (1977)

Austin, C. M. "*Preus of Missouri and the Great Lutheran Civil War* by James E. Adams." *Lutheran World* 24:4 (1977), pages 487–89.

Jewett, Robert. "*Preus of Missouri and the Great Lutheran Civil War* by James E. Adams." *The Christian Century* 94:31 (October 5, 1977), pages 885–86.

Kretzmann, Martin L. "*Preus of Missouri and the Great Lutheran Civil War* by James E. Adams." *Dialog* 16:3 (Summer 1977), pages 227–28.

Lau, D. "*Preus of Missouri and the Great Lutheran Civil War* by James E. Adams." *Lutheran Spokesman* 20:5 (November 1977), pages 6–10.

Mayer, H. T. "*Preus of Missouri and the Great Lutheran Civil War* by James E. Adams." *Currents in Theology and Mission* 4:4 (August 1977), pages 240–41.

Shurden, Walter B. "*Preus of Missouri and the Great Lutheran Civil War* by James E. Adams." *Expositor* 75:1 (Winter 1978), pages 138–39.

Stauderman, Albert P. "*Preus of Missouri and the Great Lutheran Civil War* by James E. Adams." *The Lutheran* 15:12 (June 15, 1977), page 31.

Surburg, Raymond F. "*Preus of Missouri and the Great Lutheran Civil War* by James E. Adams." *Concordia Theological Quarterly* 41:4 (October 1977), pages 103–6.

Carl E. Braaten. *Because of Christ.* (2010)

Mattes, Mark C. "*Because of Christ: Memoirs of a Lutheran Theologian* by Carl E. Braaten." *Lutheran Quarterly* 25:2 (Summer 2011), pages 178–80.

James C. Burkee. ***Power, Politics, and the Missouri Synod.*** **(2011)**

Childs, James M., Jr. "*Power, Politics, and the Missouri Synod* by James C. Burkee." *Seminary Ridge Review* 15:1 (Autumn 2012), pages 122–25.

Conkling, Martin E., and Paul R. Hinlicky. "*Power, Politics, and the Missouri Synod* by James C. Burkee." *Lutheran Quarterly* 26:3 (Autumn 2012), pages 325–33.

DeBerg, Betty A. "*Power, Politics, and the Missouri Synod: A Conflict that Changed American Christianity* by James Burkee." *Church History* 81:1 (March 2012), pages 247–48.

Menke, Wesley. "*Power, Politics, and the Missouri Synod: A Conflict that Changed American Christianity* by James Burkee." *The Journal of Religious History* 37:1 (March 2013), pages 153–54.

Nessan, Craig L. "*Power, Politics, and the Missouri Synod: A Conflict that Changed American Christianity* by James Burkee." *Currents in Theology and Mission* 38:2 (April 2011), page 149.

Schurb, Ken. "*Power, Politics, and the Missouri Synod: A Conflict that Changed American Christianity* by James Burkee." *Concordia Historical Institute Quarterly* 84:1 (Spring 2011), pages 55–57.

Todd, Mary. "*Power, Politics, and the Missouri Synod: A Conflict that Changed American Christianity* by James Burkee." *The Catholic Historical Review* 98:1 (January 2012), pages 174–76.

Concordia Seminary, Board of Control. ***Exodus from Concordia.*** **(1977)**

"*Exodus from Concordia: A Report on the 1974 Walkout* by Board of Control, Concordia Seminary, St. Louis." *Lutherans Alert National* 12:8 (August 1977), pages 12–13.

Frederick Danker. ***No Room in the Brotherhood.*** **(1977)**

Fredrich, Edward C. "*No Room in the Brotherhood: The Preus-Otten Purge of Missouri* by Fred Danker." *Wisconsin Lutheran Quarterly* 74:4 (October 1977), page 341.

Groh, J [John]. E. "*No Room in the Brotherhood: The Preus-Otten Purge of Missouri* by Fred Danker." *Currents in Theology and Mission* 4:3 (June 1977), pages 181–84.

Kurt E. Marquart. *Anatomy of an Explosion.* (1977)

Fredrich, Edward C. "*Anatomy of an Explosion: A Theological Analysis of the Missouri Synod Conflict* by Kurt E. Marquart." *Wisconsin Lutheran Quarterly* 74:4 (October 1977), pages 341–42.

Kromminga, John H. "*Anatomy of an Explosion: A Theological Analysis of the Missouri Synod Conflict* by Kurt E. Marquart." *Calvin Theological Journal* 14:1 (April 1979), pages 106–9.

Price, T. D. "*Anatomy of an Explosion: A Theological Analysis of the Missouri Synod Conflict* by Kurt E. Marquart." *Perspectives in Religious Studies* 6:2 (Summer 1979), pages 171–75.

Rynbrandt, A. "*Anatomy of an Explosion: A Theological Analysis of the Missouri Synod Conflict* by Kurt E. Marquart." *Reformed Review* 32:3 (Spring 1979), pages 173–74.

Vigness, Paul G. "*Anatomy of an Explosion: A Theological Analysis of the Missouri Synod Conflict* by Kurt E. Marquart." *Lutherans Alert National* 12:9 (September 1977), pages 15–17.

John H. Tietjen. *Memoirs in Exile.* (1990)

"*Memoirs in Exile: Confessional Hope and Institutional Conflict* by John H. Tietjen." *First Things* 9 (January 1991), page 58.

Fredrich, Edward C. "*Memoirs in Exile: Confessional Hope and Institutional Conflict* by John H. Tietjen." *Wisconsin Lutheran Quarterly* 89:1 (Winter 1992), page 71.

Habel, Norman C. "*Memoirs in Exile: Confessional Hope and Institutional Conflict* by John H. Tietjen." *Lutheran Theological Journal* 26:2 (August 1992), pages 141–43.

Jordahl, Leigh D. "*Memoirs in Exile: Confessional Hope and Institutional Conflict* by John H. Tietjen." *Dialog* 30:3 (Summer 1991), pages 256–58.

Klein, Ralph W. "*Memoirs in Exile: Confessional Hope and Institutional Conflict* by John H. Tietjen." *Currents in Theology and Mission* 18:2 (April 1991), pages 133–35.

Kolb, Robert. "*Memoirs in Exile: Confessional Hope and Institutional Conflict* by John H. Tietjen." *Lutheran Quarterly* 7:1 (Spring 1993), pages 106–9.

Leonard, Bill J. "Schism Memoirs." *The Christian Century* 107:34 (November 21–28, 1990), pages 1096–98.

Meilaender, Gilbert. "*Memoirs in Exile: Confessional Hope and Institutional Conflict* by John H. Tietjen." *First Things* 14 (June–July 1991), pages 38–42.

Preus, Robert D. "*Memoirs in Exile: Confessional Hope and Institutional Conflict* by John H. Tietjen." *Logia* 21:3 (Holy Trinity 2012), pages 89–94.

Reumann, John Henry Paul. "*Memoirs in Exile: Confessional Hope and Institutional Conflict* by John H. Tietjen." *Theological Studies* 53:1 (March 1992), pages 174–76.

Simpson, Gary M. "*Memoirs in Exile: Confessional Hope and Institutional Conflict* by John H. Tietjen." *Dialog* 31:3 (Summer 1992), page 239.

Smith, Gregory K. "*Memoirs in Exile: Confessional Hope and Institutional Conflict* by John H. Tietjen." *Concordia Journal* 18:2 (April 1992), pages 212–17.

Paul A. Zimmerman. *A Seminary in Crisis.* (2007)

Brenner, John M. "*A Seminary in Crisis: The Inside Story of the Preus Fact Finding Committee* by Paul A. Zimmerman." *Wisconsin Lutheran Quarterly* 109:1 (Winter 2012), pages 71–73.

Hannah, John R. "*A Seminary in Crisis: The Inside Story of the Preus Fact Finding Committee* by Paul A. Zimmerman." *Lutheran Forum* 41:1 (Spring 2007), pages 57–60.

Klein, Ralph W. "*A Seminary in Crisis: The Inside Story of the Preus Fact Finding Committee* by Paul A. Zimmerman." *Currents in Theology and Mission* 35:3 (June 2008), page 227.

Pahl, Jon. "*A Seminary in Crisis: The Inside Story of the Preus Fact Finding Committee* by Paul A. Zimmerman." *Lutheran Quarterly* 23:4 (Winter 2009), pages 493–94.

Scaer, David P. "*A Seminary in Crisis: The Inside Story of the Preus Fact Finding Committee* by Paul A. Zimmerman." *Concordia Theological Quarterly* 74:1–2 (January–April 2010), pages 162–63.

Schroeder, Edward H. "The Wars of Missouri that Led to Seminex: A Retrospective." Parts 1–3. [https://crossings.org/?s=zimmerman. Hardcopy available at Concordia Historical Institute and Concordia Seminary Library.]

Senkbeil, Harold L. "*A Seminary in Crisis: The Inside Story of the Preus Fact Finding Committee* by Paul A. Zimmerman." *Logia* 17:2 (Eastertide 2008), pages 47–48.

6.0 Entries in Reference Works

(alphabetical by title of work, then by author of entry)

Huber, Donald L. "John H. Tietjen (1928–)." Pages 419–29 in *Dictionary of Heresy Trials in American Christianity.* Edited by George H. Shriver. Westport, Connecticut: Greenwood Press, 1997. [Includes a short bibliography.]

Miller, Glenn T. "Concordia Theological Seminary [Springfield, Illinois] (1969–1974)." Pages 94–103 in *Dictionary of Heresy Trials in American Christianity.* Edited by George H. Shriver. Westport, Connecticut: Greenwood Press, 1997. [Includes a short bibliography.]

Becker, Matthew L. "Jacob Preus." Pages 618–19 in *Dictionary of Luther and the Lutheran Traditions.* Edited by Timothy J. Wengert. Grand Rapids: Baker Academic, 2017. [Includes a short bibliography.]

Granquist, Mark A. "Seminex and the Association of Evangelical Lutheran Churches." Pages 678–79 in *Dictionary of Luther and the Lutheran Traditions.* Edited by Timothy J. Wengert. Grand Rapids: Baker Academic, 2017. [Includes a short bibliography.]

Huggins, Marvin A. "Lutheran Church—Missouri Synod." Pages 447–50 in *Dictionary of Luther and the Lutheran Traditions.* Edited by Timothy J. Wengert. Grand Rapids: Baker Academic, 2017. [Includes a short bibliography.]

"Concordia Seminary-in-Exile." Pages 286–87 in *A Documentary History of Lutheranism: From the Enlightenment to the Present.* Edited by Eric Lund and Mark Granquist. Minneapolis: Fortress Press, 2017.

"Document of Dismissal, Concordia Seminary Board of Control." Page 285 in *A Documentary History of Lutheranism: From the Enlightenment to the Present.* Edited by Eric Lund and Mark Granquist. Minneapolis: Fortress Press, 2017. [Text of document with introductory paragraph and photograph.]

Bell, Albert A., Jr. "Seminex." Pages 423–25 in *Encyclopedia of Religious Controversies in the United States.* Edited by George H. Shriver and Bill J. Leonard. Westport, Connecticut: Greenwood Press, 1997. [Includes a short bibliography.]

Bridges, Linda McKinnish. "Missouri Synod Lutherans." Pages 296–98 in *Encyclopedia of Religious Controversies in the United States.* Edited by George H. Shriver and Bill J. Leonard. Westport, Connecticut: Greenwood Press, 1997. [Includes a short bibliography.]

Photograph by Paul Ockrassa

The processional on the day of the "walkout," February 18, 1974.

7.0 Relevant Publications for Further Investigation

7.1 Independent, Unofficial Lutheran Publications

(alphabetical by title)

Concordia Historical Institute Holdings

Affirm. Balance, Inc., Milwaukee, Wisconsin [later Saint Louis]. (1971–)

Balance. Ev. Lutheran Church of St. John, Sycamore, Illinois. (1969)

California Concerns: The 'Other Witness' for California Lutherans. California Concerns, San Leandro, California. (1973–92)

California Perspective. Evangelical Lutherans in Mission, San Francisco / Burlingame, California. (1975)

Call. Concerned Assembly, Lutheran Laity, Fort Wayne, Indiana. (1974)

Calling All Loyal Lutherans. Indiana Doctrinal Concerns Program, Lafayette / Fort Wayne, Indiana. (1974–75)

Calumet Newsletter. Evangelical Lutherans in Mission, Northwest Indiana, Calumet Chapter. (1975)

Central Illinois ELIM Newsletter. Evangelical Lutherans in Mission, Urbana / Champaign, Illinois. (1974–75)

Christian News [previously *Lutheran News*]. Lutheran News, Inc., New Haven, Missouri. (1968–)

Cincinnati Concerns. Doctrinal Concerns Program, Cincinnati, Ohio. (1973–75)

Colorado ELIM Newsletter. Colorado ELIM, Wheat Ridge, Colorado. (1975–77)

Colorado Laymen's Newsletter. Conservative Lutheran Laymen of Colorado (varies), Denver. (1973–82)

Colorado Perspective. Evangelical Lutherans in Mission, Colorado Assembly, Littleton / Wheat Ridge, Colorado. (1975–76)

Concord: A Plea for Evangelical Unity in Missouri. Concord, Indianapolis, Indiana. (1972–73)

Confessional Lutheran. Confessional Lutheran Publicity Bureau, Chicago. (1940–69)

Doctrinal Concerns. Doctrinal Concerns, Hilliard, Ohio. (1978–79)

Eastern Canada Herald [title varies]. Evangelical Lutherans in Mission, Eastern Canada, London, Ontario. (1974–76)

ELIM Eastern District Newsletter / Eastern-English ELIM District Newsletter [title varies]. Eastern District ELIM, Williamsville, New York. (1974–77)

ELIM in Missouri. ELIM in Missouri District, Saint Louis. (1974–75)

ELIM Ohio Newsletter. ELIM Ohio, Columbus, Ohio. (1975–78)

Evangelical Lutheran: Supporting the Doctrinal Stance of the LCMS in Southern California, Southern Nevada, and Arizona. Evangelical Lutheran, Rosemead, California. (1975–82)

Evangelical Lutherans in Mission. ELIM, Northern Illinois Area, Westchester, Illinois. (1974–76)

FAAL Newsletter. Free Association for Authentic Lutheranism, May City, Iowa. (1971)

Faithful Messenger. Doctrinal Concerns Program, Hilliard / Columbus, Ohio. (1975)

Forum Letter [companion publication to *Lutheran Forum*]. New York. (1972–) [See especially columns "As Missouri Turns" and "The Continuing Crisis" from October / November 1974–August 1979.]

In Touch. Lutheran Faculty Federation, Valparaiso, Indiana. (1973–75)

A major source of articles and essays on the effects of LCMS convention actions, e.g., adoption of *A Statement,* on Lutheran academe immediately before and following the "walkout," and establishment of Seminex. *In Touch* is held only at Concordia Historical Institute.

Indiana Perspective. ELIM in Indiana, Fort Wayne, Indiana. (1975)

INFO: An Information Service for Missouri Synod Lutherans, St. Louis. (1972–73)

Editorial board: Gus Bremer, Joseph J. Carter, Cordula Duerbeck, Les Kuhlmann, Kenneth A. Roffmann, Samuel J. Roth, Alvin H. Sasse, Walter M. Schoedel, and Herbert W. Schuppan.

Kansas Layman. Kansas Layman, Topeka, Kansas. (1974–78)

KYRIOS. Doctrinal Concerns Program, North Wisconsin, Eau Claire, Wisconsin. (1976–91)

Lay Voice. The Lutheran Committee, Dallas. (1974–78)

Lay Voice of Nebraska Lutherans. Doctrinal Concerns Program of Nebraska, Plainview, Nebraska. (1974–86)

Layman's Informant—Minnesota South. Concerned Lutheran Laymen, Golden Valley / Minneapolis, Minnesota. (1973–77)

Laymen's Analysis. Hope Lutheran Church, Chicago. (1974–77) ["ur text" reprinted by other organizations as below]

Laymen's Analysis. South Dakota Concerned Lutherans, Sioux Falls, South Dakota. (1976–78) [same / similar content as above for corresponding dates]

Laymen's Analysis: Northern Illinois Region. Hope Lutheran Church, Chicago. (1975–79) [same content as above for corresponding dates]

Loyal Defender. National Evangelical Lutheran Conference, Southeastern District Chapter, Newton, North Carolina / Reston, Virginia. (1979–90)

Loyal Laymen. Loyal Laymen, Miami. (1980–88) [began in 1977]

Loyal Lutheran Newsletter. Association of Loyal Lutherans / Loyal Lutheran Association, Albany / Coos Bay, Oregon. (1980–2013)

Loyal Lutheran Newsletter. National Evangelical Lutheran Conference, New Jersey Chapter, Paterson, New Jersey. (1975–79)

Lutheran News [continued as *Christian News*]. Lutheran News, Inc., New Haven, Missouri. (1962–67)

Lutheran Perspective [continues *Missouri in Perspective*]. Evangelical Lutherans in Mission, Saint Louis. (1981–87)

Lutherans United for Synod. Association of Loyal Lutherans / Loyal Lutheran Association, Albany / Coos Bay, Oregon. (1974–84)

Missouri—Free, United, Evangelical. Dick [Rev. Richard] Koenig, Amherst, Massachusetts. (1969–71)

Missouri in Perspective [continued by *Lutheran Perspective*]. Evangelical Lutherans in Mission, Saint Louis. (1973–81)

News and Commentary. Evangelical Lutherans in Mission, Minnesota North, Wyoming, Minnesota. (1975)

Newsletter of the New Orleans Doctrinal Concerns Committee [continues *Pensacola Area* publication below]. Editorial Group, New Orleans. (1981–85)

Newsletter of the Pensacola Area Doctrinal Concerns Organization. Pensacola Area Doctrinal Concerns Organization, Pensacola, Florida. (1975–80)

Northern 'Light.' Minnesota North DCP [Doctrinal Concerns Program], Crookston, Minnesota. (1974–81)

Northwest Loyal Lutheran. Doctrinal Concern [*sic*] Program, Immanuel Lutheran, Albany, Oregon. (1974–78)

Northwest Perspective. Evangelical Lutherans in Mission, Troutdale, Oregon. (1974–76)

Ohio Concerns. Ohio Doctrinal Concerns Program, Hilliard, Ohio. (1976–77)

Oklahoma Evangel. Oklahoma Doctrinal Concerns Organization, Kingfisher, Oklahoma. (1973–80)

Once Over Lightly. Dr. Harold N. Ives, Cloverdale, California. (1968–70)

Save Our Synod [SOS]. Doctrinal Laity, Saint Paul / Victoria / etc., Minnesota. (1974–78)

Selah. Evangelical Lutherans in Mission, Saint Paul, Minnesota. (1975–76)

South Wisconsin Perspective. Evangelical Lutherans in Mission, Muskego, Wisconsin. (1974–76)

Southern Concerns. Doctrinal Concerns Committee, Gretna, Louisiana. (1972–78)

Southern District ELIM Newsletter. Evangelical Lutherans in Mission / St. Paul Lutheran Church, Shreveport, Louisiana. (1975)

Southern Illinois District ELIM. Southern Illinois District ELIM, Carbondale, Illinois. (1975)

STICK Newsletter. Saints Together in Christ's Kingdom, Bayside, New York. (1976–77)

Table Talk. Continuation Committee, Watertown, Wisconsin. (1970–71)

Talking Together: Michigan Laymen's Analysis of Issues in the Missouri Synod. Michigan Lutherans United for Synod, Inc., Southgate / Wyandotte, Michigan. (1975–84)

Texas Perspective. Evangelical Lutherans in Mission, Dallas. (1976)

7.2 *Institutional Publications*

(Concordia Historical Institute holdings in brackets [ ])

7.2.1 *Christ Seminary—Seminex*

(alphabetical by title)

[Academic Catalogs] [CHI: Sum 1974, 1975–1978, 1979–1980, 1982–1983 Supp.]

Sample catalog / contents:

Christ Seminary / Seminex: Catalog 1978–1980. Saint Louis: Christ Seminary—Seminex, 1978. 63 pages. [CHI: Christ Seminary—Seminex. 120.25 MO, Box 1, "Catalogs" folder]

Catalog includes: Academic Calendar (1978–80), Statement of Purpose, requirements and procedures for MAR, MDiv, STM, and ThD programs; Curriculum; Contextual Education; Placement; Advanced Studies; Outreach Program; Black Ministries Program; Hispanic Ministries Program; Clinical Pastoral Education Program; Public Lectures Schedule (1977); Course Offerings (33–52); Directory, including Seminary Faculty (56–60) and Vicar Supervisors (62).

Christ Seminary—Seminex Community Book. Saint Louis: Christ Seminary—Seminex. 32 pages. [CHI: Christ Seminary—Seminex. 120.25 MO, Box 2, "Brochures" folder]

Contents are presented in two parts: 1. "Christ Seminary—Seminex Life"; 2. "St. Louis Life." Booklet includes a listing of local AELC, ALC, and LCA congregations (2–4), a graphic display of facilities (floors 8 through 15 of the University Club Building at 607 N. Grand Blvd.) (14), and a listing of Seminex publications (23).

Directory / Guide to the People of Concordia Seminary in Exile [title varies]. Saint Louis: Concordia Seminary in Exile / Seminex. [CHI: 1974–1983]

Focus: On the Convention and Concordia Seminary / On Chicago / On Suspension and Synod's Bylaws / On Res. 4-47; The "Omnibus Resolution." Saint Louis: Seminarians Concerned for Reconciliation under the Gospel. [CHI: 2:1–4 (July 31–November 1973)]

The Grand Fool [student publication]. Saint Louis: Christ Seminary—Seminex. [CHI: 1:1, 2:1–2, 3:2 (1981–1983)]

Resources for Ministry. Saint Louis: Office of Seminary Relations. Christ Seminary—Seminex. [CHI: 1–5 (1978–1983)]

Directory of Seminex graduates available for placement.

Sample Resources (2):

Resources for Ministry: Vol. II 1979/80. Second edition. Saint Louis: Christ Seminary—Seminex Office of Seminary Relations. 40 pages. [CHI: Christ Seminary—Seminex. 120.25 Mo., Box 2, "Brochures" folder]

Produced by Chris Eldredge. Includes listing of graduates by specialized ministry focus.

Resources for Ministry: Vol. III 1980/81. Third edition. Saint Louis: Christ Seminary—Seminex Office of Seminary Relations. 36 pages. [CHI: Christ Seminary—Seminex. 120.25 Mo., Box 2, "Brochures" folder]

This copy of *Resources for Ministry* includes a May 5, 1980, letter by Robert H. Smith, Director of Placement.

Self Study: Prepared for the Association of Theological Schools in the United States and Canada. Saint Louis: The Seminary, 1979–80. 3 volumes. [CHI Library Collection]

Seminar—in Exile. Saint Louis: Concordia Seminary in Exile. [CHI: Feb, Nov 1974, 6:2,3 (Apr, May 1975)]

Served as an "exchange of scholarly opinion for community of Concordia Seminary in Exile." Cf. *Seminar* of Concordia Seminary.

Sent. Saint Louis: Christ Seminary—Seminex, 1978. [CHI: Christ Seminary—Seminex. 120.25 MO, Box 2, "Brochures" folder]

Sent is a duotone, tabloid-sized two-sided poster with photos, names, and locations of more than 350 graduates of Christ Seminary—Seminex. "You There, . . . / You Have Only One Life, . . . / Give It Away! / From the beginning of time, there has been a plan. Unfolding ever since—every year, every day. It all began with one person, SENT to a new and strange land. Abraham went, and after him came others. They were not all heroes, nor were they all powerful, influential, rich or gifted. But they believed a promise and saw the challenge of a lifetime lived out for God and for people. History tells us they were not always welcome. It says so on their graves . . . on the walls of catacombs and prison camps, . . . and on the architectural masterpieces of the world. Some gave their blood to lions . . . fed back to the earth through the dust of the arena floor. Others spent long, unheralded and simple years of quiet toil for the good of others."

Poster includes statistics on Christ Seminary—Seminex graduate placement. Copy in CHI Collection includes an introductory letter, dated April 1978, by President John H. Tietjen, who writes: "Our seminary continues to face a twin challenge. One is to recruit new students to prepare for ministry. The second is to find ministry opportunities to which our graduates can be sent."

Spectrum in Exile [brief articles, announcements]. Saint Louis: Concordia Seminary in Exile / Seminex. [CHI: 1:4–4:13, 6:5 (March 14, 1974–May 5, 1977; December 4, 1978) issues missing]

Strivings: A Theological and Literary Journal of Seminex. Saint Louis: Concordia Seminary in Exile / Seminex. [CHI: 1:1–3 (1977)]

Together: Information and News from the Seminex Community. Saint Louis: Concordia Seminary in Exile / Christ Seminary Seminex [CHI: [1]–9:2 (1974–1983)]

Together: Information and News from the Seminex Community. Chicago: Christ Seminary Seminex. [CHI: 9:3–12:1 (1983–1986)]

Together into the Future . . . : Alumni/ae Directory: 1983/1984. Saint Louis: Christ Seminary / Seminex Development Office. 90 pages. [CHI: Christ Seminary—Seminex. 120.25 MO, Box 1, "Alumni/ae Association" folder]

This second edition of the alumni directory, edited by David Krause, includes a May 20, 1983, Constitution for Christ Seminary—Seminex and list of Alumni/ae Association Board of Directors. Includes listing of graduates by specialized ministry focus.

Signed publications (2):

Krause, David. *A Great Tradition, A Greater Future: Christ Seminary—Seminex Alumni/ae Directory, 1982/1983.* [Saint Louis: Christ Seminary—Seminex Development Office], 1983. 88 pages. [CHI Library, Geographic Collection, Missouri, Saint Louis, Concordia Seminary-in-Exile, Box 1]

Manz, John C., and Aaron Sorrels. *Seminex Community Clusters: A Proposal for Building Relationships.* [Saint Louis: s.n.], 1975. 25 leaves. [WorldCat catalog]

7.2.2 *Concordia Seminary*

(alphabetical by title)

Seminar. Saint Louis: Concordia Seminary. [CHI: 1–6 (Reformation 1968–January 1974)]

Served as an "exchange of scholarly opinion and creativity among the members of the Concordia Seminary community."

Spectrum [brief articles, announcements]. Saint Louis: Concordia Seminary. [CHI: 1–37 (1968–1999)]

7.2.3 *Concordia Senior College (Fort Wayne, Indiana)*

Triangle [student publication]. Fort Wayne, Indiana: Concordia Senior College. [CHI: 1–19 (1957–1976)] [Also held at Allen County Public Library. Fort Wayne, Indiana]

Photograph by Paul Ockrassa

Concordia Seminary president John Tietjen addresses members of the media and students assembled by the Luther Statue during the moratorium, January 1974.

8.0 Archival Resources / Collections

8.1 Concordia Historical Institute

(alphabetical by name / subject)

Organizational Records and Personal Papers

Adams (James E.) Papers. Collection ID 0003 [news reporter and author of *Preus of Missouri*]
Balzer (Martin W.) Collection. Collection ID 3365 [1974 graduate, Concordia Seminary]
Barth (Karl L.) Papers. Collection ID 0028 [member, Fact Finding Committee]
Beto (George J.) Papers. Collection ID 0205 [LCMS Board of Public Relations, 1966–76]
Biel (Kurt E.) Family Papers. Collection ID 1470 [president, Missouri District, LCMS; Board of Control, Concordia Seminary]
Bruns (Arlen J.) Sermons. Collection ID 2732 [president, Kansas District, LCMS]
Bunjes (Paul G.) Papers. Collection ID 0251 [faculty member, Concordia Teachers College, River Forest, Illinois; member, LCMS Commission on Worship]
Burgdorf (Paul H.) Files. Collection ID 0255 [editor, *Confessional Lutheran*]
Caemmerer (Richard R., Sr.) Papers. Collection ID 0264 [faculty, Seminex]
Carpenter (Milton) Papers. Collection ID 0267 [treasurer, LCMS]
Christ Seminary—Seminex (Saint Louis, Missouri). Faculty Journals. Collection ID 1484
Coates (Thomas) Papers. Collection ID 0269 [faculty, Concordia Senior College, Fort Wayne, Indiana]
Concordia Senior College (Fort Wayne, Indiana) Records. Collection ID 1090
Constable (John W.) Papers. Collection ID 1473 [faculty, Seminex]
Dissen (Walter C.) Papers. Collection ID 2046 [Board of Control, Concordia Seminary]
Eberhard (Carl Alfred) Papers. Collection ID 3177 [Board of Appeals, LCMS]
Evangelical Lutherans in Mission (Saint Louis, Missouri) Records. Collection ID 1224
Fincke (Eugene E.) Papers. Collection ID 2826 [Board of Control, Concordia Seminary]
Friedrich (Edward J.) Papers. Collection ID 0326 ["A Statement (of the Forty-Four)"]
Fuerbringer (Alfred O.) Papers. Collection ID 0335 [president, Concordia Seminary, 1953–69]
Griesse (Wilbert Elfred) Papers. Collection ID 1469 [chair, LCMS Council of Presidents]

Harms (Oliver R.) Collection. Collection ID 0062
Harnapp (Harlan) Papers. Collection ID 0406
Inter-Lutheran Commission on Worship (ILCW) Records. Collection ID 1439
Jungkuntz (Richard P.) Papers. Collection ID 0461 [faculty, Christ Seminary—Seminex]
Kalin (Everett) Recordings. 78-5-3058, 78-5-3057 [faculty, Christ Seminary—Seminex]
Kiehl (Erich H.) Papers. Collection ID 0471 [faculty, Concordia Seminary]
Klotz (John W.) Papers. Collection ID 1478 [faculty, Concordia Seminary]
Kretzmann (Paul Edward) Papers. Collection ID 0514 [faculty, Concordia Seminary; left to work with the Orthodox Lutheran Conference, Orthodox Lutheran Seminary]
Kuechle (George J.) Papers. Collection ID 0520 [Documents relating to *A Brief Statement*, "A Statement (of the Forty-Four)," and ecumenism]
LCMS. Altar and Pulpit Fellowship Collection. Collection ID 3279
LCMS. Board for Communication Services. Transcript to *Warrior of God—Man of Peace*. Collection ID 1830
LCMS. Board for European Affairs. Collection ID 0119 [contains material relating to the Bad Boll Conferences and "A Statement (of the Forty-Four)"]
LCMS. Board for Higher Education. Collection ID 0113
LCMS. Board for Higher Education. Minutes. Collection ID 2487
LCMS. Board for Mission Services (1952–1982). Collection ID 1806
LCMS. Board for Mission Services. Minutes & Agendas (1970–1980). Collection ID 2033
LCMS. Board for Mission Services. Mission Manuals (1962–1981). Collection ID 1953
LCMS. Board for Missions in North America. Collection ID 0125
LCMS. Board for North and South American Missions. Collection ID 0123
LCMS. Board for Public Relations. Collection ID 0084 [*The Lutheran Witness* correspondence]
LCMS. Board for Support and Pensions. Collection ID 0107 [minutes]
LCMS. Board for World (Foreign) Missions. Collection ID 0130
LCMS. Board of Parish Education. Collection ID 0128
LCMS. Board of Parish Education. Advance Editorial Commission (1962–1972). Collection ID 1848
LCMS. Chief Administrative Officer (1972–1998). Collection ID 2000
LCMS. Colloquy Committee for Pastoral Ministry Records. Collection ID 0027
LCMS. Commission on Theology and Church Relations (CTCR). Collection ID 0098
LCMS. Commission on Worship, Liturgics, and Hymnology. Collection ID 0103
LCMS. Committee on Doctrinal Unity. Collection ID 0099
LCMS. Committee on Organization (1969–1975). Collection ID 0059
LCMS. Council of Presidents. Collection ID 0048
LCMS. Emergency Planning Council. Collection ID 0151
LCMS. Executive Offices. Collection ID 0026

LCMS. Missions. Philippines Records. Collection ID 1432

LCMS. Office of the President. J. A. O. Preus Administration (1969–1981) Records. Collection ID 1482

LCMS. Office of the President. Ralph A. Bohlmann Administration (1981–1992) Records. Collection ID 2144

LCMS. Special Hymnal Review Committee. Collection ID 2359

Loose (George A.) Papers. Collection ID 2051 [chair, Board of Control, Concordia Seminary]

Lutheran Council in the United States of America. Collection ID 1438; 1988; 2782; 2783; 2784; 2790; 2792; 2809; 2954; 3011

Lutheran Council in the United States of America. Archives of Cooperative Lutheranism, Oral History Project (1976–1987). Collection ID 2901

Maier (Walter A.) Papers. Collection ID 0569 [faculty, Concordia Seminary; speaker, *Lutheran Hour*; editor, *Walther League Messenger*]

Meyer (Lawrence B.) Papers. Collection ID 0588 [administrator, LCMS]

Mueller (Herbert A.) Papers. Collection ID 2285 [secretary, LCMS]

Nauss (Milton J.) Papers. Collection ID 0624 [Concordia Theological Seminary, Springfield, Illinois, Board of Control (attempted to reconcile opposing parties)]

Nickel (Theodore F.) Papers. Collection ID 3048 [vice president, LCMS]

Otto (Ewald Justus) Papers. Collection ID 1481 [chair, Board of Control, Concordia Seminary]

Preus (Robert David) Collection. Collection ID 0116 [faculty, Concordia Seminary]

Roehrs (Walter R.) Papers. Collection ID 0037 [Bad Boll Conference, Reports]

Sasse (Hermann O. E.) Collection. Collection ID 0706 [correspondence]

Sauer (Alfred von Rohr) Papers. Collection ID 0708 [faculty, Seminex]

Sauer (Robert C.) Papers. Collection ID 1491 [assistant to LCMS President Preus]

Scharlemann (Martin H.) Papers. Collection ID 0710 [faculty, Concordia Seminary]

Scherer (Herman Charles) Papers. Collection ID 0712 [president, Missouri District, LCMS]

Spitz (Paul Ph.) Papers. Collection ID 1490 [vice president, Missouri District]

"Statement [of the Forty-Four], A" (1945) Collection. Collection ID 0001

Streufert (Paul William) Papers. Collection 0805 [member, Fact Finding Committee]

Walther League Records. Collection ID 1405

Weber (Edwin C.) Papers. Collection ID 0853; 1493 [first vice president, LCMS]

Wente (Walter H.) Papers. Collection ID 1489 [faculty, Concordia Senior College, Fort Wayne, Indiana]

Werning (Waldo J.) Papers. Collection ID 0033 [Board of Stewardship, LCMS]

Zimmerman (Paul A.) Records. Collection ID 1494 [chair, Concordia Seminary FFC]

Library Collections (Organizational)

American Lutheran Church (ALC) (1960)
Association of Evangelical Lutheran Churches (AELC)
Christ Seminary—Seminex (Chicago, Illinois)
Concordia Seminary (Saint Louis, Missouri) History. Controversy
Concordia Seminary in Exile—Seminex (Saint Louis, Missouri)
Concordia Senior College (Fort Wayne, Indiana)
Evangelical Lutherans in Mission (ELIM)
Grace Lutheran Church (River Forest, Illinois)
LCMS. Board of Mission Services (1965–1981)
LCMS. Commission on Constitutional Matters (CCM)
LCMS. Commission on Theology and Church Relations (CTCR). Committee on Doctrinal Unity
LCMS. Constitution and Bylaws
LCMS. *Convention Workbook / Reports and Overtures* and *Convention Proceedings*
LCMS. General History. Controversy 1970s
LCMS. Office of the President. Harms Administration (1962–1969)
LCMS. Office of the President. Preus Administration (1969–1981)
LCMS. Parish Education. *Mission:Life*
Lutheran Church in America (LCA)
Lutheran Council in the United States (LCUSA)

Audio Collections (Organizational)

"Outreach" Presentation of Faculty Majority (NOV 2020 #1)
Arlis Ehlen—New England Pastors Conference (part 3–6) (October 17, 1972: 93-09-35 A)
Arthur C. Repp—"On Dissent within the Church" (90-10-36 A)
Concordia Seminary (Saint Louis) Quad Show—The Age of the Hilarious (Graduating Class), 1970 (73-4-128)
Concordia Seminary (Saint Louis) Quad Show, 1970 (95-08-0000 A1 and 95-08-0000 A2)
Crisis at Concordia Seminary 1–2; KFUO Broadcast, August 18, 1975 (75-8-254)
Everett Kalin; Christ Seminary—Seminex Faculty (Saint Louis, Missouri) (78-5-3058)
Faith at Work—Studies in Genesis 1–4 (73-3-38 and 73-3-39)
Faith in Action—Issues Confronting the Church 1–4 (73-3-22 and 73-3-23)
Faith in Action—Mission Affirmations 1–4 (73-3-32 and 73-3-33)
Holy Scripture and the Gospel, R. Bohlmann and R. Bertram (73-3-12)
Interview of Alfred Fuerbringer by Dan Barby, Tenth Anniversary of Seminex, 1984 (11-01-04 A1)
John Tietjen et al. "A Better Way" on Theological and Political Issues (75-5-219)
LCMS Convention (New Orleans), 1973. Issues #1–3 (73-4-1525, 73-5-312; 73-5-3401)

LCMS Convention (New Orleans), 1973. Meeting Reports 1–2 (74-12-128 and 74-12-127)

Moellering and Klann; Faculty Minority (78-5-3062)

Moratorium Discussion. "Seminex Moratorium Resolution" (NOV 2020 #1)

Pastor Kohn, Board of Missions and Dr. Tietjen, Seminex (Fort Wayne, Indiana) (March 25, 1974: 03-06-16 A2)

Ralph Bohlmann (January 7, 1974: 89-01-50 A)

Rev. Dr. Martin H. Scharlemann to the Student Body of Concordia Seminary concerning the Moratorium (75-1-64)

Rudolph Meyer's Analysis of Synodical Problems by Machinske and Speaking on the Saint Louis Seminary by Everett Kalin (78-5-3057)

Seminary (Concordia Seminary) Students Presentation (January 31, 1974) and Vicar Melang, "The Real Authority," Luke 7:1–10 (June 16, 1974: 03-06-16 A1)

Theological Conference (September 1972: 89-01-50 A)

Theological Convocation (Saint Louis) (April 14–18, 1975: 75-05-396, 75-05-397, 75-05-398, and 75-05-399) J. A. O. Preus, Tepker, M. Franzmann, R. Bohlmann, H. Bouman, F. Kramer, Bertram, Huth, et al.

Reel to Reel Audio

Christ Seminary—Seminex (Saint Louis, Missouri) 14 titles

KFUO. Interviews with Dr. Arthur C. Piepkorn (1969–1971) 5 titles

KFUO. Preus Statement and Knutson Statement (1971: 1983-07-01274-000)

LCMS. Conventions (1950–1981) complete sets

Martin Scharlemann Essay (1992-06-00052-001)

Reel to Reel Films

Christ Seminary—Seminex (Saint Louis, Missouri) 96 reel-to-reel films

Other Audiocassettes

Alfred von Rohr Sauer—Address at Enid (76-6-136)

Chapel Devotions: Sueflow, Bornmann, Hopmann, Bohlmann, February–March 1975 (75-3-100)

Dr. Williams, Synod, Seminary and Seminex, Redeemer [Albuquerque] (03-06-16 A3)

Faith in Action—Why Lutheran? 1 & 2 (73-3-72)

Faith in Action—Why Lutheran? 3 & 4 (73-3-73)

Klann (78-5-3063)

Theological Convocation (Saint Louis)—Side 1: Keynote Address: J. A. O. Preus and Devotional Addresses: A. G. Kuntz. Side 2: Inspiration and Inerrancy:

H. W. Tepker with Reactors, J. M. Childs and R. D. Preus (April 14–18, 1975: 75-05-396)

Theological Convocation (Saint Louis)—Sides 3 and 4: Plenary Session, Inspiration and Inerrancy and Historical-Critical Method by Martin H. Franzmann with Reactors, H. H. Buls and R. W. Klein; Plenary Session (April 14–18, 1975: 75-05-397)

Theological Convocation (Saint Louis)—Sides 5 and 6: The Church under the Scriptures: R. A. Bohlmann and H. J. A. Bouman; with Gospel-Scripture Relationship by F. P. Kramer (April 14–18, 1975: 75-05-398)

Theological Convocation (Saint Louis)—Sides 7 and 8: Gospel-Scripture Relationship, Reactors, R. W. Bertram and H. A. Huth with Plenary Session and Sectional Reports and Closing Comments (April 14–18, 1975: 75-05-399)

Tell the People . . . to Go Forward (80-5-00167)

Vicar Melang, The Historical-Critical Method of Interpreting the Scriptures (03-06-16 A4)

Visual Tour of Campus by Dr. John Tietjen for Use with Filmstrip (76-6-67)

Winningham, Quardokus, Weinhold, Thompson, Steenbock, Todd Schulz, Gilbert Bunzel, et al. 6 tapes (76-6-262-7)

Other Films

Christ Seminary—Seminex (Saint Louis, Missouri). Tietjen Sermon (83-09-10666)

Concordia Seminary (Saint Louis, Missouri). Inauguration of Dr. John Tietjen (1970: 71-01-539)

Other Audio

Christ Seminary (Saint Louis, Missouri) (Seminex). Street Presence and Bertram's Class (1978: 1983-09-10725-000)

Christ Seminary (Saint Louis, Missouri) (Seminex). Dr. Bertram's Class and Werberig (1978: 1983-09-10726-000)

Christ Seminary (Saint Louis, Missouri) (Seminex). Student Interviews and Discussions (1978: 1983-09-10727-000)

Christ Seminary (Saint Louis, Missouri) (Seminex). Sermon in Chapel and Classroom (1978: 1983-09-10729-000)

Christ Seminary (Saint Louis, Missouri) (Seminex). Facility Interviews and Dr. Sauer Class (1978: 1983-09-10730-000)

Christ Seminary (Saint Louis, Missouri) (Seminex). Dr. Sauer Class and Dr. Tietjen Class (1978: 1983-09-10730-000)

Christ Seminary (Saint Louis, Missouri) (Seminex). Dr. Tietjen Class and Scene in Chapel (1978: 1983-09-10732-000)

Christ Seminary (Saint Louis, Missouri) (Seminex). Reel 11 (1978: 1983-09-10733-000)
Christ Seminary (Saint Louis, Missouri) (Seminex). Sent (1978: 1983-09-10722-000)
Christ Seminary (Saint Louis, Missouri) (Seminex). Miller (Columbus, Ohio) and Breese (Cleveland, Ohio) (1978: 1983-09-10736-000)
Christ Seminary (Saint Louis, Missouri) (Seminex). Hornbostel (Nursing Home, Cleveland, Ohio) and Seling (Lutheran Medical Mission Association, Cleveland, Ohio) (1978: 1983-09-10737-000)
Christ Seminary (Saint Louis, Missouri) (Seminex). Thielicke (1978: 1983-09-10647-000)
Christ Seminary (Saint Louis, Missouri) (Seminex). "In God for the World." John Tietjen (1976-07-00065-000 and 1976-07-00066-000)
Christ Seminary—Seminex (Saint Louis, Missouri). Placement Committee and Service; Sermon in Chapel (1978: 1983-08-10723-000)
An Evening with J. A. O. Preus (1970: 1985-03-00272-000)
J. A. O. Preus. Meeting with the Concerned Lutheran Laymen (1968: 1992-11-00045-002)
KFUO. Interview with Dr. A. C. Piepkorn (1969: 1989-01-00050-005)
KFUO. Interview with Dr. A. C. Piepkorn. (1970: 1972-06-00281-000)
KFUO. Interview with Dr. A. C. Piepkorn. (1971: 1972-06-00282-000)
KFUO. Interview with Dr. A. C. Piepkorn. "Authority in the Church" (1970: 1972-06-00279-000)
KFUO. Interview with Dr. A. C. Piepkorn. "The Papacy" (1970: 1972-06-00280-000)

8.2 Other Archival Collections

(alphabetical by name / subject)

Association of Evangelical Lutheran Churches (U.S.), Delegate Assembly. Workbooks, Proceedings and Files, 1976–1987. Elk Grove Village, Illinois: Evangelical Lutheran Church in America (ELCA) Archives.

Buelow, Leonard P., Harlan L. Harnapp, and John H. Tietjen. Conversations and Discussions of Pastors L. P. Buelow, H. L. Harnapp, and Others with Dr. John H. Tietjen (1973). Evanston, Illinois: Ernest and Bernice Styberg Library Collection at Northwestern University.

Christ Seminary in Exile—Seminex, Robert W. Bertram (1921–2003) Papers [1943–2008]. Elk Grove Village, Illinois: Evangelical Lutheran Church in America (ELCA) Archives.

Concordia Seminary, Saint Louis Board of Control and Office of the President Documents. Concordia Seminary, Saint Louis Archives.

Ewald, Elwyn, Executive Secretary. Association of Evangelical Lutheran Churches (U.S.), General Subject Files, 1973–1985 (bulk dates 1979–1984). Elk Grove Village, Illinois: Evangelical Lutheran Church in America (ELCA) Archives.

Jaech, Emil G., President, Northwest District, LCMS. Emil G. Jaech Papers (1973–1976). Portland, Oregon: Concordia University Portland Archives.

Lieske, Henry L. (1932–1989) Papers [by LCMS pastor documenting the conflict between moderate and conservative members of the LCMS resulting in schism in 1976 and formation of Seminex]. Oberlin, Ohio: Oberlin College Library.

Piepkorn, Arthur Carl (1907–1973), John Albert Piepkorn, Bertha Taenzer Piepkorn, and others. Papers, 1905–1978. Elk Grove Village, Illinois: Evangelical Lutheran Church in America (ELCA) Archives.

Tietjen, John H., Administrative Files (1965–1987). Elk Grove Village, Illinois: Evangelical Lutheran Church in America (ELCA) Archives.

Tietjen, John H., Evidence [one volume, loose-leaf]. Chicago: JKM Library, Lutheran School of Theology at Chicago. Also Saint Paul, Minnesota: Concordia University Library.

Tietjen, John H. *Expectations of Ministry: A Speech to Prospective Students.* "Weekend in Exile," March 20, 1976. Austin, Texas: Booher Library, Seminary of the Southwest.

"Tietjen Case Documents [1974]." Commission on Theology and Church Relations. Concordia Seminary, Saint Louis, Board of Control. Faculty Hearings Committee. The Lutheran Church—Missouri Synod. [These documents are held at Kroemer Library at Concordia Theological Seminary, Fort Wayne, Indiana, and also at Southern Baptist Theological Seminary Library, Louisville, Kentucky.] (OCLC 22936839)

Zimmermann, Elwood H. *A Brief Report: Ever Only All for Thee* [selected resolutions of the 1973 convention of the LCMS, with introductory letter from E. H. Zimmermann, president of the Indiana District]. Fort Wayne, Indiana: Kroemer Library, Concordia Theological Seminary.

Appendix

Seminex, from Early Signs to Formation

As Reflected in Overtures to and Resolutions of Conventions of The Lutheran Church—Missouri Synod 1962–1975

In the early 1960s, concerns regarding teaching at Concordia Seminary, Saint Louis, were already troubling the Missouri Synod. Whether or not the overtures / resolutions on theology, doctrine, and Holy Scripture mentioned the seminary, it was clear that teaching—sometimes of specific professors—at the seminary often underlay the concerns. In addition to overtures / memorials and the resulting resolutions, substantive reports of commissions and special committees dealing with the controverted issues were printed in the Synod's convention *Workbooks*.

To illustrate the early stages of the growing controversy, relevant overtures / memorials, and the resulting resolutions from four conventions (1962, 1965, 1967, 1969) are shown in detail. For conventions at the height of the controversy in 1971 and 1973, when overtures numbered in the hundreds, summaries and descriptions along with representative key documents and actions are provided. Following the "walkout" and formation of Seminex, the 1975 convention of the Missouri Synod in Anaheim had much to deal with, as reflected in the many overtures and resolutions listed in this appendix.

Note that actions on the resolutions are generally not included, as amendments and other complications are often involved. Researchers are urged to use the information in this section as a guide to the relevant convention documents, including *Today's Business*, which are available at Concordia Historical Institute and, to some extent, in the libraries of the seminaries and many of the schools in the Concordia University System.

Overtures designated "unprinted" or "unpublished" or "mimeographed" did not appear in the *Workbooks* proper but were independently supplied to delegates at the conventions. (Copies of many of these "unprinted" resolutions are available from Concordia Historical Institute.)

Cleveland (June 20–30) **1962**

Memorials

326 – **To Censor Publication of Articles in Student Periodicals** [re *Seminarian* at Concordia Seminary, Saint Louis] (*Reports and Memorials*, page 157)

331 – **To Request the Convention to Give Clear and Simple Answers to Certain Questions** [re specific teachings about Scripture taught at Missouri Synod churches and schools] (*Reports and Memorials*, pages 161–63)

335 – **To Maintain the Synod's Doctrinal Standards, Etc.** [re articles and public teachings by seminary professors and others] (*Reports and Memorials*, pages 164–65)

336 – **To Reiterate Agreement with Certain Principles regarding Discipline** [in cases of public errant teaching] (*Reports and Memorials*, page 165)

337 – **To Declare "A Statement on the Form and Function of Holy Scriptures" Unacceptable** [re statement of the Concordia Seminary faculty published in *The Lutheran Witness*, April 4, 1961] (*Reports and Memorials*, page 166)

344 – **To Forbid Attacks on Doctrinal Position of the Synod, Etc.** ["even under the guise of exploratory work or of theological opinion"] (*Reports and Memorials*, page 170)

350 A (Unprinted Memorial) – **To Urge the Praesidium to Act with More Dispatch, Etc.** [re doctrinal deviation by professors] (*Unprinted Memorials Referred to Floor Committee #3* [1962], page 5)

350 B (Unprinted Memorial) – **To Request Synodical Officials to Carry Out Discipline, Etc.** [re false public teaching] (*Unprinted Memorials Referred to Floor Committee #3* [1962], page 10)

351 – **To Restudy the Question: "What Is a Doctrine?"** [overture critical of report printed in *The Lutheran Witness*, May 8, 1956, and supporting the Concordia Seminary faculty document "A Statement on the Form and Function of the Holy Scriptures" printed in *The Lutheran Witness*, April 4, 1961] (*Reports and Memorials*, page 178)

354 (Unprinted Memorial) – **To Elect a Special Committee to Conduct an Investigation of Theology Taught at Saint Louis Seminary, Etc.** (*Unprinted Memorials Referred to Floor Committee #3* [1962], pages 3–4)

356 (Unprinted Memorial) – **Expression of Concern That "Statement on the Form and Function of the "Holy Scripture" "Is Not Sufficiently Clear," Etc.** [re the

Saint Louis faculty statement printed in *The Lutheran Witness*, April 1961] (*Unprinted Memorials Referred to Floor Committee #3* [1962], page 6)

363 (Unprinted Memorial) – **To Instruct Concordia Publishing House to Remove a Bible Class Editor** [re Oscar E. Feucht's claim that "Dr. Scharlemann has taught me a great deal. Everything I write is to a greater or lesser extent informed or affected by his statements."] (*Unprinted Memorials Referred to Floor Committee #3* [1962], pages 12–13)

Resolutions

3-09 – **To Supervise Doctrine and Practice** (Memorials 335, 343, 344, 348; Unprinted Memorials 350 A, 350 B, 354) (*Proceedings*, pages 102–3)

3-16 – **Questions on Doctrine of Scripture** (Memorials 331, 338, 339, 340) (*Proceedings*, pages 104–5)

3-18 – **To Emphasize the Sure Truth and Comfort of Scripture regarding the Immortality of the Soul and the Resurrection of the Flesh** (Memorial 331; Unprinted Memorials 357, 361) (*Proceedings*, page 106)

3-19 – **To Relieve Dr. M. Scharlemann of His Office as Teacher, Etc.** (Memorial 335; Unprinted Memorial 356) (*Proceedings*, pages 106–7)

3-22 – **To Restudy "What Is a Doctrine?"** (Memorial 351) (*Proceedings*, page 108)

3-29 – **To Continue Study of Statement on "The Form and Function of Scripture"** (Memorial 337; Unprinted Memorial 356A) (*Proceedings*, page 111)

3-31 – **Removing a Bible Class Editor** (Unprinted Memorial 363) (*Proceedings*, pages 111–12)

3-32 – **Principles regarding Discipline** (Memorial 336) (*Proceedings*, page 112)

Detroit (June 16–26) **1965**

Overtures

2-06 – **To Ask the Commission on Theology and Church Relations to Give a More Precise Definition of "Inspiration of the Scriptures"** (*Convention Workbook / Reports and Overtures*, pages 49–50)

2-07 – **To Request Convention to Distinguish Clearly between Position One and Position Two in Report on Revelation, Inspiration and Inerrancy** (*Convention Workbook / Reports and Overtures*, pages 49–50)

2-08 – To Reject Report of the Commission on Theology and Church Relations—"A Study Document on Revelation, Inspiration, Inerrancy" (*Convention Workbook / Reports and Overtures*, page 51)

2-09 – To Reaffirm Unwavering Loyalty to the Scriptures as the Inspired and Inerrant Word of God, Etc. (*Convention Workbook / Reports and Overtures*, page 52)

2-10 – To Petition the 1965 Detroit Convention to Reaffirm the Historic Christian and Lutheran Doctrine of the Mosaic Authorship of the First Five Books of the Bible, Etc. (*Convention Workbook / Reports and Overtures*, pages 52–54)

2-11 – To Petition the Detroit Convention to Request . . . Resignation of All . . . Professors, Pastors, Teachers Who Continue to Maintain that the . . . Prophet Isaiah Did Not Write the Entire Book of Isaiah (*Convention Workbook / Reports and Overtures*, pages 54–56)

2-12 – To Petition the Detroit Convention to Reaffirm the Historicity of the Jonah Account (*Convention Workbook / Reports and Overtures*, pages 56–57)

2-13 – To Petition the Detroit Convention to Reaffirm the Historic Christian Doctrine that the Old Testament Directly Predicts a Personal Messiah (*Convention Workbook / Reports and Overtures*, pages 57–60)

2-14 – To Relieve of Their Position . . . Professors . . . Who Reject Literal Interpretation of Genesis 1 and 2 (*Convention Workbook / Reports and Overtures*, page 60)

2-15 – To Petition the Detroit Convention to Have the Synod Affirm Its Conviction that Adam and Eve Were Historical Personages, Etc. (*Convention Workbook / Reports and Overtures*, pages 60–62)

2-16 – To Petition the Detroit Convention to Reaffirm that It Accepts the Doctrine that God Made Heaven and Earth in Six Days, Etc. (*Convention Workbook / Reports and Overtures*, pages 62–64)

2-17a – To Petition the Detroit Convention to Declare that the Theory of the Evolutionary Origin of Man and the World Will Not Be Accepted within the Synod, Etc. (*Convention Workbook / Reports and Overtures*, pages 64–66)

2-18 – To Instruct Officials to Disciplinary Proceedings against Clergymen Who Allow Possibility that Man Was Created by Process of Evolution (*Convention Workbook / Reports and Overtures*, page 66)

2-19 – To Insure that Convention Committees Will Respect Scripture (*Convention Workbook / Reports and Overtures*, pages 66–67)

2-20 – **To Have the Synod Acknowledge Openly that Antiscriptural Teaching Has Made Inroads within the Synod** (*Convention Workbook / Reports and Overtures*, pages 68–70)

2-22 – **To Reaffirm Our Traditional Beliefs and Interpretations** [re Genesis, Jonah, etc.] (*Convention Workbook / Reports and Overtures*, page 72)

2-25 – **To Declare . . . that There Shall Not Be Taught in the Synodical Institutions of Learning . . . Anything that Contradicts the Synodically Adopted Statements Mentioned Above, Etc.** [re *Thirteen Theses on Election and Conversion*, *A Brief Statement of the Doctrinal Position of the Missouri Synod*, *Common Confession*] (*Convention Workbook / Reports and Overtures*, page 73)

2-30 – **To Ask the Synod to Declare Its Doctrinal Position without Equivocation, Etc.** [re authorship of books of the Bible, words of Scripture to be understood in their natural sense, etc.] (*Convention Workbook / Reports and Overtures*, pages 74–77)

2-31 – **To Have the Synod Declare Its Determination Faithfully to Obey the Lord's Instruction, Etc.** [re the doctrinal turmoil and its effects in the Synod] (*Convention Workbook / Reports and Overtures*, pages 77–78)

2-37 – **To Have the Synod Require Innovators to Admonish the Synod concerning the Synod's Alleged Error before Teaching in the Classroom, Etc.** (*Convention Workbook / Reports and Overtures*, pages 81–82)

2-45 Un [published Overture] – **To Request that Five Overtures Not Submitted to the 1962 Convention Be Submitted to the 1965 Convention of The Lutheran Church—Missouri Synod** [re writings of some professors at Concordia Seminary, Saint Louis, and Concordia, Bronxville, New York] (*Unpublished Reports and Overtures*, pages 4–6)

2-47 M [imeographed Overture] – **Resolutions Passed by the Special Conference Called in Iowa District West to Hear Dr.** [Norman] **Habel's Essay "The Form and Meaning of the Fall Narrative" and Held at Holiday Inn, Fort Dodge, Iowa, on May 25, 1965** (*List of Overtures Received Too Late to Be Included in the "Unpublished" Overtures . . . and Therefore Being Presented to the Detroit Convention in Mimeographed Form*, page 6)

4-55 M [imeographed Overture] – **To Authorize a Program of Emergency Action . . . to Restore Purity of Scriptural Doctrine within the Synod, Etc.** (*List of Overtures Received Too Late to Be Included in the "Unpublished" Overtures . . . and*

Therefore Being Presented to the Detroit Convention in Mimeographed Form, pages 12–17)

5-29 Un [published Overture] – **To Request the Detroit Convention to Ask the President of the District in which Dr. Martin Scharlemann Now Holds Membership to Deal with Him according to the Synodical "Handbook," Etc.** (*Unpublished Reports and Overtures*, pages 17–19)

5-30 Un [published Overture] – **To Petition that the Detroit Convention Request the President of the District in which Dr. Gilbert Thiele Now Holds Membership to Deal with Him according to the Synodical "Handbook," Etc.** (*Unpublished Reports and Overtures*, pages 19–21)

5-31 Un [published Overture] – **To Ask that the Detroit Convention Require the President of the District in which Dr. Robert Scharlemann Now Holds Membership to Deal with Him according to the Synodical "Handbook," Etc.** (*Unpublished Reports and Overtures*, pages 21–23)

5-33 Un [published Overture] – **To Petition the Detroit Convention to Request the Praesidium to Seek, according to Proper Procedure, the Removal of Dr. Alfred Fuerbringer from Presidency of Concordia Seminary, St. Louis** (*Unpublished Reports and Overtures*, pages 24–26)

5-44 Un [published Overture] – **To Take More Effective Steps to Bring about a Satisfying and God-Pleasing Solution of the Present Offensive Situation in the Synod with Respect to Doctrine** (*Unpublished Reports and Overtures*, pages 33–34)

Resolutions

2-01 – **To Reaffirm Unwavering Loyalty to the Scriptures as the Inspired and Inerrant Word of God** (Overture 2-09) (*Proceedings*, page 94)

2-02 – **To Request Commission on Theology and Church Relations to Give a More Precise Definition of "Inspiration of the Scriptures"** (Overture 2-06) (*Proceedings*, page 94)

2-06 – **To Take No Action on Overture Not Submitted to the 1962 Convention (Concordia Collegiate Institute, Bronxville, N.Y.)** (Overture 2-45) (*Proceedings*, page 95)

2-07 – **To Propose that the Commission on Theology and Church Relations Plan and Produce a Comprehensive Study of Biblical Hermeneutics** (Report 2-01) (*Proceedings*, pages 95–96)

2-08 – **To Uphold and Honor the Doctrinal Content of Synodically Adopted Statements** (Report 2-01; Overtures 2-14, 2-25, 2-26, 2-27, 2-28, 2-29, 2-30, 2-31, 2-37; Unpublished Overture 4-49) (*Proceedings*, page 96)

2-09 – **To Make a Clear Distinction between Position One and Position Two of "A Study Document on Revelation, Inspiration, Inerrancy" and to Reject the Document** (Overtures 2-07, 2-08) (*Proceedings*, page 96)

2-14 – **To Respect Scripture** (Overtures 2-19, 2-24, 2-43) (*Proceedings*, page 97)

2-17 – **To Reaffirm "Quia" Subscription to Lutheran Confessions, Etc.** (Overtures 2-21, 2-23) (*Proceedings*, page 98)

2-23 – **To Have the Synod Openly Acknowledge that Antiscriptural Teaching Has Made Inroads within the Synod** (Overture 2-20) (*Proceedings*, pages 99–100)

2-26 – **To Reaffirm Our Belief that the Old Testament Prophecies of the Savior Are Fulfilled in Jesus Christ** (Overture 2-13) (*Proceedings*, page 100)

2-27 – **To Reaffirm the Historicity of the Jonah Account** (Overture 2-12) (*Proceedings*, page 100)

2-29 – **To Concur in Response by Commission on Theology and Church Relations to Propositions 1 and 2 of Memorial 331 Cleveland "Proceedings"** (Report 2-01; Overtures 2-15, 2-16, 2-17a, 2-18) (*Proceedings*, page 101)

2-33 – **False Doctrine Must Be Acknowledged and Retracted** (Overture 2-45 Un) (*Proceedings*, page 102)

2-34 – **Re Publication "What Is Troubling the Lutherans?"** (Overture 2-45 Un) (*Proceedings*, page 102)

2-35 – **Re Authorship of the Pentateuch and the Book of Isaiah** (Overtures 2-10, 2-11, 2-22) (*Proceedings*, page 103)

2-37 – **Re Resolutions by Iowa District West on the Habel Essay** (Overture 2-47 M) (*Proceedings*, pages 103–4)

New York (July 7–14) **1967**

Overtures

2-07 – **To Reject "A Lutheran Stance toward Contemporary Biblical Studies"** [re CTCR document] (*Convention Workbook/Reports and Overtures*, pages 60–61)

2-08 – **To Reject "A Study Document on the Witness of Jesus and Old Testament Authorship"** [re CTCR document] (*Convention Workbook / Reports and Overtures*, pages 61–62)

2-09 – **To Make Certain Declarations regarding Authorship and Inspiration of Various N. T. Books** [re Pauline authorship of Romans and Petrine authorship of 1 Peter] (*Convention Workbook / Reports and Overtures*, page 62)

2-10 – **To Reaffirm Position on the Scriptures** [re Scriptures as the inspired, infallible, inerrant Word of God] (*Convention Workbook / Reports and Overtures*, page 62)

2-11 – **To Reaffirm Stance toward "Proper Meaning" of Words of Scripture** [re maintaining the "plain, clear words" of Scripture] (*Convention Workbook / Reports and Overtures*, page 63)

2-12 – **To Answer Specific Questions re Scripture** [re stance of Synod and synodical catechism that the entire Scripture is the inspired, inerrant, and infallible Word of God] (*Convention Workbook / Reports and Overtures*, page 63)

2-13 – **To Reaffirm Scriptural Stance** [re Law and Gospel and "all doctrines revealed in Scripture as confessed in the Symbolical Books of the Lutheran Church"] (*Convention Workbook / Reports and Overtures*, page 63)

2-14 – **To Reaffirm Status of Holy Scripture** [as detailed in Missouri Synod Constitution, catechism, and *Brief Statement*—in contrast to higher-critical method presented in February 1967 issue of *Concordia Theological Monthly*] (*Convention Workbook / Reports and Overtures*, page 64)

2-15 – **To Reaffirm Doctrine of Verbal and Plenary Inspiration** [as detailed in synodical catechism and *Brief Statement*] (*Convention Workbook / Reports and Overtures*, pages 64–65)

2-16 – **To Reaffirm Position on Scripture** [re theological, historical, geographic, scientific truth of Scripture] (*Convention Workbook / Reports and Overtures*, page 65)

2-17 – **To Acknowledge Openly that Antiscriptural Teaching Has Made Inroads within the Synod** [re "the inerrancy of Scripture is attacked in the *Concordia Theological Monthly* for September 1965." Petrine authorship of 1 Peter and "inspiration of Scripture is attacked in 'Doxology: God's People Called to Celebrate His Glory.'" Synodical Bible study *A Man to Follow*, January 1967 article in *Concordia Theological Monthly*, and Martin Scharlemann essay also given as examples.] (*Convention Workbook / Reports and Overtures*, pages 65–68)

2-18 – **To Either Discipline or Divide** [re discipline of Missouri Synod members "who are not true to the condition of membership"] (*Convention Workbook / Reports and Overtures*, page 68)

2-19 [see also 2-20–2-44] – **To Elect a Board of Inquiry** [re formation of board to hold hearings and report to the next synodical convention on "problems in the area of doctrine and discipline which are disturbing the church"] (*Convention Workbook / Reports and Overtures*, pages 68–69)

2-45 – **To Form Lay Commission on Doctrine and Practice** ["to examine teaching materials . . . at any and all synodical or Synod-supported institutions of higher learning, including . . . lecture notes taken by students" "and to publish . . . what they have examined and observed," "and any recommendations for corrective action"] (*Convention Workbook / Reports and Overtures*, pages 69–70)

2-46 – **To Direct Proper Officials to Exercise Doctrinal Discipline** [re antiscriptural and destructive teachings that have made inroads within the Missouri Synod; examples given: essay delivered by faculty member of Concordia, River Forest; article in Spring 1962 issue of *Dialog*; interpretations of first chapters of Genesis; "The Shape of Faith in Jesus Christ" in May 1965 issue of Walther League *Arena*; a "much disputed essay [of a] professor of our St. Louis seminary" re: soul of a believer after death] (*Convention Workbook / Reports and Overtures*, pages 70–71)

2-47 – **To Deal More Firmly with Disturbances** [in doctrine and practice "contrary to Article VI of the Constitution of Synod"] (*Convention Workbook / Reports and Overtures*, page 71)

2-48 – **To Take Steps to Expedite Action in Present Controversies** [causing "an ever widening breach between so-called liberal and conservative elements in the Synod"] (*Convention Workbook / Reports and Overtures*, page 71)

2-49 – **To Make Various Declarations and Take Various Steps in Theological Matters** [re church discipline of those who persistently promote false doctrine of "new theology which follows dialectical thought forms" and teaches "that there is no absolute truth," following the "dialectical middle-of-the-road" example of the "later Melanchthon"; list of eleven areas of false doctrine included] (*Convention Workbook / Reports and Overtures*, pages 71–72)

2-50 [also 2-51] – **To Ask Those Who Deny Historicity of Jonah Account and of Gen. 1–3 to Seek Fellowship Elsewhere** [re "the clear meaning of Scripture," particularly the events in Jonah and details of the creation and fall into sin] (*Convention Workbook / Reports and Overtures*, page 73)

2-52 – **To Declare that God Created the World in 6 days of 24 Hours Each** [as teaching of Scripture and binding upon Missouri Synod members] (*Convention Workbook / Reports and Overtures*, page 73)

2-53 [also 2-105 U] – **To Reject Symbolical Interpretation of Gen. 1–3** [re essay "The Form and Meaning of the Fall Narrative" by Norman Habel, associate professor of biblical studies, Concordia Seminary, Saint Louis] (*Convention Workbook / Reports and Overtures*, pages 73–74)

2-54 [also 2-55, 2-56, 2-57, 2-58, 2-59, 2-60] – **To Declare Certain Teachings False Doctrine** [re "the questioning or denial of the inerrancy of Scripture," "the denial of the vicarious atonement," "the denial of the physical resurrection of Christ," "the denial of the immortality of the soul," allowing "the possibility that man may have evolved from a primary organism and the denial of the 6-day creation"] (*Convention Workbook / Reports and Overtures*, pages 74–75)

2-61 – **To Define More Precisely the Synod's Stand on Creation** [re doctrine of creation as presented in articles in the May 1965, September 1965, September 1966 issues of *Concordia Theological Monthly*] (*Convention Workbook / Reports and Overtures*, page 75)

2-62 [also 2-63, 2-64, 2-65] – **To Deal with Valparaiso U. regarding Evolution** [as taught in printed material and textbooks used] (*Convention Workbook / Reports and Overtures*, pages 75–76)

2-66 [also 2-67, 2-68] – **To Reconsider Previous Memorials on Doctrinal Matters** ["that have been ignored, rejected, and emasculated" by previous conventions of Synod as documented in The State of the Church, Inc., materials] (*Convention Workbook / Reports and Overtures*, page 76)

2-69 – **To Submit** [Concordia Teachers College] **River Forest Seminar Papers for Study and Recommendation** [re eight study papers presented to the River Forest faculty by members / former members of the theology division from September 27–December 6, 1965] (*Convention Workbook / Reports and Overtures*, pages 76–77)

2-92 – **To Declare "Brief Statement" Scriptural and Binding** ["since the *Brief Statement* received adverse action at the Cleveland convention, the Synod may . . . take formal action to change this"] *Convention Workbook / Reports and Overtures*, pages 84–85)

2-94 – **To Require False Teachers to Repent** [re "pastors, teachers, and professors . . . who publicly teach and profess doctrines and positions contrary to Holy Scripture"; *Cresset* (Valparaiso), *Arena* (Walther League), and other "published essays, Sunday school literature, and confirmation manuals" cited] (*Convention Workbook / Reports and Overtures*, page 85)

2-95 U [npublished Overture] [also 2-96, 2-97, 2-98, 2-99, 2-100, 2-101] – **To Exercise Doctrinal Discipline** [re "pastors, teachers, and professors . . . who publicly teach and profess doctrines and positions contrary to Holy Scripture"; Dr. Martin Scharlemann (Concordia Seminary, Saint Louis), Dr. Robert Hoyer, Dr. Gilbert Thiele (Concordia Seminary, Saint Louis), Rev. Ronald C. Starenko, Rev. Richard E. Koenig, Rev. Wayne Saffen, Rev. Ralph Moellering, Dr. Karl Krekeler, Dr. William Bloom, Dr. Alfred von Rohr Sauer, Dr. Norman C. Habel (Concordia Seminary, Saint Louis) cited] (*Unpublished Reports and Overtures*, pages 16–17)

2-105 U [npublished Overture] - See 2-53 above

2-106 U [npublished Overture] – **To Reaffirm Historicity of Jonah Account** [essay of Dr. Alfred von Rohr Sauer cited] (*Unpublished Reports and Overtures*, pages 17–18)

2-107 U [npublished Overture] – **To Reaffirm Historicity of Adam and Eve** [re Missouri Synod teachers continuing to teach evolution; October 1965 Northwestern Indiana Pastors and Teachers Conference cited] (*Unpublished Reports and Overtures*, page 18)

2-109 U [npublished Overture] – **Not to Establish a Board of Doctrinal Review** [argues that the Missouri Synod *Handbook* charges the faculty of Concordia Seminary with the responsibility for being the Synod's official doctrinal censor of all manuscripts of religious or theological nature before they are published by the Synod or any of its agencies; any new board of review would replace the faculty as Synod's official doctrinal censor] (*Unpublished Reports and Overtures*, pages 18–19)

2-114 U [npublished Overture] – **Supplementary Report of Commission on Theology and Church Relations: A Review of the Question, "What Is a Doctrine?"** [I. History of the Question; II. Use and Meaning of the Term "Doctrine"; III. Conclusions and Applications] (*Unpublished Reports and Overtures*, pages 19–25)

Resolutions

2-02 – **To Commend "A Lutheran Stance toward Contemporary Biblical Studies" for Study and Discussion** [CTCR document] (Report 2-01; Overture 2-07) (*Proceedings*, page 88)

2-03 – **To Reexamine and to Clarify "The Witness of Jesus and Old Testament Authorship"** (Report 2-01; Overture 2-08) (*Proceedings*, page 88)

2-04 – **To Adopt "A Declaration on the Status and Use of Synodically Adopted Doctrinal Statements"** [CTCR document on the status and use of *Brief Statement*, *Common Confession*, and *Doctrinal Declaration*] (Report 2-01; Overture 2-92) (*Proceedings*, pages 88–89)

2-16 – **To Reaffirm Position on Scriptures** (Overtures 2-10, 2-11, 2-12, 2-13, 2-14, 2-15, 2-16) (*Proceedings*, page 92)

2-22 – **To Continue Study of Issues Involving Authorship and Inspiration of Various New Testament Books** [CTCR to continue exploration of issues and share findings] (Overture 2-09) (*Proceedings*, page 93)

2-24 – **To Adopt New Procedures for Doctrinal Censorship** [report and recommendation of the Study Committee on Censorship adopted; appreciation to faculty of Concordia Seminary, Saint Louis, for previous responsibilities as official censor of Missouri Synod publications] (Report 2-03; Overtures 2-45, 2-109 U, 2-110 U) (*Proceedings*, page 94)

2-26 – **To Follow Proper Procedures in Doctrinal Discipline** (Overture 2-48) (*Proceedings*, page 94)

2-27 – **To Decline to Reconsider Previous Overtures on Doctrinal Matters** [president cannot act on issues documented in The State of the Church, Inc., materials until CTCR completes studies] (Overtures 2-66, 2-67, 2-68) (*Proceedings*, page 94)

2-30 – **To Reaffirm Our Position on Certain Doctrines** [Holy Scripture is the inerrant Word of God, Christ made atonement for sins of whole world and propitiated God's wrath against sin, Christ rose from the dead glorified in His flesh, soul does not cease to exist after death, and only those who believe in Christ receive eternal life] (Overtures 2-54, 2-55, 2-56, 2-57, 2-58, 2-59, 2-60) (*Proceedings*, page 95)

2-31 – **To Reaffirm Our Position on Creation, Fall, and Related Subjects** [six-day creation; man is the principal creature of God; Adam and Eve were real, historical human beings; the fall of Adam and Eve into sin was a historical fact, the subsequent inherent corruption of all human beings] (Overtures 2-50, 2-51, 2-52, 2-53, 2-61, 2-62, 2-63, 2-64, 2-65, 2-54, 2-55, 2-56, 2-57, 2-58, 2-59, 2-60, 2-105 U, 2-106 U, 2-107 U) (*Proceedings*, page 95)

2-32 – **To Decline to Submit River Forest Seminar Papers for Study and Recommendation and to Refer This Matter to River Forest Board of Control** [because of unavailability of papers for convention and due process] (Overture 2-69) (*Proceedings*, pages 95–96)

2-33 – **To Decline to Elect Board of Inquiry or Lay Commission but to Seek Better Solutions** [for fear that creating a board of inquiry would cause more unrest in the Synod, resolution requests the LCMS Council of Presidents to carefully investigate improving structure re doctrinal supervision and report to next convention] (Overtures 2-19–2-45) (*Proceedings*, page 96)

2-36 – **To Refer "A Review of the Question 'What Is a Doctrine?'" to 1969 Convention** [CTCR document commended to membership for study and discussion and document be referred to 1969 convention for adoption] (Report 2-114 U) (*Proceedings*, page 97)

2-37 – **To Deal Decisively in Cases of Alleged False Teaching** [deal with accusers and accused in love] (Overtures 2-17, 2-18, 2-46, 2-47, 2-49, 2-50, 2-51, 2-93, 2-94, 2-95 U–2-101 U) (*Proceedings*, page 97)

Denver (July 11–18) **1969**

Overtures

2-03 – **To Have All Convention Actions Conform to "Scripture Alone" and "Justification by Faith Alone"** [re "*heilsgeschichtliche* theology" presented by Concordia Seminary, Saint Louis, professor in February 1965 issue of *Concordia Theological Monthly*; article opposing belief that John 10:35 expresses Christ's teaching re infallibility and inerrancy of Scripture in October 1964 issue of *Concordia Theological Monthly*; opposition of Law and Gospel "propositions" of Scripture in June 1968 article in *The Lutheran Witness*; LCUSA document stating, contrary to Philippians 2:5ff., that "Jesus … [emptied] himself of any aspiration to be as God"] (*Convention Workbook / Reports and Overtures*, pages 72–73)

2-04 – **To Produce Substitute for "Christian Discipline" Document** [re document of "regulations" issued by the Office of the President of Synod that "completely ignores several Bible passages … highly pertinent to the subject treated" in cases where "the committing of a sin has become generally known and public offense has been given, it is not necessary to observe the three degrees of remonstrance prescribed in Matthew 18"] (*Convention Workbook / Reports and Overtures*, pages 73–74)

2-05 – **To Reject All Heterodoxy** (*Convention Workbook / Reports and Overtures*, page 74)

2-06 – **To Reaffirm Statements on Inerrancy of Scripture** [re "every word of the Bible is God's Word," according to John 10:35, *Brief Statement*, and Luther's Small Catechism] (*Convention Workbook / Reports and Overtures*, page 74)

2-07 – **To Recognize the Real Theological Issue of Our Day (Interpretation of Scripture)** [the recognition that "the interpretation of Holy Scripture (anti-historical and anti-supernatural interpretation) is the great and overriding issue within Christendom and Lutheranism in our day"] (*Convention Workbook / Reports and Overtures*, pages 74–75)

2-08 – **To Reaffirm Position on the Scriptures** ["as the inspired, infallible, inerrant Word of God"] (*Convention Workbook / Reports and Overtures*, page 75)

2-09 [also 2-10, 2-11, 2-12, 2-13] – **To Remove from Office Those Who Deny Mosaic Authorship of Pentateuch** [contrary to Overture 2-10 presented at Detroit Convention, "some professors in the LCMS continue to deny the Mosaic authorship of the Pentateuch"] (*Convention Workbook / Reports and Overtures*, pages 75–76)

2-14 [also 2-15, 2-16, 2-17, 2-18] – **To Remove from Office Those Who Deny Unity of Isaiah** [re "some professors in the LCMS continue to deny the unity of Isaiah"] (*Convention Workbook / Reports and Overtures*, page 76)

2-19 [also 2-20, 2-21, 2-22, 2-23] – **To Affirm Historicity of New Testament** ["Whereas, some professors within The Lutheran Church—Missouri Synod agree with these liberal scholars" re teaching that Jesus never said some of the words which are attributed to Him in the New Testament and some miracles recorded in the New Testament never actually happened "in ordinary calendar history"] (*Convention Workbook / Reports and Overtures*, pages 76–77)

2-24 – **To Deal with Doctrinal Unrest** ["because some of the members of our Synod teach that the original and ancient texts of the Holy Scriptures contain errors"; examples given: Genesis account of creation is not correct; Book of Jonah is a parable; the Bible contains myths; Bible text does not correctly reflect the actual words of Jesus; Daniel did not write Daniel; evolution may be possible] (*Convention Workbook / Reports and Overtures*, page 77)

2-25 – **To Deal with Those in Conflict with Doctrinal Position** [president of the LCMS to use the power of his office to admonish, correct, and discipline those who express themselves contrary to the doctrinal and confessional position of our Synod"] (*Convention Workbook / Reports and Overtures*, pages 77–78)

2-26 [also 2-27] – **To Introduce Corrective Measures** [re developments including "acceptance of God's Word as God's inerrant Word" and "teaching practices at preparatory and terminal schools"] (*Convention Workbook / Reports and Overtures*, page 78)

2-28 – **To Remove Disunity** [in the Synod where "two different theologies of the Word of God and the Gospel exist" and "lack of disciple" exists; published comments of Valparaiso Chancellor O. P. Kretzmann cited. "That this convention direct the President of Synod to proceed with all possible haste . . . to correct the erring and to remove them from office if they will not be corrected."] (*Convention Workbook / Reports and Overtures*, pages 78–79)

2-29 – **To Eliminate Special System of Theological Censorship** [in favor of doctrinal supervision by District and synodical presidents through already-established channels of administration] (*Convention Workbook / Reports and Overtures*, page 79)

2-31 – **To Clarify an Apparent Conflict regarding the Public Doctrine of the Church** [re granting tenure to Concordia Seminary, Saint Louis, professor Norman Habel by the seminary's Board of Control despite the positions and conclusions stated in his printed essay "The Form and Meaning of the Fall Narrative" (Concordia Seminary Print Shop, 1965)] (*Convention Workbook / Reports and Overtures*, page 81)

2-49 – **To Stand on the "Brief Statement" as in 1932** [reaffirmation of adherence to *Brief Statement*, "that pastors, teachers, and professors . . . teach nothing contrary" to it] (*Convention Workbook / Reports and Overtures*, pages 89–90)

2-50 [also 2-51] – **To Require Adherence to "Brief Statement"** [that all Synod officers and boards "permit nobody under their authority to teach falsely but to be prompt and diligent in administering due admonition" in accord with rules to be established for suspending a pastor or teacher found guilty of teaching false doctrine] (*Convention Workbook / Reports and Overtures*, page 90)

2-52 – **To Reaffirm "Brief Statement," Especially Certain Sections at This Time** [paragraphs 1, 5, and 29; Bible as inerrant Word of God, six-day creation, orthodox character of a church body by what is actually taught in its pulpits and theological seminaries] (*Convention Workbook / Reports and Overtures*, pages 90–91)

2-53 – **To Reaffirm Doctrinal Position of "Brief Statement"** ["and exercise proper, God-pleasing discipline with those who reject *Brief Statement*"] (*Convention Workbook / Reports and Overtures*, page 91)

2-54 – **To Require Assent to "Brief Statement"** [by "all pastors, professors, teachers, and congregations of our Synod" and "that the President of the Synod, the District Presidents, the Circuit Counselors, and the Boards of Control of our institutions to take disciplinary action against all . . . who teach contrary to the Scriptural position of our Synod as set forth in the *Brief Statement*"] (*Convention Workbook / Reports and Overtures*, page 91)

2-62 U [npublished Overture] – **To Establish Facts on Alleged Unfaithfulness in Doctrine among Clergy** ["that we require the clergy of our church body to be faithful to the Gospel of Christ in all points in keeping with . . . their ordination vow"; allegations from March 27, 1969, issue of *Balance* re Messiah Lutheran Church, Sterling, Illinois, cited] (*Unpublished Reports and Overtures*, page 6)

2-63 U [npublished Overture] – **To Exercise Discipline** [re the inerrancy of Scripture] (*Unpublished Reports and Overtures*, pages 6–7)

2-68 U [npublished Overture] – **To Require Adherence to Doctrinal Statements** [adopted by Synod, such as *Brief Statement* and *Statement on Scripture*] (*Unpublished Reports and Overtures*, page 8)

2-72 U [npublished Overture] – **To Investigate Theological Change Reported by "CTM"** [reform measures, including funding of $25,000, to "investigate . . . inclusive of Concordia Seminary, St. Louis," "another type of theology [that] has gained prominence in our circles" as reported in the February 1965 issue of Concordia Seminary, Saint Louis, *Concordia Theological Monthly*] (*Unpublished Reports and Overtures*, page 10)

Resolutions

2-01 – **To Answer Concerns re Authorship of Pentateuch and Book of Isaiah** (Overtures 2-09 to 2-18) (*Proceedings*, page 84)

2-02 – **To Urge Concern for Continued Exercise of Doctrinal Discipline** (Overture 2-03) (*Proceedings*, pages 84–85)

2-03 – **To Reaffirm Position on Word of God** (Overtures 2-08, 2-58 U, 2-59 U, 2-60 U) (*Proceedings*, page 85)

2-04 – **To Receive "Answers to Questions Raised regarding the Document 'A Lutheran Stance toward Contemporary Biblical Studies'"** (Report 2-01) (*Proceedings*, page 85)

2-05 – **To Receive "A Response to Questions on 'The Witness of Jesus and Old Testament Authorship'"** (Report 2-01) (*Proceedings*, page 85)

2-06 – **To Preserve Doctrinal Unity through Proper Supervision** (Overtures 2-09 to 2-28, 2-62 U, 2-63 U, 2-72 U) (*Proceedings*, pages 85–86)

2-13 – **To Answer Concerns of Overture 2-07 (Interpretation** [of Scripture]**)** (Overture 2-07) (*Proceedings*, page 87)

2-16 – **To Affirm Historicity of New Testament** (Overtures 2-19 to 2-23, 2-58 U, 2-59 U, 2-60 U, 2-69 U) (*Proceedings*, pages 87–88)

2-20 – **To Decline Overture to Produce Substitute for "Christian Discipline" Document** (Overture 2-04) (*Proceedings*, page 89)

2-21 – **To Commend and Refer "A Statement on Death, Resurrection, and Immortality"** (Report 2-01) (*Proceedings*, pages 89–90)

2-24 – **To Accept and Commend "A Review of the Question 'What Is a Doctrine?'"** (Report 2-01) (*Proceedings*, page 90)

2-27 – **To Honor and Uphold Doctrinal Statements** (Overtures 2-31, 2-49, 2-50, 2-51, 2-52, 2-53, 2-54) (*Proceedings*, page 91)

2-29 – **To Study Materials Distributed by Hermeneutics Study Committee and to Request Board of Directors to Consider Providing Funds for Workshops** (Report 2-01; Overture 2-61 U) (*Proceedings*, pages 91–92)

2-30 – **To Receive Expression of Concern to Remain Faithful** (Overture 2-30) (*Proceedings*, page 92)

2-31 – **To Review System of Theological Censorship** (Overture 2-29) (*Proceedings*, page 92) [*referred to the president for action*]

2-33 – **To Affirm Desire to Follow Orthodoxy** (Overture 2-05) (*Proceedings*, page 92)

2-38 – **To Answer Concerns of Trinity Lutheran Church, Austin, Texas** [We "affirm our belief in the plenary, verbal inspiration of Scripture, the inerrancy of Scripture, and that Scripture is in all its words and parts the very Word of God" as taught in the Scriptures and in the Lutheran Confessions] (Overture 2-06) (*Proceedings*, page 93)

Milwaukee (July 9–16) 1971

In 1971, some seventy overtures (2-07 to 2-74) submitted to the convention in Milwaukee continued to reflect disagreements in how to view and / or enforce doctrinal and confessional statements and resolutions (*Convention Workbook / Reports and Overtures*, pages 52–71). It was clear that the issues generally (and some specifically) related to the teaching at Concordia Seminary. A lengthy and complicated resolution, Resolution 2-21 **To Uphold Synodical Doctrinal Resolutions** (*Proceedings*, pages 117–20) attempted to deal with the concerns of Overtures 2-07 to 2-11, 2-13 to 2-19, 2-21, 2-22, 2-25 to 2-33, 2-35 to 2-44, 2-46 to 2-48, 2-52, 2-54 to 2-56, 2-59 to 2-64, 2-66, 2-70, 2-112, 2-113. Also relevant was Resolution 5-24 **To Define Status of Synodically Adopted Doctrinal Statements** (*Proceedings*, pages 163–65).

In addition to these overtures and resulting resolutions, another group under the category of "Seminary Inquiry" consisted of almost forty overtures and focused specifically on matters involving Concordia Seminary, commending or reprimanding the seminary faculty vis-à-vis President Preus's appointing of a Fact Finding Committee to investigate the teaching of Concordia Seminary faculty subsequent to the 1969 convention in Denver. Several resolutions attempted to deal with this group of overtures, including Resolution 2-23 **To Support the Judgment of the President of the Synod** (Overtures 2-57, 2-75, 2-78, 2-80, 2-82 to 2-87, 2-89, 2-90, 2-92 to 2-95, 2-97 to 2-11) (*Proceedings*, page 120) and Resolution 2-24 **To Call to Repentance** (Overtures 2-71, 2-73, 2-74, 2-80, 2-88) (*Proceedings*, pages 120–21). While the report of the Fact Finding Committee had not been made public before the Milwaukee convention, the voting delegates adopted Resolution 2-28 **To Direct the Board of Control of Concordia Seminary, St. Louis, to Act** (Overtures 2-84, 2-85, 2-99, 2-100, 2-107, 2-108, 2-110, 2-111, 2-229, 2-230, 2-232) (*Proceedings*, page 122). This resolution directed the seminary Board of Control to "take appropriate action" on the basis of the Fact Finding Committee report, and also to report progress to the president of Synod and the LCMS Board for Higher Education. The president of Synod was also instructed to report "on the progress of the Board of Control within one year." Also relevant was Resolution 5-23 **To Adopt "Statement on Ethics"** (Overtures 2-71, 2-73, 2-74, 2-80, 2-88, 5-83) (*Proceedings*, pages 162–63). This resolution concerned the "Statement on

Ethics" adopted unanimously by the LCMS Council of Presidents in April 1971 which condemned public attacks on Synod leaders (especially the president of Synod) in view of the Eighth Commandment.

New Orleans (July 6–13) 1973

By the time the Missouri Synod commemorated its 50th Regular Convention in the summer of 1973, both synodwide issues and specific issues at Concordia Seminary had come to a head.

Dozens of overtures were submitted expressing continued concern over general doctrinal issues confronting the whole of Synod. Under the heading "Confessions, Resolutions, Discipline" (*Convention Workbook / Reports and Overtures*, pages 51–60), overtures proposed Synod reaffirmation of doctrinal statements while others called for Synod action on a wide variety of proposals that advocated either a loosening or tightening of ecclesiastical discipline in regards to instances of public expressions of doctrine. Additionally, under the heading "Other Concerns" (*Convention Workbook / Reports and Overtures*, pages 70–79), more than twenty overtures continued to press the Synod on affirming its stand on specific doctrinal positions such as the inerrancy of Scripture, the Law-Gospel distinction, Adam and Eve, the Genesis creation accounts, accounts of miracles in the Bible, original sin, and the *almah* of Isaiah 7:14. Opposing overtures also advocated strict limits on the boundaries of "doctrine" that would add anything to the simple words of the second article of the Synod's Constitution and thereby "frustrate the Spirit of God who seeks to lead us into all truth" (78).

Many of these overtures, along with related matters presented in printed convention reports, were subsumed under a resolution submitted to the convention delegates by Committee 2 (Theology and Church Relations) and Committee 3 (Seminary Issues). Resolution 2-12 **To Understand Article II of the Synod's Constitution as Requiring the Formulation and Adoption of Synodical Doctrinal Statements** (based on Overtures 2-12 to 2-34, 2-104, 2-105, 3-24A to 3-29B, 3-99A, 3-190, 3-193A, 3-195B, 5-47) (*Proceedings*, pages 111–15) began with a two-page preamble arguing for the ongoing need of the church to provide "*up-to-date* and *binding interpretations* of her official Confessions" (111–12). In the resolution's five concluding paragraphs, the resolution argues for the appropriateness and necessity of "statements of doctrine which apply the teachings of Scripture and the Confessions to controverted issues" (114); that Article II of the Synod's Constitution permits—and at times even requires—"the formulation and adoption of doctrinal statements as definitive of the

Synod's position relative to controverted issues" (114–15); and that such statements are "binding upon all its members" (115).

A resolution directly related to the Synod's "colleges and seminaries" was submitted by Committees 2 and 3. Resolution 2-38 **To Repudiate the Historical-Critical Method of Interpreting Scripture** (*Proceedings*, pages 121–22) was not enacted but was referred to the Synod's Board of Directors under omnibus Resolution 4-47.

The real story of the 1973 convention was Concordia Seminary, Saint Louis. An entire convention floor committee (Committee 3), headed by Lewis Niemoeller, was charged with reviewing overtures and formulating appropriate resolutions for the convention's consideration. The gravity of the situation is reflected in the reports, recommendations, and memorials presented in the 66-page section in the *Workbook* entitled "Seminary Issues" (*Convention Workbook/Reports and Overtures*, pages 99–165). The following documents were submitted by the president of Synod:

> Report 3-01A – **Report of Board of Control of Concordia Seminary, St. Louis, to The Lutheran Church—Missouri Synod, the President of the Synod, and the Board for Higher Education on Action Taken in Response to the Directive of the Synod in Milwaukee Convention Resolution 2-28** (*Convention Workbook/Reports and Overtures*, pages 99–100). The Board of Control of Concordia Seminary received the Fact Finding Committee report in September 1971 and subsequently issued its Progress Report in June 1972. "In this report the board listed the issues which it had isolated on the basis of its study of the Fact Finding Committee Report and announced its intention of discussing those issues with faculty members" (99). Personal interviews with the twenty-nine faculty members were conducted between September 1972 and January 1973 and included questions concerning the historical-critical method; creation;, original sin; prophecy and fulfillment; miracles; the meaning of inspiration, infallibility, and inerrancy; the nature of the authority of Scripture; the relationship between Law and Gospel; and subscription to the Lutheran Confessions and synodically adopted doctrinal statements. However, "the board did not consider the interview process to be an investigation of charges of false teaching. Rather it considered the interviews to be fraternal discussions" (99). "The Board of Control voted by ballot individually on 44 members of the faculty. . . . By majority action the board voted to commend 44 professors" (100).
>
> Report 3-01B – **Report of Some Members of Board of Control of Concordia Seminary, St. Louis** (*Convention Workbook/Reports and Overtures*, pages 100–102). "Minority" report of Concordia Seminary Board of Control members Walter C. Dissen, Edwin C. Weber, with Charles H. Burmeister, Eugene E. Fincke, who argue that, first, some important details of the interview process and reporting of that process were left out of Dr. John Tietjen's reports of each of the interviews, and subsequently his report to the convention. Second, the Board of Control "ignored the following requests of the synodical President" to deal first with Dr. Tietjen's own confessional stance and failure to exercise supervision of the doctrine of the faculty under his responsibility as the executive officer of the institution. Third, the board has ignored the synodical president's *A Statement of Scriptural and Confessional Principles* in using the document to judge the appropriateness of the teachings of members of the

faculty. The report references and includes **Exhibit A—Items of Deep Concern regarding the Doctrine Taught at the St. Louis Seminary** (*Convention Workbook / Reports and Overtures,* pages 102–4). "The majority of the board . . . concluded that it was aware of many problems. However, it has to date not settled any of the issues. Nevertheless it has declared the faculty free of false doctrine without referring to any criteria applied to the admittedly many problems" (101).

Report 3-01C – **Supplemental Report** (*Convention Workbook / Reports and Overtures,* pages 104–7). Two lay members of the Board of Control (Eugene E. Fincke and Charles H. Burmeister) document conflicts of interest in regards to individual members of the Board of Control (for example, accreditation of Concordia Seminary by the AATS), undocumented handling of gifts and grants by President Tietjen, inappropriate financing of projects by President Tietjen that should have had prior board approval (for example, hiring of attorneys, the publication and distribution of *Fact Finding or Fault Finding* and *Faithful to Our Calling, Faithful to Our Lord* without the board's knowledge), President Tietjen's hiring and use of public relations staff of the seminary, President Tietjen's use of awarding honorary degrees (even to currently serving Board of Control members) without committee or board approval, and procrastination by President Tietjen and the board majority on investigating and disciplining faculty charged with doctrinal errors while exonerating faculty members by one or two vote margins.

Proposed [Synod] ***Handbook* Changes** (*Convention Workbook / Reports and Overtures,* pages 111–17). The proposed changes by the Special Task Force on Accreditation related to boards of control, tenure, removal from office, ecclesiastical supervision, academic accreditation at Synod colleges and seminaries. These changes were subsequently adopted by the convention in Resolution 3-02 **To Change Bylaws of the "Handbook" as Recommended by the Special Task Force on Accreditation** (*Proceedings,* pages 128–31).

Additionally, Overtures 3-11 to 3-196 dealt with a panoply of seminary-related issues: the acceptance of the official Board of Control report; teaching of individual faculty members; doctrinal, confessional, and constitutional issues; the historical-critical method and Scripture; "Gospel reductionism"; removal of certain faculty members and the president of Concordia Seminary; and Board of Control issues.

While some resolutions at the 1973 convention dealt with technical matters (such as retaining accreditation), two substantive resolutions were adopted:

Resolution 3-01 – **To Adopt "A Statement** [of Scriptural and Confessional Principles]**"** (*Proceedings,* pages 127–28). This 1972 document was the most relevant to and critical of certain teachings at Concordia Seminary, Saint Louis.

Resolution 3-09 – **To Declare Faculty Majority Position in Violation of Article II of the Constitution** (*Proceedings,* pages 133–39). In this seven-page resolution, two documents reflecting the position of the faculty majority are prominently referred to: (1) *Fact Finding or Fault Finding,* President Tietjen's response to the *Report of the Synodical President* (also known as the "Blue Book") on the teachings at Concordia Seminary (both the report and the response were published in September 1972); and (2) *Faithful to Our Calling, Faithful to Our Lord* (published in November 1972).]

Two other relevant resolutions came before the convention and were handled as follows:

Resolution 3-10 – **To Deal with the St. Louis Board of Control** [re their perceived failure to "carry out its responsibilities"] (*Proceedings*, page 139). This proposed resolution was "referred under omnibus Resolution 4-47 to the Board of Directors."

Resolution 3-12A – **To Deal with Dr. John Tietjen under the Provisions of Synod's "Handbook"** (*Proceedings*, page 140). This resolution was offered by the floor committee during one of the last sessions of the convention as a replacement for the much more lengthy Resolution 3-12 (*Proceedings*, pages 140–42). Resolution 3-12A was adopted as amended.

Aftermath of the Resolutions Adopted at New Orleans

The convention that charged the Concordia Seminary Board of Control to deal with the issues discussed ended on July 13, 1973. Ten days later, forty-nine faculty and staff members of Concordia Seminary issued the document "A Declaration of Protest and Confession," in which they "rejected charges of teaching false doctrine, declared that the Synod's convention had violated procedures for evangelical discipline and had violated the 'Scripture Alone' principle of the Reformation and charged the convention had used 'coercive power' to establish doctrine" (*The Lutheran Witness*, October 7, 1973, page 23). Five professors also released "An Appeal," rejecting "A Declaration" (23). Subsequently, Concordia Seminary's Board of Control suspended Dr. Tietjen as president and faculty member at their August 18 meeting, but then delayed implementation of its action on September 29 (21). Many protesting the actions of the Synod in convention organized a "Conference on Evangelical Lutheranism," held on August 28–29, 1973, where a legal corporation was begun, later named "Evangelical Lutherans in Mission (ELIM)" (*The Lutheran Witness*, September 16, 1973, page 22). President Preus included, in the same *Lutheran Witness* issue, his strong critique of the convention. Later, President Preus published his after-convention report to the Synod in *The Lutheran Witness* in five installments (December 16, 1973; January 6, January 27, February 17, and March 17, 1974).

At its November 19 meeting, the Concordia Seminary Board of Control "announced it would review the teaching outlines for all seminary courses offered during the remainder of the present academic year" (*The Lutheran Witness,* December 16, 1973, page 23). The board also "asked that instructors state in writing how they 'propose to deal with' topics and methods affected by two New Orleans synodical convention resolutions [Resolution 3-01 and 3-09]" (23). "Another action directed the seminary president, Dr. John Tietjen, to explain in writing some of his recent actions and decisions in the light of his position under synodical policies" (23). Delayed by the sudden death of Concordia Seminary professor Arthur Carl Piepkorn on December 13, the Concordia Seminary Board of Control suspended Dr. Tietjen as president the following month, at its January 20 meeting. Note several references to convention resolutions in the article announcing Dr. Tietjen's suspension (*The Lutheran Witness*, January 27, 1974, page 25). On January 21, a majority of the student body declared a moratorium on class attendance, and a majority of the faculty announced that they considered themselves to also be suspended. Twenty-eight days later, the Board of Control required faculty members either to return to class or to be held in breach of their teaching contracts. The next day, February 18, 1974, faculty and students staged a "walkout" procession off the Concordia Seminary campus. Seminex / Seminary-in-Exile was formed shortly thereafter and thus would be a major issue for the 1975 convention in Anaheim.

Anaheim (July 4–11) **1975**

Overtures specifically regarding Seminex submitted for publishing in the 500-page *Convention Workbook / Reports and Overtures* included those that either urged recognition of Seminex and its graduates (6-33A, 6-34A, 6-35A, 6-36A, 6-37, 6-38, 6-39A, 6-40, 6-41A, 6-42, 6-43, 6-44A, 6-52A to 6-52H) or urged repudiation of Seminex—especially as a source of pastors for Missouri Synod congregations (3-45A, 3-47, 3-187A, 3-198A, 6-53, 6-54, 6-55A, 6-56A, 6-57A, 6-58A, 6-59A, 6-60, 6-61A&B, 6-62, 6-63, 6-64, 6-65A, 6-66A, 6-67, 6-68).

Two specific resolutions at the 1975 convention dealt specifically with Seminex and its graduates:

> Resolution 6-02 – **To Clarify Status of Seminex** (*Proceedings*, page 141). "*Resolved*, That the Synod, by the mercies of God, would beseech those engaged in conducting and supporting Seminex to close the institution in the interest of promoting peace and harmony in our midst; and be it further *Resolved*, That the Synod herewith indicate that the J.P.T.E [Joint Project for Theological Education] (Seminex), if it continues to exist, will be regarded as any other theological school not affiliated with The Lutheran Church—Missouri Synod." The resolution was adopted.

> Resolution 6-05 – **To Clarify Status of Seminex Graduates** (*Proceedings*, page 144). "Resolved, That the Synod encourage those graduates of the Joint Project which have not been endorsed by the faculty of a synodical seminary to request admission to the pastoral ministry of the Synod by making their desire known to the Colloquy Board for the Pastoral Office." The resolution was adopted.

A number of overtures urged the convention to rescind Resolution 3-09 of the 1973 convention in New Orleans that had declared the Saint Louis faculty majority in violation of Article II of the Synod's Constitution. Resolution 3-10 – **To Decline to**

Rescind N.O. Resolution 3-09 "died since it failed to receive action before adjournment" (*Proceedings,* page 100). That many related matters remained to be addressed and resolved was reflected in the number of resolutions dealing with ELIM, the status of doctrinal statements, and specific issues of scriptural interpretation that also failed to receive action before adjournment.

Photograph by Paul Ockrassa

Student body president Gerald Miller explains "Operation Outreach," a plan to communicate the plight of the faculty and students to the church at large, Koburg Hall, January 1974. More than 250 students participated in the public relations effort, logging more than 118,000 miles as they traveled throughout the country to share their message.

Index

C

D

G

H

I

J

K

L

M

N

O

P

Q

R

S

T

Y

Z

Photograph by Paul Ockrassa

Concordia Seminary students plant crosses with names of seminary faculty members in the Main Quadrangle of the campus.